# THE PRIVATE PILOT'S
# HANDY REFERENCE MANUAL

## Other TAB Books by the Author:

# THE PRIVATE PILOT'S HANDY REFERENCE MANUAL

BY JOE CHRISTY

MODERN AVIATION SERIES

## TAB BOOKS Inc.

BLUE RIDGE SUMMIT, PA. 17214

FIRST EDITION

SIXTH PRINTING

Printed in the United States of America

Reproduction or publication of the content in any manner, without express permission of the publisher, is prohibited. No liability is assumed with respect to
the use of the information herein.

Library of Congress Cataloging in Publication Data

Christy, Joe.
    The private pilot's handy reference manual.

    Includes index.
    1. Private flying—Handbooks, manuals, etc.
I. Title.
TL721.4.C48      629.132'5217      80-21002
ISBN 0-8306-9663-6
ISBN 0-8306-2325-6 (pbk.)

# Preface

This manual is a digest of data often referenced by private pilots—or data that should be referenced—but which normally must be tracked down from a variety of sources. Included are a review of certain fundamentals and a new approach to the "go, no-go" decision, because the decade of the 1980s will demand an ever greater degree of proficiency from every pilot-in-command. However, this is not an instruction book. It is intended as a handy reference on subjects directly related to the operation of private aircraft in the United States Federal Airways System.

A good deal of space is devoted to a glossary of the terms employed by air traffic controllers and Flight Service Station specialists. Complete understanding between those who operate the Air Traffic Control (ATC) systems and those who use the systems is a safety factor that affects all who fly.

Aviation weather is also dealt with at length and is entirely pilot-oriented, based upon experience and practical considerations. Every pilot must firmly establish for himself his own personal weather minimums, fully understand how to recognize these minimums in any situation, and stick rigidly to them. Realistic guidelines are offered to aid in this critical determination.

Joe Christy

# Contents

# Federal Aviation Regulations for Pilots

There are three medical standards for pilots. The third-class medical certificate is valid for 24 months and expires on the last day of the calendar month in which it was issued. For example, a third-class medical certificate issued July 10, 1980, would expire July 31, 1982. The third-class medical validates the Private Pilot's Certificate, and is also issued in combination with the Student Pilot's Certificate.

## Medical Certificates

To be eligible for a third-class medical certificate, an applicant must have distant visual acuity of 20/50 or better in each eye separately, without correction. If the vision in either or both eyes is poorer than 20/50 and is corrected to 20/30 or better in each eye with corrective glasses, the applicant may be qualified on condition that he wear glasses while acting as an airman. He must be able to hear the whispered voice at 3 feet, and have no acute or chronic diseases of the internal ear or disturbances in equilibrium. He must have no established medical history or diagnosis of *personality disorders, psychosis, alcoholism, drug dependency, epilepsy,* unexplained loss of *consciousness, convulsive disorders, angina pectoris* or other evidence of coronary heart disease. A history of diabetes that requires insulin or similar agents for control may be also be disqualifying.

A second-class medical certificate is required for commercial pilots and flight instructors. It is good for a period of 12 calendar months after date of issue. For example, if issued on July 15, 1980, the certificate is in force until July 31, 1981. However, the holder of a commercial pilot's certificate may fly as a private pilot (not for hire) for an additional 12 months—in this example until July 31, 1982—if the second-class medical is not renewed prior to its 12-month expiration period. To be eligible for a second-class medical certificate, an applicant must have distant visual acuity of 20/20 or better in each eye separately, without correction; or at least 20/100 in each eye separately corrected to 20/20 or better with corrective glasses, in which case the glasses must be worn when operating an aircraft. In addition, the applicant must be able to distinguish aviation red, green and white and meet certain other requirements related to *bifoveal fixation* and *vergencephoria*. A whispered voice must be heard at 8 feet with each ear separately. Other requirements are the same as those for the third-class certificate.

The first-class medical certificate consists of all the requirements of the second-class certificate with additional emphasis on sight, hearing and heart condition. This certificate is intended for airline pilots (more accurately the holder of an airline transport rating, which is needed to obtain most corporate flying positions), and is valid for a period of six months as a first-class certificate, six additional months as a second-class certificate, and an additional 12 months as a third-class certificate. To be eligible for a first-class medical certificate, an applicant must have distant visual acuity of 20/20 or better in each eye separately, without correction; or at least 20/100 in each eye separately corrected to 20/20 or better with corrective glasses. Also, he must have near vision of at least $V=1.00$ at 18 inches with each eye separately, normal color vision, normal fields vision, and no acute or chronic condition in either eye. The wearing of glasses is permitted. The applicant must be able to hear the whispered voice at a distance of at least 20 feet with each ear separately, or demonstrate a hearing acuity of at least 50 percent of normal in each ear throughout the effective speech and radio range as tested with a standard audiometer. After age 35, the applicant is subject to an electrocardiographic exam.

Blood pressure limits are specified only for the first-class medical certificate. However, as a general guide to the second and third-class certificates, a maximum reading of 170/100 is typical. The applicant's age, weight and total physical condition is considered in cases of elevated blood pressure readings. Blood pressure limitations for the first-class medical certificate are in Table 1-1.

In certain instances the medical standards may be waived for private pilot applicants. This is even legally possible for second and first-class medical certificates. Any person who is

Table 1-1. Blood Pressure Limitations for First-Class Medical Certificate.

| AGE | MAXIMUM RECLINING | | ADJUSTED MAX RECYCLING | |
|---|---|---|---|---|
| 20-29 | 140 | 88 | | |
| 30-39 | 145 | 92 | 155 | 98 |
| 40-49 | 155 | 96 | 165 | 100 |
| 50 & up | 160 | 98 | 170 | 100 |

denied a medical certificate may, within 30 days after the date of the denial, apply in writing, in duplicate, to the Federal Air Surgeon, Attention: Chief, Aeromedical Certification Branch, Civil Aeromedical Institute, Federal Aviation Administration, P.O. Box 25082, Oklahoma City, OK 73125, for reconsideration of that denial. It may take a little time, but you will be heard.

The FAA appoints medical doctors throughout the country to perform airmens' medicals. Most FBOs, flight schools, Flight Service Stations or any pilot in your area will have a list of such doctors in your area.

### Airmens' Certificates

To clear up any possible misunderstanding over terms, it should be mentioned that the FAA issues "Airmens' Certificates," not "Pilots' Licenses." The student pilot obtains a combination medical certificate and Student Pilot Certificate, although this is often referred to as a "Student Permit."

### Student Pilot

In addition to a third-class medical certificate, one must be at least 16 years of age, able to read, speak and understand English in order to obtain a Student Pilot Certificate (Fig. 1-1). The FARs specify the minimum training the student must have prior to solo which includes aircraft pre-flight inspection, engine operation, taxiing, take-off, landing, traffic pattern procedures, level flight, turns, climbs, stalls, glides and emergency landings. Upon completion, and when the flight instructor is satisfied with the student's level of competence, the instructor may endorse the student's certificate for solo flight. The student may solo only such aircraft as the instructor designates on the student's certificate and in the student's log book. Except for special cases, this endorsement is valid only for a period of 90 days.

The solo student will fly only within an area designated by his flight instructor. Prior to student solo cross-country, the student must have additional dual instruction in cross-wind and

Fig. 1-1. One may obtain a Student Pilot's Certificate at age 16, but must be 17 to qualify for a Private Pilot's Certificate.

simulated soft-field landings and take-offs, climbing and gliding turns at minimum safe airspeeds, cross-country navigation and simple maneuvers by reference only to instruments. He must be able to handle two-way radio communications and to understand cross-country planning, the use of weather reports and emergency procedures. He must have also obtained an FCC Radio-Telephone Operator's Permit. Most FBOs will have on hand the form 753-A which the student sends, along with $4, to the Federal Communications Commission for this permit. Student pilots may not make international flights, carry passengers, or operate an aircraft for hire or the furtherance of a business.

### Private Pilot Certificate

Eligibility for a Private Pilot's Certificate includes the provisions that one must be at least 17 years of age, able to read, speak, and understand the English language, must have passed the Private Pilot's Written Examination within the preceding 24 months, and must have at least 40 hours of instruction in-flight including 20 hours of solo time (Fig. 1-2). Of the solo time, at least 10 must be cross-country. One cross-country flight must include three landings at places more than 100 miles from the point of departure.

When the above qualifications are met to the satisfaction of the student's instructor, the CFI (Certified Flight Instructor) may provide the student with a written recommendation for the Private Pilot Flight Test, which is administered by an FAA Designated Pilot Examiner or by an FAA Inspector. This test consists of three phases: an oral quiz, an in-flight test of basic piloting techniques, and a cross-country flight test. A student who fails his flight test may apply for a re-test upon presentation of a statement from his flight instructor that he has been given additional instruction, and that the instructor now regards the applicant ready for re-testing.

The Private Pilot's Written Examination is normally given at the local Federal Building, GADO (General Aviation District Office), or at a place designated by the FAA. The student's flight instructor will advise time and place. This examination includes multiple-choice questions on flight theory, meteorology, the Airman's Information Manual, the FARs, the flight computer, navigation, pre-flight planning, radio procedures and emergency procedures. The minimum passing grade is 70, and no notes or other aids are allowed in the test room. The student is expected to supply a navigation computer and plotter (Fig. 1-3).

Do not make an appointment with an FAA Inspector or Designated Pilot Examiner and fail to keep it or turn up late. Also, never attempt flattery or try to "snow" one of these people. They've heard it all before and they resent it. If you do not know the answer to a question, say so. They do appreciate honesty.

### Commercial Pilot Certificate

The applicant for a Commercial Pilot's Certificate must be at least 18 years of age. He must be able to speak, read and

Fig. 1-2. The first V-tail Bonanza was delivered in 1947. Today it remains the Mercedes of its class (courtesy of Beech Aircraft Corp).

Fig. 1-3. Use of the flight computer (actually a circular slide rule) is permitted when taking FAA written examinations for pilot's certificates (courtesy of Cessna Aircraft Company).

understand English, hold a valid second-class medical certificate, and must have the required flying experience. The experience includes: 250 hours minimum total flight time, 100 hours of which must be as pilot in command (PIC); a minimum of 50 hours cross-country experience, which must include take-offs and landings from two different airports under two-way radio instruction from an airport tower; as well as one cross-country flight of at least 350 miles and including three landings, one of which is at least 150 miles from the point of departure. The applicant must have had at least 10 hours of instrument flight instruction and 10 hours of flight instruction devoted to maneuvers required in the commercial pilot flight test. A minimum of five hours of night flight, including at least 10 take-offs and landings, is also required, as PIC.

The applicant must have also passed a written examination within the preceding 24 months, which the student may request with a written endorsement from his instructor. Such endorsement or recommendation is valid for 60 days.

The commercial pilot flight test is administered in four phases: an oral examination, basic flying techniques, precision maneuvers and a cross-country flight. The maneuvers include gliding spirals, pylon-8s, lazy-8s, steep turns, chandelles, maneuvering at minimum controllable airspeed, and stalls from all normally anticipated flight attitudes with an without power. Accuracy landings within 200 feet beyond a designated mark are also required.

## General Requirements

Pilot certificates for the private and commercial rating are permanent and are kept valid by proper renewal of the associated medical certificates. These certificates must be carried at all times while one is acting as PIC, and must be shown to any law enforcement officer or FAA inspector upon request.

Flight Instructor's Certificates and Student Pilot Certificates automatically expire at the end of the twenty-fourth calendar month after the month in which they were issued.

Lost or destroyed pilot certificates may be replaced for a fee of $2 by sending your name, permanent mailing address, social security number, date and place of birth, and any available information regarding the grade, number and date of issue of the certificate to: Federal Aviation Administration, Airman Certification Branch, P.O. Box 25082, Oklahoma City, OK 73125. Lost or destroyed medical certificates may be replaced in similar fashion and an equal fee by applying to: Federal Aviation Administration, Civil Aeromedical Institute, Aeromedical Certification Branch, P.O. Box 25082, Oklahoma City, OK 73125.

Table 1-2. Airplane Subdivisions.

| ITEM | CATEGORY | CLASS | TYPE |
|------|----------|-------|------|
| Aircraft | Transport<br>Normal<br>Utility<br>Acrobactic<br>Limited<br>Restricted<br>Experimental<br>Provisional | airplane<br>rotorcraft<br>glider<br>Balloon<br>landplane<br>seaplane | Cessna 150<br>Beech B19<br>etc. |
| | Airplane<br>Rotorcraft<br>Glider<br>Lighter-than-air | single-engine, land<br>single-engine, sea<br>multi-engine, land<br>multi-engine, sea<br>gyroplane<br>helicopter<br>airship<br>free balloon | |

Fig. 1-4. A separate rating must be added to a pilot's certificate for seaplane operation (courtesy of Cessna Aircraft Company).

## Aircraft and Pilot Ratings

The FARs subdivide airplanes into category, class and type. Airmen ratings employ the same terms but the meanings are different. Table 1-2 clarify these differences.

## Type Ratings

A pilot's certificate describes the category, class, and type of aircraft the holder is rated to fly. For example, a Commercial Pilot's Certificate may read "Airplane, multi-engine, land, Douglas DC-9." That describes the category, class and type of aircraft the pilot is rated to fly.

Since type ratings are required only for aircraft over 12,500 pounds, turbojets and certain helicopters, they are not usually found on Private Pilot's Certificates. In order to obtain a type rating, an applicant must hold or concurrently obtain an instrument rating and demonstrate proficiency in a flight test.

## Class Ratings

In general aviation, a class rating normally covers transition to twin-engined aircraft. For example, a pilot whose certificate reads "Airplane, single-engine, land," wishes to have a class rating added to his ticket so he can fly, say, a *Piper Seminole*. In order to obtain the class rating, the applicant must have made at least five take-offs and landings in the Seminole in solo flight, or as the only manipulator of the controls accompanied by a pilot rated to carry passengers in that aircraft. In addition, he must obtain a flight instructor's written recommendation and pass a flight test in the aircraft (Fig. 1-4). Normally, five or six hours of dual are considered the minimum for adequate light-twin transition from single-engine aircraft. Since 1 November 1974, flight instruction has been required in high-performance single-engine aircraft (over 200 hp) if one is to act as PIC—that is, for holders of an SEL rating.

### Recency of Experience

In order to carry passengers a pilot must have a category and class rating for the aircraft employed, and must meet recency of flight experience as per Part 61 of the FARs. Within the preceding 90 days he must have made at least three take-offs and landings to a full stop. This now applies to aircraft type as well (Fig. 1-5). Also, if a passenger-carrying flight is to be made at night, he must have had five take-offs and five landings at night during the preceding 90 days. Night experience may be counted as day experience, but not vice versa. Only that flight time required to meet experience standards toward a pilot certificate or rating, or to meet recency requirements, must be logged.

### Change of Address

When a pilot changes his mailing address (permanent), the FAA must be notified within 30 days. This notice should go to: Federal Aviation Administration, Airman Certification Branch, P.O. Box 25082, Oklahoma City, OK 73125.

### Biennial Flight Review

Since 1 November 1974, a *biennial flight review* has been required of all pilots not engaged in airline or commercial flight operation where the FAA does not otherwise require periodic flight checks. The biennial flight review is not a test and no

Fig. 1-5. The "recency of experience" rule requiring three takeoffs and landings within the past 90 days applies to both class and type of aircraft.

grade is given. Its purpose is merely to assure that at least once every two years each pilot rides with a competent instructor who will comment on the pilot's technique and look for any possible bad or lazy flying habits. Also, the pilot will be examined for his knowledge of the FARs that pertain to the certificate held. The flight review will also be administered according to the pilot certificate and rating held, including an instrument rating. The CFI (or CFII) who administers the review will sign the pilot's logbook so stating.

## Pilot in Command

The pilot in command of an aircraft is directly responsible for, and is the final authority as to, the operation of that aircraft (FAR 91.3).

A student pilot is the pilot in command during any legal solo flight of his training, and during the flight test for a pilot certificate.

A private or commercial pilot is the pilot in command during that time that he is the sole manipulator of the controls of an aircraft for which he is rated, or when he is the sole occupant of the aircraft. He is also the pilot in command when acting as PIC of an aircraft on which more than one pilot is required under the type certification of that aircraft.

A certificated flight instructor is the pilot in command during all flight time in which he acts in the capacity of a flight instructor.

FAA inspectors or other authorized flight examiners are not pilots in command during a flight test unless they so state. In other words, they may take command if they see fit. Otherwise, the applicant is the pilot in command.

## Pilot Responsibility

Each pilot in command shall before beginning a flight, familiarize himself with all available information concerning that flight (FAR 91.5). Now there's a regulation that covers a lot of ground.

"All available information" includes weather reports, fuel requirements, alternate landing fields for flights extending more than 25 miles from the departure airport, current air charts and a study of the ground elevation along the intended and possible alternate routes, along with careful notation of obstacles (TV towers, etc.), runway conditions at destination, and point of departure conditions including density altitude.

Review all radio aids available along the intended route, referencing air charts and Part 3 of the *Airman's Information Manual*.

Part 2 of the Airman's Information Manual (AIM) contains the U.S. Airport Directory listing airports of entry, Flight Service Stations and weather office phone numbers. Part 4 of AIM contains a listing of VOR check points, restrictions to enroute navaids and special notices of interest to airmen.

The pilot in command is also responsible for a thorough pre-flight check of the aircraft and a determination that its 100-hour inspection (if rented) or annual inspection is not past due (Fig. 1-6). The loaded weight and balance computation is an additional responsibility of the PIC.

The weather briefing will be discussed in the section of this manual devoted to weather. Flight planning will be covered in the section on air navigation.

## The National Airspace

The *national airspace* is divided into two main categories, *controlled* and *uncontrolled*. Since uncontrolled airspace repre-

Fig. 1-6. A thorough preflight check of the aircraft is possibly one of the most ignored FARs.

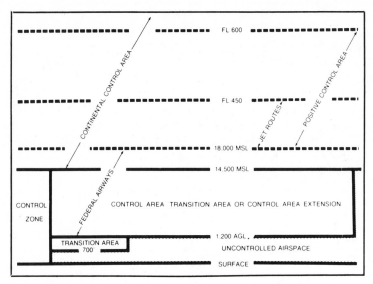

Fig. 1-7. Vertical extent of airspace segments (courtesy of FAA).

sents a minimal regulation condition, it contains no sub-categories. Controlled airspace, however, is subdivided into a number of special use blocks. East of the Mississippi River about 70 percent of the airspace is controlled; in the West about 25 percent is controlled, and along the West Coast about 70 percent. A subdivision is voluntary flight procedure airspace. Typically, volunteer flight procedure airspace is located over national parks or major cities. Pilots are requested to fly at greater altitudes than the FAR minimum over such areas for ecology and noise abatement reasons.

Note that FAR 91.105 provides basic VFR visibility, cloud clearance and ceiling limits for flight in both controlled and uncontrolled airspace. See Table 1-3 and Fig. 1-7.

The single exception to the information in Table 1-3 is Special VFR. In this instance, certain airports are permitted to authorize an aircraft to enter a controlled area when conditions are less than three miles visibility and/or a 1,000-foot ceiling. Under Special VFR the minimums are reduced to one mile visibility and clear of the clouds.

### Uncontrolled Airspace

*Uncontrolled airspace* is that airspace in which minimal VFR visibility and cloud restrictions apply. This airspace is generally located in remote areas and extends in altitude from the surface nominally to 14,500 feet MSL (floor of the Continental Control Area). Often, the ceiling of uncontrolled airspace is limited to 700 or 1,200 feet AGL by an overlaying transition area or control area. Aerobatics are permitted in uncontrolled airspace.

## Controlled Procedure Airspace

The following common airspace allocations are characterized by various FAR procedures but are technically uncontrolled airspace from the standpoint of ceiling and visibility limits. Air traffic area is the airspace within a horizontal radius of five statute miles from the geographical center of any airport at which a control tower *is operating*, extending from the surface of the airport up to 3,000 feet above the elevation of the airport. Within an airport traffic area the following regulations apply:

● Flight operations are intended for the purposes of take-off and landing only. Should it be desirable to penetrate an airport traffic area, it is necessary to obtain an ATC clearance from the tower before entering the area. Initial call-up should be made 15 miles out. Two-way communications with the tower are required while in an airport traffic area, unless landing at a non-tower airport within an airport traffic area of another airport.

● Turbine powered aircraft shall maintain a traffic pattern altitude of at least 1,500 feet above the surface when operating to an airport within an airport traffic area. Now, except for

Table 1-3. Altitude, Visibility and Cloud Clearance Limits.

| ALTITUDE | VISIBILITY | CLOUD CLEARANCE |
|---|---|---|
| 1,200 feet or less above the surface within con-trolled airspace | 3 statute miles | 500 feet below 1,000 feet above 2,000 feet horizontal |
| Outside controlled airspace | 1 statute mile | Clear of clouds |
| More than 1,200 ft above the surface but less than 10,000 feet MSL within con-trolled airspace | 3 statute miles | 500 feet below 1,000 feet above 2,000 feet horizontal |
| Outside controlled air space | 1 statute mile | 500 feet below 1,000 feet above 2,000 feet horizontal |
| More than 1,200 feet above the surface and at or above 10,000 feet MSL | 5 statute miles | 1,000 feet below 1,000 feet above 1 mile horizontal |

Fig. 1-8. ATC personnel in the tower control the airspace within the defined air traffic area and the movement of aircraft on the airport.

special cases, FARs do not specify traffic pattern altitudes. Convention has established such altitudes which have been proven in practice and in the interest of safety. Recommended traffic pattern altitude for aircraft other than turbine powered is 1,000 feet if the airport is located in a control zone, and 800 feet for an airport located in uncontrolled airspace. If a 1,000-foot ceiling were to exist, the pattern altitude in controlled airspace would become 500 feet (minimum cloud clearance), but would remain 800 feet in uncontrolled airspace (clear of clouds).

● The traffic pattern shall be flown as a left-hand pattern unless noted otherwise by a segmented circle, instructions from tower, a flashing amber light or as listed in the AIM.

● Speed limits within an airport traffic area are: reciprocating engine aircraft, 156 kts (180 mph); and turbined powered aircraft, 200 kts (230 mph). If located within a TCA, the speed limit is 250 kts (288 mph).

● Departure routing shall comply with procedures established for that airport. Turbine powered airplanes and large aircraft shall climb to an altitude of 1,500 feet above the surface as rapidly as practicable.

● At an airport with an operating control tower, no pilot may taxi an aircraft on a runway, take-off or land an aircraft unless he has received a clearance from ATC (Fig. 1-8). A clearance to taxi to a runway is a clearance to cross all intersecting runways, but it is not a clearance to taxi onto the assigned runway.

● In the event of an aircraft radio failure in flight, a pilot may continue to operate the aircraft and land at a tower controlled airport if weather conditions are at or above VFR minimums. He must maintain visual contact with the tower and adhere to the following light signals in Table 1-4 as a means of communication.

● The dimensions of airport traffic areas are not shown on sectional charts. The letters CT in the airport data description block indicate that an airport traffic area is located at that airport.

### Airport Advisory Area

The *airport advisory area* is that area within five statute miles of an airport where a control tower is not operating but where a Flight Service Station is located in (a ceiling limit is not specified). At such locations the FSS provides advisory service to arriving and departing aircraft, and the following regulations apply.

● Arriving aircraft shall make all traffic pattern turns to the left unless the airport displays light signals (flashing amber) or has visual markings indicating that turns should be made to the right.

Table 1-4. Light Signals.

| SIGNAL | ON THE GROUND | IN FLIGHT |
|---|---|---|
| Steady green | cleared for take-off | cleared to land |
| Flashing green | cleared to taxi | return for landing |
| Steady red | stop | give way to other traffic; circle |
| Flashing red | taxi clear of landing area (runway) in use | airport unsafe; do not land |
| Flashing white | return to starting point | exercise extreme |
| Alternating red and green | A general warning signal; caution | |

● Departing aircraft shall comply with FAA traffic patterns for taht airport.

● Participation in the airport advisory program is not mandatory.

● Aircraft operating VFR will contact the FSS 15 miles out when landing, and will again call the FSS for pre-taxi advisories when preparing to leave. This same procedure is useful at airports that possess neither a control tower nor a FSS, but which has a *Unicom* (122.8 Mhz) in operation.

The pilot will understand that an airport traffic area is technically not controlled airspace; FARs apply only to communications, speed limits and landing/take-off procedures. Visibility and cloud clearance limits in an airport traffic area are the same as for uncontrolled airspace—unless the airport traffic area is located in a control zone.

## Control Zones and Control Areas

Airspace which extends upward from the surface nominally to 14,500 feet (the base of the Continental Control Area) constitutes a *Control Zone*. In general, Control Zones are located about airports and are normally circular in shape with a radius of five statute miles, plus extensions as necessary for instrument departure and arrival paths. A Control Zone may encompass more than one airport. Control Zones are shown on charts by a dotted blue line.

*Control Areas* consist of all *Federal Airways* plus airspace areas needed to interconnect the system. A Federal Airway is eight nautical miles in width and typically extends from 1,200 feet above ground level (AGL) to 18,000 feet mean sea level ((MSL). Sectional charts use a shaded blue outline to denote Control Area floors of 1,200 feet AGL. Control Area floors other than that are noted with the appropriate numerical value.

## Transition Area

A *Transition Area* is controlled airspace which extends upward generally from 700 or more AGL to the floor of the overlying controlled airspace. The basic function of the Transition Area is to provide a zone of controlled airspace for IFR operations in the process of descent or climb while in the near vicinity of the airport. Transition Areas are noted by a magenta-colored outline on sectional charts.

## Continental Control Area

The *Continental Control Area* consists of the airspace above the United States (excluding the Alaska Peninsula) at and above 14,500 feet MSL, but does not include the airspace less than 1,500 feet above the surface or certain prohibited or restricted areas. For all practical purposes, the Continental Control Area may be thought of as a large blanket covering the United States (including Alaska) with provisions for a 1,500 feet clearance where it passes over mountainous regions. The ceiling of the Continental Control Area is infinity.

## Positive Control Area

*Positive Control Areas* consist of airspace in which flight must be conducted only under instrument flight rules. For operations within Positive Control Areas, aircraft must be:

● Equipped with instruments and equipment for IFR operation and flown by a pilot rated and current for instrument flight.

● Equipped with a coded radar beacon *transponder*.

● Equipped with communications radio transmitter-receiver equipment necessary to the flight.

● Equipped with Distance Measuring Equipment (DME) if the operation is above flight level 240 (24,000 feet).

Positive Control Area exists from 18,000 feet MSL to flight level 600 throughout the United States.

## Terminal Control Area

*Terminal Control Areas* (TCAs) are "super air traffic control areas." In a TCA *all* aircraft are subject to direction by ATC. The TCAs vary in shape in that they are designed to accommodate the particular airport they service. In general, they extend from the surface to an altitude of 7,000 feet MSL. Group I TCAs are located at the busiest airports. Group II TCAs are at less congested locations. The following regulations apply to Group I TCAs:

—Clearance is required prior to flight in a TCA.

—Student flights are prohibited.

—An operable two-way radio for communicating with ATC is required.

—An operable VOR (or TACAN) receiver is required.

—An operable beacon transponder having at least a mode

A/3, 409B-code capability, replying to A/3 interrogations is required.

Group II TCAs are similar in their requirements to Group I. The exception is that student flight is permitted and that radar beacon transponders are not required for VFR aircraft.

The Terminal Control Area is basically an anti-collision flight procedure. Fundamentally, this is accomplished by radar control of *all* aircraft within the boundaries of a TCA. As a VFR pilot you must obtain a clearance from ATC (approach control) before entering the TCA. Be prepared to hold outside the TCA at times of heavy traffic. If VFR, remember that you have the obligation of remaining in VFR conditions.

## Special Use Airspace

Special Use Airspace consists of airspace where airborne activity must be confined because of the specialized nature of the activity. There are various classes of specialized use airspace.

**Prohibited Area.** A *Prohibited Area* is airspace within which the flight of aircraft is not allowed for reasons of national security or national welfare, unless prior permission has been granted by the proper government authority. Such an area is the location of White House and Capitol Buildings in Washington, D.C. Also, some wildlife areas are similarly protected. These will be clearly shown on air charts.

**Restricted Area.** *Restricted Areas* confine or segregate flight activities regarded as hazardous to other aircraft. These activities may be artillery firing, aerial gunnery or guided missile firing. Normally, such activities take place within certain hours. You may penetrate only with permission of the controlling authority.

## Warning Area

A *Warning Area* is airspace, within international airspace, established to contain hazardous operations conducted by U.S. military forces. No restriction to flight is imposed, because flight within international airspace cannot be legally restricted. Most Warning Areas lie within three statute miles of the coast line and are located over ocean areas.

## Alert Area

An *Alert Area* is airspace in which there is a high volume of pilot training activity or an unusual type of aeronautical activity, neither of which is normally hazardous to aircraft. (Fig. 1-9). No unique flight restrictions or communications are imposed. Within a Control Zone, the floor of an Alert Area is established at least 4,000 feet AGL and the ceiling no higher than the beginning of Positive Control airspace (18,000 feet MSL).

### Intensive Student Jet Training Area (ISJTA)

An ISJTA imposes no special restrictions on VFR flights, although pilots transiting the area are equally responsible with the military pilots for collision avoidance. Restriction is on IFR flight. Information on training areas may be obtained from any FSS within 100 miles of the area.

### Special Operations

Airspace devoted to military training routes is termed *Olive Branch Routes*. Refer to the Airman's Information Manual Parts 3 and 4 for route descriptions. Treat Olive Branch Routes as Alert Areas.

### Terminal Area Graphic Notice

This references high density terminal area suggested routes for transiting aircraft. Refer to AIM, Part 4, Area Notices, for route descriptions.

### Special Air Traffic Rules and Air Traffic Patterns

Special rules or procedures apply to some airspace area. Pilots must obtain an ATC advisory before entering such areas.

### Temporary Flight Restrictions

Temporary airspace flight restrictions may be placed in effect in the vicinity of any incident or event that is likely to

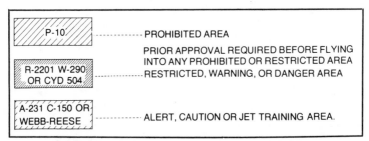

Fig. 1-9. Certain blocks of airspace may not be freely transited. Airspace reservations below 18,000 MSL are numbered and indicated on the charts.

generate hazardous congestion of air traffic, such as air shows, floods, forest fires, etc. Pilots are notified through NOTAMS and FSS.

## Voluntary Flight Procedure Airspace

When flying over national parks and wilderness areas administered by the U.S. Forest Service, National Park Service or the Fish and Wildlife Service, maintain a minimum altitude of 2,000 AGL. At present, this is a voluntary program. However, the controlling agency in each case has the legal authority to impose minimum altitude limits. No landings or take-offs may be made in these areas except at officially designated airports.

## Air Defense Identification Zones

*Air Defense Identification Zones* (ADIZs) are areas of airspace over land or water in which the ready identification, location and control of civil aircraft is required in the interest of national security. There are four such zones that surround the continental United States off the East and West Coasts, Gulf of Mexico, and along the United States border with Mexico. These are shown on air charts. In addition to the ADIZ, *Distant Early Warning Identification Zones* (DEWIZs) are established to provide similar aircraft identification at lone ranges. Such a zone is in Alaska. If your route of flight requires penetration of an ADIZ or DEWIZ the following regulations in general apply:

● A flight plan is required for both IFR and VFR flight, and a VFR flight plan shall be designated as DVFR.

● Two-way radio is required. Between Mexico and the United States a flight may be made without radio, but one must land at a designated airport-of-entry nearest the point of entry and file an arrival notice.

● Position reports are required. All DVFR flights must report estimated time of penetration of an ADIZ at least 15 minutes prior to penetration. Reports must include the time, position, altitude and estimated time of arrival at the next reporting point. Time estimates should be within five minutes. Course position estimates should be within 10 miles of the center line for a domestic ADIZ and within 20 miles of course center line for a coastal ADIZ or DEWITZ.

● Except for flight between Mexico and the United States, coastal or domestic ADIZ requirements do not apply if operating north of 25 degrees latitude or west of 85 degrees west longitude at a true airspeed of less than 180 kts. The DEWIZ procedures do not apply in Alaska when operating at a true airspeed of less than 180 kts while the pilot maintains a listening watch on an appropriate frequency. ADIZ procedures do not apply within the continental United States over or within three miles of an island in Hawaii, and for flights that remain within 10 miles of a departure point.

● In an emergency situation the PIC may deviate from ADIZ or DEWIZ procedures to the extent required by the emergency to insure flight safety, but must report the reason for the deviation to the proper communications facility as soon as possible.

### Airway Routes

The national airspace is divided into two major airways systems. The low altitude system of Victor Airways extends up to 18,000 feet MSL. The airspace from 18,000 feet MSL to flight level 600 (60,000 feet MSL on a standard day) contains the high altitude *Jet Airway* system. There are operational differences between the *Victor and Jet Airways*. Altitudes flown on Victor Airways are MSL. It is necessary for a pilot to correct the altimeter setting during the course of a flight. FARs require that the aircraft altimeter be set to stations along the route within 100 miles of the aircraft.

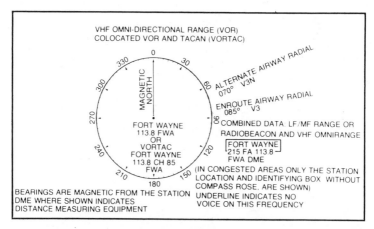

Fig. 1-10. Sectional and World Aeronautical Charts contain an exceptional amount of navigational data. Every pilot should be accomplished in interpreting it.

For flights in the Jet Airways system, the altimeter is set to a constant pressure altitude of 29.92 inches of mercury (Hg). Flight in the high altitude structure is thus conducted at a constant pressure altitude instead of a constant mean sea level altitude as in the low altitude structure (Fig. 1-10). On non-standard days (when the altimeter is other than 29.92 Hg), flight levels will not be located at their numerically equivalent MSL altitudes. Flight level 190 will not be at 19,000 feet MSL, for example. To maintain the division between the Jet Airway system and the Victor Airway system at 18,000 feet MSL, the lowest usable flight level is determined by the atmospheric pressure in the intended area of operation. See Table 1-5.

## The Hemispheric Rule

As a collision avoidance measure, our airspace is divided into a series of layers to segregate VFR and IFR traffic as well as east and west bound traffic. Altitude separation is accomplished according to the so-called hemispheric rule.

VFR aircraft operating in level cruising flight above 3,000 feet above the surface and less than 18,000 feet MSL shall maintain odd 1,000-foot MSL altitudes plus 500 feet when eastbound (a magnetic course of zero degrees through 179 degrees), and even thousand-foot MSL altitudes plus 500 feet when westbound (a magnetic course of 180 degrees through 359 degrees). In other words, maintain 3,500 feet, 5,500 feet, 7,500 feet, etc., when on magnetic headings between zero degrees and 179 degrees and 4,500 feet, 6,500 feet, etc., when on magnetic headings between 180 degrees and 359 degrees.

IFR aircraft operating in uncontrolled airspace in level cruising flight above 3,000 feet above the surface and below 18,000 feet MSL shall fly at odd thousand-foot levels (3,000, 5,000, etc.) when eastbound (zero degrees through 179 degrees magnetic). Fly even thousand-foot levels when westbound (180 degrees to 359 degrees magnetic).

## Special VFR

Special VFR weather minimums allow a lower cloud clearance and visibility minimum in certain Control Zones if a Special VFR clearance is first obtained from ATC. For fixed-wing aircraft Special VFR minimums are one statute mile visibility and clear of the clouds. This may be the determination of the PIC except for operations in a Control Zone where ground

Table 1-5. Lowest Usable Flight Levels.

| CURRENT ALTIMETER SETTING | LOWEST USABLE FLIGHT LEVEL |
|---|---|
| 29.92 or higher | 180 |
| 29.91 thru 29.42 | 185 |
| 29.41 thru 28.92 | 190 |
| 28.91 thru 28.42 | 195 |
| 28.41 thru 27.92 | 200 |
| 27.91 thru 27.42 | 205 |
| 27.41 thru 26.92 | 210 |

visibility is reported. Such a clearance may be authorized by a control tower in a Control Zone, the nearest tower, FSS or Air Route Traffic Control Center. Control Zones that permit Special VFR are identified on Sectionals by a dotted blue line. Those that do not are identified by the letter "T". Special VFR is not allowed at night in all Control Zones unless the pilot is instrument rated and the aircraft IFR equipped.

## Minimum Legal Altitudes

The minimum allowable altitude over a congested area is 1,000 feet above the highest obstacle within a horizontal radius of 2,000 feet of the aircraft (Fig. 1-11). A congested area may be interpreted by the FAA to mean anything from a city to groups of people on a beach.

When over other than "congested areas," a minimum of 500 feet above the surface must be maintained. Again, exactly what constitutes a non-congested area is open to FAA interpretation and may vary from region to region.

Over open water or sparsely populated areas, aircraft may not be operated closer than 500 feet to any person, vessel, vehicle or structure. Again, the term "sparsely populated" is not precisely defined in the FARs, but is obviously intended to mean areas that are less populated than "non-congested" areas. These are not the only generalities or somewhat vague terms in the FARs. Others exist with regard to aircraft maintenance. Common sense, however, will usually be the pilot's best guide when confronted with a FAR that, perhaps by necessity, is open to more than one interpretation.

In general, the altitude minimums for IFR operation require 2,000 feet above the highest obstacle within a horizontal distance of five miles from the course to be flown in mountainous areas. In flat areas there is a minimum of 1,000 feet above the

Fig. 1-11. The minimum allowable altitude over a congested area is 1,000 feet above the highest obstacle within a horizontal radius of 2,000 feet of the aircraft. One six Quebec appears to be in violation of the FAR.

highest obstacle within a horizontal distance of five statute miles from the planned course.

### Right-of-Way

● An aircraft in distress has the right-of-way over all other air traffic.

● When aircraft of different categories are converging, the least maneuverable has the right-of-way. Balloons have the right-of-way over all other aircraft. Gliders (sailplanes) have the right-of-way over all except balloons. Blimps and Zeppelins (airships) have the right-of-way over an airplane or rotorcraft. And an aircraft towing or refueling other aircraft has the right-of-way over all other engine-driven aircraft.

● When two aircraft are approaching each other head-on, or nearly so, each aircraft shall alter course to the right.

● When two aircraft are converging at approximately the same altitude at a right angle (or nearly so), the aircraft to the pilot's right has the right-of-way. The FARs do not differentiate in right-of-way rules between small or large aircraft. However, one must consider that visibility from the cockpit of an airliner is very restricted. As a practical matter you will do well to keep out of the way even though you may have the right-of-way. It

Fig. 1-12. The FARs define aerobatic flight as a roll or bank exceeding 60 degrees and/or a climb or dive that exceeds 30 degrees (courtesy of Don Downie).

may even be argued that, since light aircraft are more maneuverable than airliners, the big ones have the right-of-way in any case.

● An aircraft that is being overtaken by a faster machine has the right-of-way, and the pilot of the overtaking aircraft must alter course to the right and pass well clear.

● Aircraft, while on final approach to land or while landing, have the right-of-way over other aircraft in flight or on the surface. When two or more aircraft are approaching an airport for a landing, the aircraft at the lowest altitude has the right-of-way, but shall not take advantage of this rule to cut in front of one which is on final approach or to overtake that aircraft.

●Aircraft operating over water shall keep clear of all surface vessels and avoid impeding their navigation.

## Aerobatics

*Aerobatics* are not permitted over any congested area, settlement or over an open assembly of persons. Aerobatics are not permitted within a Control Zone or Federal Airway. Minimum altitude for aerobatic flight is 1,500 feet above the surface, and minimum visibility is three statute miles. Airshow performers obtain special waivers. The FARs define aerobatic flight as a roll or bank exceeding 60 degrees and/or a climb or dive that exceeds 30 degrees (Fig. 1-12).

## Formation Flying

Civilian *formation flight* is forbidden except by previous arrangement with the PICs in the formation. No paying passengers may be carried in formation flights. Pilots flying in formation must not operate their aircraft so close to others as to create a collision hazard.

## Reckless Flying

You may not operate an aircraft in the air or on the ground in a reckless manner so as to endanger the lives and property of others. No object may be dropped from an aircraft in flight that creates a hazard to persons or property.

No person may act as a crew member of a civil aircraft within eight hours after the consumption of any alcoholic beverage, while under the influence of alcohol, or while using any drugs that affect his faculties in any way that may compromise the safe operation of the aircraft. Furthermore, except in an emergency, no pilot may allow a person who is obviously under the influence of intoxicating liquors or drugs (except a medical patient under proper care) to be carried in that aircraft. We're tempted to comment at length on that one; but perhaps it's better to merely report what the regs say and leave it at that.

## Aircraft Lighting

Aircraft position lights must be turned on from official sunset to official sunrise, both on the ground and in the air when the aircraft is being operated (Fig. 1-13). Rotating beacons and/or strobes are also turned on during these hours. If you are in doubt as to exactly when such official times occur, the tower, FSS or ATC facility will advise. In Alaska, position lights must also be turned on when prominent unlighted objects cannot be seen from a distance of three statute miles, and when the sun is more than six degrees below the horizon.

Fig. 1-13. Aircraft position lights and beacons must be turned on from official sunset to official sunrise. If in doubt, check with the tower or FSS.

## ATC Clearances

An ATC clearance must be followed without deviation, except in an emergency, unless an amended clearance is obtained from the air traffic controller. If you are given a clearance that you cannot accept, say so at once. If you do not completely understand the clearance, the controller will catch your error when you read it back to him.

Whatever the situation, uncertainty, alert or distress, the PIC has three actions at his disposal to bring the ATC network to his assistance. First, there is Squawk Code 7700 on the transponder. This alerts ATC radar facilities to your location and identifies you as the aircraft in trouble.

He can contact the ATC facility nearest you (tower, center, FSS). If unsure of the proper frequency, transmit on the emergency frequency, 121.5 MHz.

The PIC must declare an emergency. Otherwise, ATC cannot give you priority.

## Speed Limits

The following aircraft speed limits apply:

—Surface to 10,000 feet MSL, 250 kts maximum.
—Below layers of a TCA, 200kts maximum
—Within an Airport Traffic Area, 156 kts for reciprocating-engine aircraft; 200 kts for jet aircraft. If located within a TCA, 250 kts for all aircraft.

## International Flights

For flights outside the United States, it is recommended that pilots obtain the current edition of the "Customs Guide for

Private Flyers," Stock No. 4802-0029 (25 cents) from Superintendent of Documents, U.S. Government Printing Office, Washington, D.C. 20402. The procedures for flying to Canada are simple; but the drug smuggling scene of the recent past ensures that new rules are soon to be enacted with regard to flying to Mexico.

## Accident Reports

Legally, all aviation accident investigation is the responsibility of the *National Transportation Safety Board* (NTSB). The NTSB also reviews airmen appeals relating to suspension, amendment, revocation or denial of pilot's certificates.

The NTSB delegates authority to the Board from which the NTSB may determine the probable cause of the accident. Authority is granted to the FAA to investigate and furnish reports to the NTSB on all non-fatal general aviation accidents, all aerial application accidents, all amateur-built aircraft accidents and all restricted category aircraft accidents. The FAA is also granted authority to investigate and report on fixed-wing aircraft accidents for vehicles which are not engaged in air carrier or air taxi operations and weight less than 12,500 pounds.

The NTSB establishes rules pertaining to the handling of aircraft accidents, incidents, overdue aircraft and safety investigations. The operator of an aircraft is required to immediately notify the NTSB, Bureau of Aviation Safety Field Office, of the following:

- Aircraft accidents
- Flight control system malfunction or failure.
- Inability of any required flight crew member to perform his/her normal flight duties as a result of injury or illness.
- Turbine engine rotor failures excluding compressor blades and turbine buckets.
- In-flight fire.
- Aircraft colliding in flight.
- An aircraft which is overdue and believed to have been involved in an accident.

The notification shall contain the following information if available:

- Type, nationality and registration marks of the aircraft.
- Name of owner and operator of the aircraft.

36

- Name of pilot-in-command.
- Date and time of accident.
- Last point of departure and planned destination.
- Position of the aircraft with reference to some easily defined geographical point.
- Number of persons aboard, number killed and number seriously injured.
- Nature of the accident, including weather and the extent of damage to the aircraft as far as is known.
- A description of any explosives, radioactive materials or other dangerous articles carried.

The NTSB may be notified through the local FAA office or, in major cities, by direct telephone contact with the NTSB field office. A formal report is required within 10 days after an accident or reportable incident has occurred, or when after seven days an overdue aircraft is still missing.

An "aircraft accident" is an occurrence associated with the operation of an aircraft which takes place between the time any person boards the aircraft with the intention of flight, until such time as all persons have disembarked the aircraft. An accident is defined as a situation in which any persons suffer death or serious injury as a result of being in an aircraft, or by direct contact with the aircraft or anything attached thereto. An accident also results when the aircraft receives substantial damage.

"Fatal injuries" imply any injury which results in death within seven days. A "serious injury" means any injury which requires hospitalization for more than 48 hours, commencing within seven days from the date the injury was received; results in the fracture of any bone (except simple fractures of the fingers, toes or nose); involves lacerations which cause severe hemorrhages, nerve, muscle or tendon damage; involves injury to any internal organ; or involves second or third-degree burns, or any burns affecting more than five percent of the body surface.

The term "substantial damage" means aircraft damage which adversely affects structural strength, performance or flight characteristics of the aircraft resulting in a major repair.

A report on an "incident" for which notification is required shall be filed only if requested by the FAA or NTSB. "Incidents," of course, are less than accidents and cover such things as damage to landing gear, failed engine accessories and ground damage to propellers. Many such notifications are undoubtedly skipped, and of those that are, a report is filed only if the FAA asks for it. Accident reports should be made on NTSB form No. 6120.1 for aircraft under 12,500 pounds in weight.

## FAR Enforcement

There are teeth in the FARs. The FAA and NTSB have all the legal powers necessary to cause offending pilots substantial discomfort—including high fines and prison terms up to 20 years or more. It is possible to be sentenced to death (for aircraft piracy). Most violations are minor, however, and the penalty, if it may be called that, is a heart-to-heart talk with an FAA safety expert, with the FAA type doing most of the talking. If the offender is wise, he will listen carefully.

Safety, economic and postal offenses are subject to civil penalties. Falsification of certificates, false aircraft marking, interference with air navigation, falsification of records, transportation of dangerous articles, aircraft piracy and the like are subject to criminal penalties.

Most cases are handled by the FAA. If you don't like their decision in the matter, you may appeal to the NTSB. If still not satisfied, you may then take your case to Federal Court (and all the way to the Supreme Court).

For what might be called "medium-serious" offenses, one may be subject to a fine or temporary suspension of his pilot's certificate (but not both). Normally, it seems that the FAA chooses the one that hurts the most, although they will usually opt for the fine if the offender's job is at stake. A pilot cited for flying while under the influence of alcohol can expect to have his certificate lifted for up to a year. A thorough investigation will be initiated to determine whether or not he is a problem drinker. He may also have to obtain a new medical certificate and pass all of the written and flight examinations again before reinstatement. This recertification process may be part of the penalty for other offenses as well. The point is that Uncle Friendly has all the power he needs to enforce the aviation regulations, so don't take the FARs too lightly.

# 2

# VFR Cross-Country

If you have been flying for any length of time, it will come as no surprise to learn that, according to the FAA, the number one cause of general aviation accidents is poor planning. Presumably, "poor planning" includes most of the weather-related accidents (we'll discuss weather and the "go, no-go" decision in a separate section); but it also includes such things as a cavalier attitude toward one's fuel supply, in attention to the aircraft's weight and balance, and even lack of proper air charts. Have you ever noticed that those people who have all those scary adventures in airplanes are simply poor planners?

### Preflight Planning

Following are suggested steps to be used in flight planning:

● Assemble the materials which will be needed on the flight such as current air charts for the route to be flown, the latest copy of the Airman's Information Manual (AIM) or Jeppesen J-AID, along with plotter and computer. It is wise to take along charts that adjoin those for the route of the flight. Then you are prepared in case it becomes necessary to circumnavigate bad weather, or in case you inadvertently fly off the chart on which your course is drawn.

● On the Sectional Chart, draw the course to be flown. Study the terrain and select appropriate check points. Note the restricted, caution and prohibited areas, as well as Air Defense Identification Zones. Study the airport information, including en route airports that can be used in case of emergency. Choose refueling stops. List radio frequencies of towers and navigational aids and also Flight Service Stations reporting the weather.

● Review weather maps and forecasts, current weather reports, winds aloft forecasts, pilot weather reports (PIREPs), SIGMETS, AIRMETS and NOTAMS. Although you can get

## Table 2-1. A Flight Plan Form.

FEDERAL AVIATION AGENCY

# FLIGHT PLAN

FORM APPROVED
BUDGET BUREAU NO. 04-R072.2

| 1. TYPE OF FLIGHT PLAN | 2. AIRCRAFT IDENTIFICATION | 3. AIRCRAFT TYPE | 4. TRUE AIRSPEED | 5. DEPARTURE TIME |
|---|---|---|---|---|
| ☐ FVFR ☐ VFR  ☐ IFR ☐ DVFR | | | KNOTS | PROPOSED (Z) / ACTUAL (Z) |

| 6. INITIAL CRUISING ALTITUDE | 7. POINT OF DEPARTURE | 8. ROUTE OF FLIGHT |
|---|---|---|
| | | |

| 9. DESTINATION (Name of airport and city) | 10. ESTIMATED TIME EN ROUTE HOURS / MINUTES | 11. FUEL ON BOARD HOURS / MINUTES | 12. ALTERNATE AIRPORT(S) |
|---|---|---|---|
| | | | |

13. REMARKS

| 14. PILOT'S NAME | 15. PILOT'S ADDRESS OR AIRCRAFT HOME BASE | 16. NO. OF PERSONS ABOARD |
|---|---|---|
| | | |

| 17. COLOR OF AIRCRAFT | 18. FLIGHT WATCH |
|---|---|
| | |

**FAA Form 398** (7-64)
USE PREVIOUS EDITION                    **CLOSE FLIGHT PLAN UPON ARRIVAL**    GPO 1964 OF—739-500    SEE REVERSE    (7233)

weather information by telephone, it is strongly recommended that a personal visit be made to the nearest weather office, Flight Service Station (FSS) or other flight service facility.

● File a flight plan (Table 2-1).

A flight plan filed with the nearest FSS is excellent insurance if you are ever forced down. It costs nothing but a few minutes of your time and is best to file in person or by telephone. You should not file by radio from your airplane unless it is impractical to file otherwise.

Part 91.82 of FAR states, "When a flight plan has been filed, the pilot in command, upon canceling or completing the flight under the flight plan, shall notify the nearest FAA Flight Service Station or ATC facility." Pilots are urged to file arrival notices with the nearest FSS when practical to reduce congestion on control tower communications channels.

On every long cross-country flight, you should take advantage of the FSS scheduled broadcasts along your route. Call them for weather reports, changing altimeter settings, etc. These services are available to you whether you are on a flight plan or not.

## VFR Cruising Altitudes

Let's assume that you plan to make a VFR cross-country flight over terrain which has a constant elevation of 2,900 feet. After charting the course, you determine that the true course is 188 degrees and the magnetic variation is 12 degrees E. Accord-

40

ing to the latest aviation weather reports, there is a broken layer of clouds at 7,000 feet all along the route. The visibility is unlimited along your intended route. The winds aloft forecast indicates that the higher the altitude, the more favorable the wind direction and speed. You wish to take advantage of the most favorable wind and, of course, comply with the FAR Cardinal Altitude rule.

The following factors must be considered:

—You wish to fly as high as legally possible to take advantage of the favorable wind.

—The base of the broken clouds is reported in height above the surface. Therefore, the base is approximately 2,900 feet plus 7,000 feet, or 9,900 feet above sea level.

—Cruising altitute is a level above mean sea level (MSL). The rules pertaining to the selection of a cruising altitude appropriate to the flight's magnetic course are applicable only when flying at or above 3,000 feet above the ground (Fig. 2-1).

—This flight will be made at an altitude of 3,000 feet or more above the surface in order to take advantage of the winds aloft. Since you will be flying at an altitude of 3,000 feet or more above the surface, you must, according to the FARs, fly at an altitude appropriate to the magnetic course. In this instance the magnetic course is 176 degrees (188 true, minus 12 degrees easterly variation).

—A magnetic course of 176 degrees in this case requires that you fly at an altitude (above sea level) of odd thousands plus 500 feet.

—In this example, you must maintain a vertical distance under the base of any cloud formation of at least 500 feet. This rules out a cruising altitude of 9,500 feet. You do not choose 5,500 feet since

Fig. 2-1. The Beechcraft Duchess is a light twin designed for training and personal transportation (courtesy of Beech Aircraft Corporation).

you want to take advantage of better tail winds at higher altitudes. You eliminate 6,500 feet because you must be at an odd thousand altitude plus 500 feet. Therefore, you select a cruising altitude of 7,500 feet, which meets legal requirements and gives you the advantage of more favorable winds.

## The Weather Briefing

Flight Service Stations provide aviation weather briefing service. At major strategically located cities weather briefings are also available through both the FSS and National Weather Service station. At many locations, the Weather Service furnishes *Pilot's Automatic Telephone Weather Answering Service* (PATWAS), which means that the weatherman records a briefing that is available to the pilot over his local telephone. Pilots may receive continuous broadcasts of weather information over certain VORs, VORTACs and many of the low and medium frequency navigational aids, known as *Recorded Weather Briefings* (TWEB). TWEB and PATWAS are similar in that they provide weather information for a radius of 250 miles.

The weather station and FSSs provide weather briefings through both listed and unlisted telephone numbers. The unlisted numbers are published in Part 3 of the Airman's Information Manual.

For long cross-country flights or flights in marginal weather, the pilot may choose to obtain an "eyeball-to-eyeball" briefing by FSS or weather station personnel. If a planned flight is short (250 miles or less), a visit with a weather briefer may be unnecessary except in marginal or poor weather situations. Often, a briefing by telephone or the information contained in recorded weather briefings (PATWAS or TWEB) will fill a pilot's needs. At the conclusion of a PATWAS recording, you may get additional information by holding the phone and waiting for the weather briefer to answer (Fig. 2-21).

You will get faster service and greatly assist the weather briefer by telling him the following when requesting service by telephone:

● Say that you are a pilot. If you are a student, private or commercial pilot, say so. The weather briefer needs to know that you are a pilot.

● The type of airplane you are flying.

● Your destination. If you plan to stop en route or deviate from the normal course, say so.

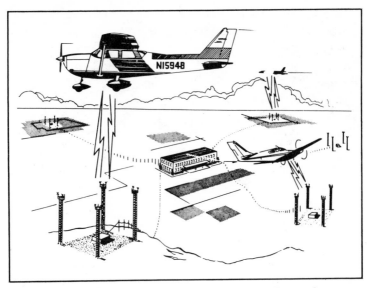

Fig. 2-2. The voices and ears of the Air Route Traffic Control Center are extended over a wide area by using remote center air/ground transmitter/ receiver sites linked to the Center by telephone lines.

- Your estimated departure time.
- Say whether or not you can go IFR.

A preflight weather briefing will be incomplete unless it includes weather synopsis (position of lows, fronts, ridges, etc.), current weather conditions, forecast weather conditions, alternate routes, hazardous weather and forecast winds aloft. Obtaining sufficient information concerning en route and destination weather before beginning a flight is one of the most important parts of preflight action. The telephone conversation that follows is an example of an individual who "thinks" he has checked the weather.

*Pilot*: "This is Elmer Zilch. Will you give me the latest Garden City, Goodland and Denver sequence reports and the winds at 8500 feet?"

*Briefer*: "Yes sir; at 1100 Central Time, Garden City was reporting clear skies, visibility more than 15, surface wind 140 degrees at 20 knots. At Goodland the visibility is still good and they report scattered cirriform clouds. Their wind is 150 degrees at 20 knots. At 1000 Mountain Time, Denver is clear, visibility 50 miles, surface wind is from 040 degrees at 10 knots. Winds at 8500 feet will average 220 degrees at 30 knots. Sir,

Fig. 2-3. Inadequate preflight planning is a chief cause of general aviation accidents, most of which are weather-related.

would you like a weather briefing for your flight? A front lies..." (the pilot interrupts at this point).

*Pilot*: "No, that's all right, thank you. I'm in a hurry. I'll check the weather along the way."

Our pilot is in a hurry to fly his family on an extended cross-country flight of approximately 463 miles (Oklahoma City to Denver). The weather looks good at his departure point and the hourly sequence reports indicate that present weather conditions are favorable along the route. However, this pilot is too anxious to get into the air—too anxious to be on his way. He probably doesn't realize how rapidly the weather can deteriorate in the three hours that will be required to reach his destination. He may be a careless or inexperienced pilot whose flying is characterized by poor judgement. If Mr. Zilch had stayed on the phone for perhaps another minute, the briefer would have given him information (Terminal and Area Forecasts, AIRMETS, etc.) which should have changed his mind about attempting the flight. He would have learned that the proposed flight would take him into rapidly deteriorating ceilings and visibilities as well as freezing drizzle (Fig. 2-3). The briefer offered the pilot more information, and it may have appeared to him that the briefer was questioning his competence. Nevertheless, the pilot should have listened to what the briefer had to offer. Sometimes it may be superfluous. Often it is vitally important (Fig. 2-4).

*Pilot*: "...Goodland Radio, I am five miles east of Goodland at 8,500. Will you give me the latest Denver weather?"

*Goodland Radio*: "...At 1200 Mountain Time, Denver was measured 1500 overcast, visibility 10, very light drizzle, temperature 38, dewpoint 34, wind 040 degrees at 15, altimeter 29.98, low clouds northeast approaching station...Denver AIRMET ALPHA 2, moderate icing in precipitation in northern third of Colorado east of the Rockies, conditions continuing beyond 1500 Mountain and moving southward...Pilot Report at 50 northeast of Denver, moderate rime icing 6,000 to 9,000 feet MSL, type aircraft unknown..."

*Pilot*: "I believe that I can Denver okay VFR, don't you?"

*Goodland Radio*: "Negative. The conditions have dropped rapidly during the past hour. I'll give you the Denver forecast."

*Pilot*: "That's okay, I'll take a look and I'll turn around if it gets too bad. It's 1500 and 10 at Denver; I think I can make it."

A CAP search plane found the wreckage the next afternoon. There were no survivors.

So often pilots are given SIGMETS, AIRMETS or Pilot Reports, but they do not realize the significance of the information. Nor have they gained a lasting respect for the forces of weather. Even though this pilot was made aware of the potential weather hazards on the flight from Goodland to Denver, he did

Fig. 2-4. Omni receiver at left; nothing to listen to over eastern Arizona at 7,350 feet. ADF extreme right, but no commercial stations in Hopi-land. The 122.9 on radio was for plane-to-plane communications with nearby pilot (courtesy of Don Downie).

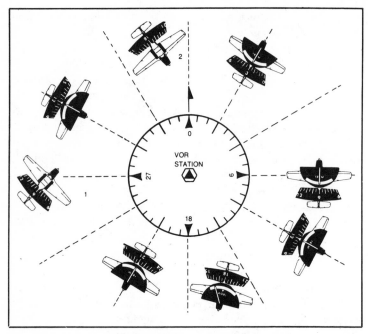

Fig. 2-5. Can you glance at the drawing and immediately tell where the To-From indicator should read in airplane 1? How about the Left-Right needle in airplane 2? Do you agree with the readings in the other airplanes?

not heed the warning. It is not unusual for a pilot to be motivated to continue flight into deteriorating weather in order to keep a speaking engagement, attend a party with friends, get home to the family, or to do a number of other seemingly important things. An almost predictable number of fatalities result from such pressures every year. I'll try to offer some useful guidelines for making the "go; no-go" decision in a subsequent section.

### How to Use VOR

The components of the VOR receiver are the *course* (or *omnibearing*) *selector*), the *left-right* (or *vertical*) *needle* and the *to-from indicator* (Fig. 2-5). The course selector permits the pilots to choose any course.

The left-right needle shows the position of the aircraft in relation to the course selected. If the course line is drawn on the chart, passing through the VOR station to which tuned, the L-R needle indicates on which side of the aircraft the desired course lies.

The to-from (T-F) indicator indicates the position of the aircraft in relation to the VOR station. It shows whether the course selected on the course selector, if intercepted and flown will take you to or from the station.

A *radial* is a line of magnetic bearing extending from the VOR station. Note the easterly-westerly line in Fig. 2-6. East of the VOR station, this line is the 080-degree radial; west of the station, this line is the 260-degree radial.

*Proper sensing* means simply if the L-R needle is to the right, the desired course is to your right. If the L-R needle is to the left, the desired course is to your left. In other words, the desired course is on the same side as the L-R needle. With reverse or opposite sensing, the course is on the opposite side from the L-R needle.

You can be sure that the L-R needle is giving proper sensing by ensuring that the heading of the aircraft is approximately the same as the course selected on the CS. Assume that you wish to maintain a course of 260 degrees which passes over PAGE VOR station. Your heading naturally will be approximately 260 degrees depending on wind direction and velocity. In this case your CS should be adjusted to 260 degrees regardless of whether you are east or west of the VOR station. In other words, always set the CS on the course you are flying, not the reciprocal of your course. Note that the L-R needle in both airplanes in Fig. 2-6 labeled "A" give the proper sensing.

When does the L-R needle give reverse sensing? This happens when the aircraft heading and course selected on the CS are approximately reciprocals (actually, anytime the angle between heading and radial selected is greater than 90 degrees). For example, both airplanes labeled "B" are trying to maintain an easterly course of 080 degrees; however, the CS is set on 260 degrees (the reciprocal of 080 degrees). Note that the L-R needle gives reverse sensing in both airplanes labeled "B." The CS should have been set on 080 degrees to get proper sensing.

Is the indication on the to-from indicator dependent on the heading of the aircraft? Absolutely not. It is dependent only on the setting of the CS and the direction of the aircraft from the station. In the two airplanes east of the VOR station the to-from indicates "to," while west of the station the to-from indicates "from." You could pivot any of the four aircraft in Fig. 2-6 through 360 degrees and there would be no change in the indication on the T-F indicator.

The to-from indicator will give a neutral indication when an unreliable signal is being received (you are either too far from the station or at too low an altitude, or the station is not properly tuned in), when you pass directly over the station, or when you cross the radials perpendicular to the course selected on the CS. For example, as the airplanes in Fig. 2-6 cross the 350-degree or 170-degree radials (and a short distance on either side), the to-from would have a neutral indication.

### Flying Directly To a Station

A VOR station may be used as a navigation aid in three general ways: to fly a course directly to a station (airplane 1), to fly a course directly away from a station (airplane 2), and to determine the direction or bearing of your aircraft *from* a particular station or stations (airplane 3).

Assume that you are flying from Stephan Airport to Hartington Airport; en route you decide to fly to O'Neill Airport (Fig. 2-7). Visualizing your position, you know you are east of the O'Neill VORTAC. Here is the step-by-step procedure.

● Tune in and aurally identify the station (O'Neill VORTAC).

● Turn course selector until the L-R needle is centered and to-from indicator shows "to" (airplane 1).

● Turn to a heading approximately the same as the setting on the CS (airplane 2).

● The L-R needle now has proper sensing (i.e., it is displaced in the direction of the desired course). Keep it centered by making turn corrections toward the needle.

● After completing the third step, you could re-center the L-R needle by readjusting the CS. Then follow this new course inbound.

### Flying Directly Away From a VOR Station

● As you pass over the station "to" will change to "from" (airplanes 1, 2A and 2B) (Fig. 2-8).

● At this time turn the CS to the radial which you wish to follow outbound (airplane 2B).

● Turn the aircraft to a heading which approximates the new setting of the CS.

● The L-R needle now has proper sensing. Keep it centered by making correcting turns toward the needle. If the

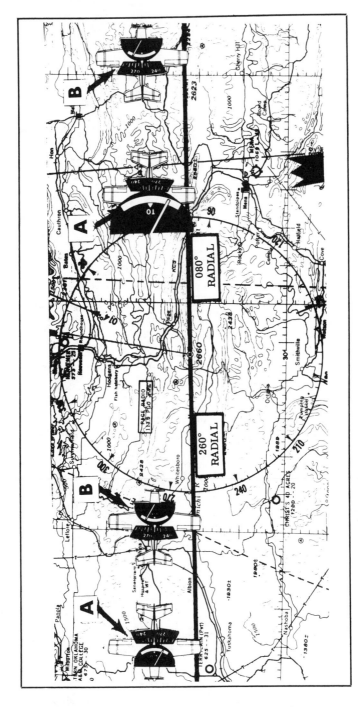

Fig. 2-6. East of the VOR station, this line is the 080-degree radial; west of the station, it is the 260-degree radial.

49

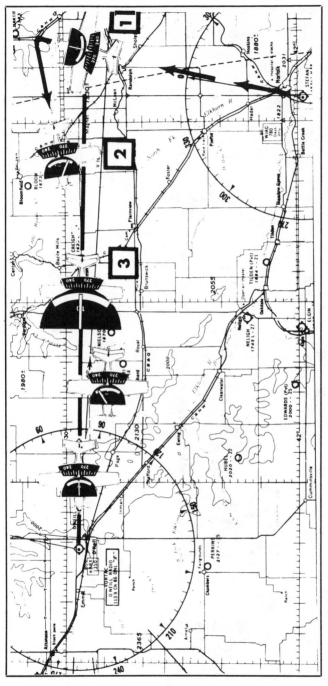

Fig. 2-7. Navigating directly to a station (airplane 1). Flying a course directly away from a station (airplane 2). Determining bearing from a station (airplane 3).

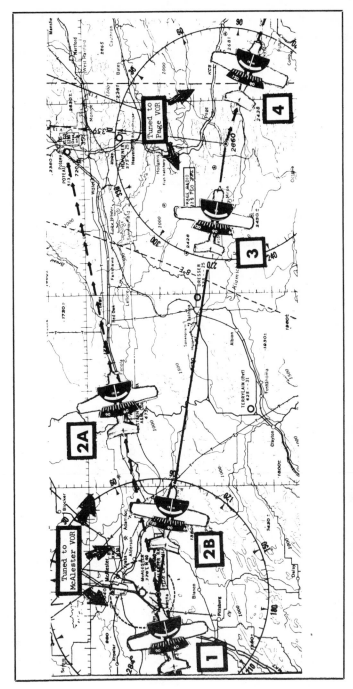

Fig. 2-8. Flying directly away from a VOR station.

needle is displaced to the left, the desired course is to the left and a correcting turn should be made to the left. If the needle is displaced to the right, the desired course is to your right and a turn correction should be made to the right.

If your outbound course from the station is the same as the inbound course, then make no change in the CS in the second step and continue on your same general heading (airplanes 1 and 2A). Two common situations in which you may be flying directly away from a VOR station are the first half of a flight between stations (airplane 2B), and also to help you find an airport located in the vicinity of a VOR station by flying outbound from the station along the radial on which the airport is located (airplane 2A or 4).

### Determining Your Direction or Bearing From a Station

Tune in and aurally identify the station. We have tuned Columbia VOR (Fig. 2-9).

Rotate the CS until the L-R needle is centered and the to-from indicator shows "from" (airplanes 2 and 3). The setting of the CS represents the radial on which you are located (185 degrees for airplane 2 and 220 degrees nor airplane 3. Draw the radial on the chart and you will have your Line of Position Visualize your position. You are south and southwest, respectively, from the station. You do not know how far south or southwest of the station without additional information.

### The Advantage In Knowing Your Bearing From a Station

See Fig. 2-9. If you are flying a course from VOR to the Augusta VOR station (airplanes 1,2,3 and 4), you can determine your position along this route by finding your bearing from a VOR station on either side of your route (airplanes 2 and 3). If you are uncertain of your position, you may determine your bearing from two or more VOR stations. Draw these radials on the chart and your position will be where they intersect. Actually, you are doing this in Fig. 2-9. You are maintaining a specific radial *from* Vance VOR and *to* Augusta VOR. You determine your radial from the Colombia VOR. The intersection of the two radials is your position. You would keep your radio tuned to Vance during the first half of the flight and to Augusta during the second half, except when determining your radial from the Colombia VOR. Knowledge of your exact position during the second half of this flight becomes very important so

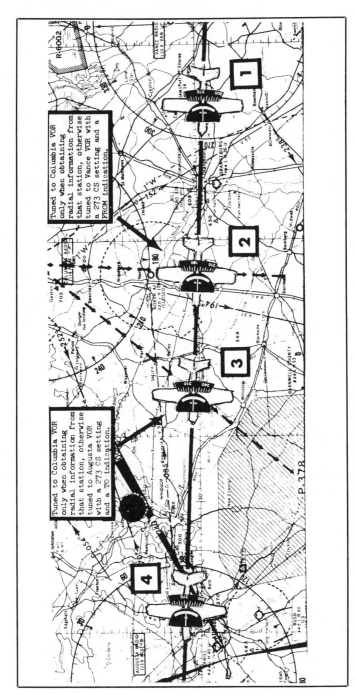

Fig. 2-9. Determining your direction or bearing from a station.

53

that you may be sure of avoiding the prohibited area southwest of airplane 3.

## Procedure When Your Position Relative to a VOR Station Is Unknown

Tune in and aurally identify the station (Liberal VOR, see Fig. 2-10). Turn the CS until the L-R needle is centered and "From" appears on the to-from indicator (airplane 1). Remember, the heading of your aircraft will not affect the reading of the to-from indicator. The resulting setting of the CS tells you the radial on which the aircraft is located or, in other words, your bearing or direction *from* the station. If the CS reads 225 degrees, you are southwest of the station; if the CS re ds 090 degrees, you are east of the station, etc. In Fig. 2-10 you are on the 093-degree radial; however, you do not know how far east of the station you are.

Visualize your position relative to the station—always do this! After determining your bearing and visualizing your position, if you wish to fly directly away from the station along the radial on which you are located, you merely turn to a heading approximately the same as the setting on the CS (airplane 2). The L-R needle will have proper sensing and you should make corrections (toward the needle) to keep the L-R needle centered.

After determining your bearing and visualizing your position, if you wish to fly directly *to* the station from your present position, you rotate the CS (approximately 180 degrees) until the L-R needle is centered and the to-from indicates "to". Turn the aircraft to a heading approximately the same as the setting on the CS and make corrections (toward the needle) to keep the L-R needle centered (airplane 3). Since the heading of the aircraft and the setting on the CS are approximately the same, the L-R needle will have proper sensing.

### Lost Procedure

It seems that most who fly cross-country are destined to lose their way or become "temporarily misplaced" at one time or another. Therefore, we should give some forethought to procedures and practices that may be used to lead wandering birdmen out of the wilderness. Confining our problems to the typical VFR dilemma, we can start with the general and then proceed to more specific rules.

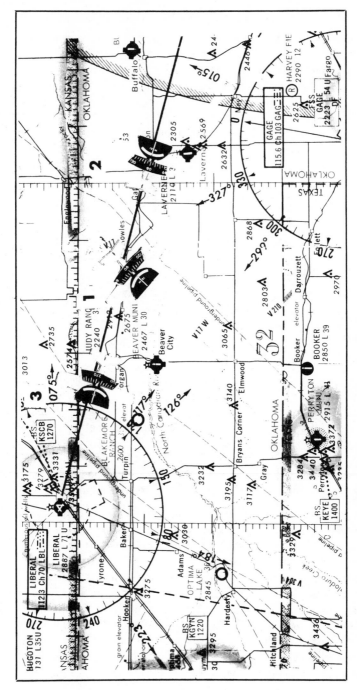

Fig. 2-10. Procedure when your position relative to a VOR station is unknown.

First of all, don't fight the problem. Try to solve it:

—Analyze and evaluate as to fuel availability and its consumption rate. How much longer can you fly with the fuel you have? Don't stretch it; a conservative estimate is best.

—Is the weather good, bad, improving or deteriorating?

—Are operating systems functioning? Do you have lights, radio and survival gear?

—Is the terrain open, flat, mountainous, swampy, semi-desert, or sparsely or heavily populated?

—How many hours of daylight remain? How much cross-country experience do you have?

—Is help available if needed?

It only takes a minute to calmly and methodically assess your situation. Spend that minute. Then, if you have planned for such a problem, you already know what to do. Just do it; and you'll be too busy to panic.

Let's say you have no radio and your position is unknown. You are low on fuel. You have inadequate experience. Darkness is imminent. The weather is deteriorating and the engine or other critical system is malfunctioning. The solution is to get the plane on the ground.

Most accidents are the product of mistakes which have multiplied over a period of time. Getting lost is no exception. Don't push your luck. It may well be that in doing so you have added the *final* mistake. It's much better to be on the ground than in it. Find a usable field and land. Don't waste time looking for the perfect place; anything usable will do. Never fly until the fuel runs out, or until it is too dark. Under any of the above mentioned conditions, you want to get down under control and with maximum visibility.

Assume you have no radio and your position is unknown. You have plenty of fuel and there is plenty of daylight. Weather is good. You must use knowledge of your last known position, elapsed time, approximate wind and ground speed (airspeed is better than nothing) to establish how far you may have traveled since your last check point. Use this distance as a radius and draw a semi-circle on your chart. For example, you estimate your ground speed at 120 kts. If you have been flying 20 minutes since your last check point, then the no-wind radius of your semi-circle is 40 nm projected along the direction of your estimated track. If you believe your wind is from the right, then you are most probably in the left quadrant of your semi-circle. Of course, unless you are sure about the wind, you cannot ignore the right quadrant.

If you've been flying a reasonably steady compass heading and noting checkpoints, you don't have much of a problem. But if you've been flying with your brain "up and locked" too long, your search may be more difficult.

In either case, uncage your eyeballs and begin some first class pilotage. Often, you'll be closer to your intended track than you think. First, look for something big. Don't concern yourself with the minute or trivial at this point unless nothing better is available. Usually, there will be linear features such as rivers, mountain ranges or prominent highways and railroads easy to spot and identify.

Once you have utilized such features to the fullest extent possible, double check all landmarks. Compare and analyze, matching identifiable features with their counterparts on your Sectional or WAC chart. But don't go down on the deck and stay there. As a general rule, it is both safer and easier at higher altitudes (Fig. 2-11).

You must always carry up-to-date charts, including those adjacent to the one in use. Everything which appears on the chart will usually be on the ground, but no chart is so detailed that everything you can see on the ground can also be found on the chart.

### Emergency Procedures With Radio

If you have two-way radio, you have something over 40,000 FAA traffic controllers, tower operators and FSS specialists—to

Fig. 2-11. The 1964 Cessna 182 cruises at 159 mph (139 kts) with 230-hp. By 1980, it had gained 160 lbs in weight and five knots in cruising speed (courtesy of Cessna Aircraft Company).

say nothing of the military controllers—about the country to re-orient you, give you a fix, steer or whatever assistance is appropriate. With good air/ground communications, you can't remain lost for long.

Don't wait until you're down to your last 15 minutes of fuel before asking for help. It isn't necessary to go to the emergency frequency 121.5, create a lot of paper work and perhaps risk a violation to get yourself out of trouble. When in doubt, ask for help and ask early.

There's no single system to get you off the hook when you get lost. If you have radios operating, the best procedure is to grab some altitude and get an Omni (VOR) or ADF bearing. Climb high enough to reach any two stations. Plot them on your chart and you have it made. If you can reach only one station, tell them your problem and then home on that station. Don't fly in circles.

The Airman's Information Manual (AIM) lists three procedures for a pilot in any emergency phase (uncertainty, alert and distress). With two-way radio operative, he should contact a controlling agency, give the nature of the problem and his intentions. If unable to contact any ground station on assigned frequencies, transmit and receive using the 121.5 emergency frequency.

First of the standard emergency procedures, with two-way radio operating, is as follows:

● Transmit "Mayday, Mayday, Mayday" (if distress), or "Pan, Pan, Pan" (if uncertain or alert).
● Aircraft identification repeated three times.
● Type of aircraft.
● Position or estimated position (state which).
● Compass heading, true or magnetic (state which).
● True air speed or estimated true air speed.
● Altitude.
● Fuel remaining, in hours and minutes.
● Nature of distress.
● Pilot's intentions.
● Assistance desired (fix, steer, bearing, escort, etc.).
● Two 10-second dashes with mike button, followed by aircraft identification once, and "over."

Comply with instructions received. Accept the "communications control" offered to you by the ground station, silence interfering radio stations, and do not change frequency or change to another station unless absolutely necessary.

My copy of AIM still lists another emergency procedure, a tri-angular pattern that one is supposed to fly in cases of radio failure or other distress situations when on instruments or on top of the weather. I will not detail it here because ground stations simply do not respond to these patterns. By the time this reaches print, that procedure will probably be discontinued.

The FAA recommends that you remember the "Four Cs" when lost (or perhaps into weather beyond your ability to handle). *Confess* your predicament to any ground station and don't wait too long. *Communicate* with your ground link and pass as much of the distress message as possible in your first communication. *Climb* if possible for better radar and DF detection. *Comply* with the instructions you receive.

One point should be kept in mind. Ground-based radar is not maintained for the purpose of getting careless pilots out of trouble. Its purpose is to aid controllers in expediting the safe flow of air traffic. As far as ATC is concerned, they must assume that every pilot is competent to perform the navigation attendant to whatever flight is undertaken. Nevertheless, if the time should ever come when you need ground-based radar, use it.

Fig. 2-12. A pair of Burt Rutan's highly efficient designs. Many believe that the safety and performance of Rutan's airplanes will force other aircraft manufacturers to follow his lead (courtesy of Don Downie).

## Performance Charts

Performance charts describe or predict the performance of an aircraft under a given set of conditions. They may be in tabular or graph form. These charts will be in the aircraft Owner's Manual, furnished by the aircraft's manufacturer. The information obtainable includes takeoff and landing distance (ground roll, and to clear an obstacle 50 feet high, fuel consumption, rate-of-climb, true airspeed, etc, for any given condition.

It isn't necessary to consult the airplane's performance charts before every takeoff and landing (Fig. 2-12). Obviously, if you are operating a light airplane from a 10,000 foot runway, it doesn't matter much how long your takeoff or landing run happens to be. But there is a dividing line, and you must be able to compute it in advance when smaller airfields and other conditions can conspire to make it a tight squeeze. Density altitude, gross weight, wind, condition of the runway and the kind of airplane you are flying all make a difference. When should you check the airplane's performance charts? Anytime you are in doubt.

As an example of what the charts can do for you, assume that you are at an airfield the elevation of which is 4,000 feet above sea level. There's no wind. The temperature is 24 degrees C (75 degrees F). Maximum gross weight for this airplane is 2,300 pounds. The performance chart shows a predicted ground run under these conditions of 1,380 feet, with 2,065 feet required to clear an obstacle 50 feet high. However, the chart also shows that these distances would be reduced by 30 percent to 966 feet and 1,445 feet, respectively, by reducing the gross weight by 200 pounds.

The performance charts will give any number of performance figures for varying conditions. Those in graph form will, of course, cover all temperature ranges and aircraft loading conditions. Other performance charts offer climb speeds and fuel consumption. Still others provide cruise and range performance that will allow you to select the most efficient rpm settings for a given altitude.

One final word about aircraft performance charts/graphs— it's wise to always pad them a little. These figures were worked out by the airplane manufacturer's engineering test pilots— highly proficient aviators—in brand new airplanes. You should assume that you may not be able to get quite as much from the airplane as they did.

## Airspeed and Groundspeed

*Airspeed* is the only speed which holds any significance for an airplane. Once it is off the ground, an airplane feels nothing out its own speed through the air. It makes absolutely no difference what its speed happens to be in relation to the ground. The aircraft in flight feels no wind. It simply proceeds, operating with the same mechanical efficiency, upwind, downwind, crosswind or in no wind at all (Fig. 2-13).

Some people seem to easily grasp this simple fact; others never do. I recently spent a fruitless half-hour trying to impart this basic bit of aeronautical knowledge to a 5,000-hour helicopter pilot. He had written a book, and in it he made the statement that, ". . .hovering in a crosswind, the wind was blowing across my rotors . . ." Since my job was to edit the book, I tried to convince this pilot that the wind could not be blowing across his rotors. If he was hovering over a given spot on the ground in a crosswind, what he was actually doing was flying sideways in the direction from which the wind was blowing.

Unfortunately, I was never able to phrase myself in a way that he understood. His nervous system had long since memorized the feel of a helicopter. He was doing all the right things with hands and feet to make a helicopter hover in a crosswind, but intellectually he literally did not know what he was doing.

A few weeks later, I edited a manuscript written by a newly-minted private pilot. This fellow wrote that, due to a "side-wind," he had been forced to fly from one city to another cross-country "holding left rudder, and my leg got very tired."

Fig. 2-13. A 1931 homebuilt design that is still built by amateur plane builders is the Pietenpol Air Camper. The airframe is all wood.

Remember, airspeed is the speed at which your airplane travels through the air. Even though the air mass through which you are traveling may also be moving (wind), the relationship of the airplane's movement to the air mass remains unchanged. This may be explained by assuming a person is walking forward at five mph inside a railroad train which is traveling 60 mph. Regardless of the train's speed, the person is walking five mph in relation to the train. If the train slows to a stop, he is still walking five mph in relation to the train. If the person turns around and walks toward the rear of the train, he continues to walk five mph in relation to the train, whatever its speed, because he is contained in the train. Similarly, you are, when airborne, contained within the air mass which supports your wings (or rotors). You will, in relation to the air mass, move through it independently of whatever velocity and direction of movement the air mass may have.

Let us further assume that our man in the train runs 15 mph toward the rear of the train while the train is moving forward at 10 mph. Another train, on a parallel track, is moving by in the opposite direction at 10 mph.

Let's consider the runner's relationship to each train. He is moving 15 mph through train A that contains him. But in relation to train B on the adjacent track (which is travelling 10 mph in the same direction he is running), he is moving at the rate of five mph—backward. If this conclusion tends to heat up your brain circuits, ask yourself how fast he is traveling in relation to train B if train B is not moving. He's traveling five mph, right?

Let's say that if our runner moves slower than 10 mph in relation to whichever train contains him, he will fall. What happens if he is able to instantly transfer from train A to train B while continuing to run 15 mph?

You got it; he will fall. He will fall because, at the instant of transition, he is moving only five mph in relation to his new environment (if train B is stopped). He is moving backward at the rate of five mph if the train B is traveling 10 mph. Perhaps this analogy will help explain the phenomenon of *wind shear*.

### Wind Shear

A wind shear occurs when two different air masses are adjacent to one another, or one above the other, and the two move at different velocities and/or in different directions. A weather condition knows as an *inversion* may set up this situation. The classic example of a trouble-causing wind shear is one that exists over or near an airport at low altitude.

Usually, an inversion is created when a warm, moist air mass moves over a relatively colder air mass. In a typical case, nighttime radiational cooling forms a pocket of very cold air in a valley or basin where the airport is located. This air, only a few hundred feet thick, is beneath a moving layer of warmer air. Due to the difference in speed between the warm air and the trapped air, a narrow zone of wind shear forms their boundaries. An aircraft penetrating this zone may suffer a quick and substantial loss of airspeed. If the transition from one air mass to the other leaves the aircraft in the air mass that is moving in the same direction as the aircraft, this abrupt change can well cost more altitude than the pilot has to spare.

## Wind and Groundspeed

So far we have not mentioned *groundspeed* because groundspeed has nothing to do with why or how an airplane flies. Groundspeed is useful only in navigation and fuel planning. As we have just seen, wind has no effect on an airplane's airspeed—except in a wind shear. Wind does, of course, affect groundspeed.

Again consider the case of a man walking inside a railroad train. If the train is moving 60 mph in relation to the ground and the man is walking forward inside the train at a speed of five mph, he is actually traveling 65 mph in relation to the ground. Conversely, if he walks toward the rear of the train at a rate of five mph and the train is moving 60 mph, he is actually traveling at a rate of 55 mph in relation to the ground (groundspeed). Similarly, an airplane flying at an airspeed of 120 mph through an air mass that is traveling in the same direction at 20 mph will have a groundspeed of 140 mph. After turning around so that the wind is now a "headwind" of 20 mph, the airplane would be traveling 100 mph in relation to the ground, or with a 40 mph reduction in groundspeed. Since groundspeed is not a factor in stalling speed, the airplane is no closer to a stall flying into the wind than flying with the wind.

Groundspeed is not always changed by an amount equal to the wind velocity. Groundspeed is increased or decreased by the full amount of the wind velocity only when a direct headwind or direct tailwind exists. As the angle between the nose of the airplane and the wind direction increases (up to approximately

90 degrees on either side), the headwind component decreases, resulting in a gradual reduction in the effect of wind on the airplane's groundspeed. As the angle increases from approximately a 90-degree crosswind to 180 degrees, the tailwind component increases with a corresponding increase in groundspeed.

Wind always takes more from you than it gives back. A cross-country round trip, with a headwind for half the flight and a tailwind of equal velocity for the remaining half of the flight, is not the same as a round trip with no wind.

The reason for this is that you are exposed to the headwind for a longer period of time. For example, let's say that your normal true airspeed in cruising flight is 100 kts. You fly a round trip between two cities that are 100 nm apart. Outbound you have a 20-kt headwind, and on the return flight a 20-kt tailwind. Therefore, outbound you have a groundspeed of 80 kts, which means that the first half of your trip requires one hour and 15 minutes. One the return flight you will have a groundspeed of 120 kts, which results in a flight of 50 minutes duration. The 20-kt wind took away 15 minutes flying against it, and gave back only 10 minutes flying with it.

### Drift

An airplane in flight does not necessarily travel in the direction it is headed. The airplane moves forward because of engine thrust pulling (or pushing) in the direction it is headed. However, if the air mass containing the airplane is also moving (wind), the airplane, in addition to its forward movement, is carried in the same direction and at the same speed as the air mass which supports it. Thus, we have two directional forces acting upon the airplane—the *thrust component* and the *wind component*. If the thrust is moving the airplane forward toward the east, and the air mass is moving it sideward toward the south (a north wind), then the resultant path over the ground will be east-southeasterly. This sideward movement of the airplane in relation to the ground, caused by the wind, is called *drift*.

We must always compensate for drift in order to make good a desired course over the ground. We must head the airplane into the wind at an angle at which the direction of the thrust component will compensate for the wind component. This wind correction angle should be sufficient to make the resultant path over the ground (ground track) coincide with the desired course over the ground. The necessary heading can be determined by trial and error, or by wind triangle computations based on true airspeed, true course, and wind direction and speed.

You may also calculate the wind correction angle with a pocket flight computer such as the venerable E-6B, or Jeppesen CSG. If you really are to comprehend what these circular slide rules are doing for you, you should first master the simple *wind*

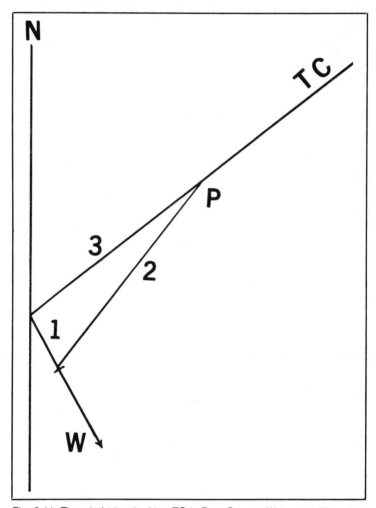

Fig. 2-14. The wind triangle. Line TC is True Course; W is wind. The wind line at 1 is wind velocity. Line 2 represents airspeed. Since the wind triangle is drawn to scale, the angle at P is wind correction angle, and line 3 is ground speed.

*triangle* (Fig. 2-14). If your ground instructor has not or did not teach you to draw wind triangles to determine wind correction angles, he cheated you. If he did not administer periodic tests to see how much of the course material you were absorbing, he did not do his job. A principal cause of the unacceptable general aviation accident rate of the immediate past is directly traceable to the pilots' lack of understanding of the *basics*.

On the ground, wind has a different effect on an airplane. In addition to being moved forward through the air by its own power, an airplane in flight is carried in the same direction and at the same speed as the movement of the air mass that supports it. Since it is free to move with the air mass, the airplane in flight does not "feel" this movement of the surrounding air (except when wind shear or sudden lulls or gusts are encountered). Therefore, after the proper correction for drift is established, control pressure need not be maintained for directional control. However, during ground operation, the friction of the airplane's wheels in contact with the ground resists drifting, creating a pivot point at the main wheels. Since a greater portion of the airplane's surface is presented to a crosswind aft of the wheels than is presented forward of the wheels, airplane tends to "weathervane" or turn into any crosswind. In this case, corrective control pressures must be applied and maintained for directional control on the ground. This weathervaining occurs in tricycle-gear airplanes as well as tailwheel aircraft.

### Crosswind Takeoffs and Landings

While the airplane is free of the ground, the wind has the effect as explained in preceding paragraphs for an airplane in flight. However, on takeoffs and landings an airplane should never be allowed to contact the ground while drifting or while headed in a direction other than that in which it is moving over the ground. Unless proper action is taken to prevent this from occurring, severe side stresses will be imposed on the landing gear. A sudden swerve or ground loop may occur. When this develops, we have an almost uncontrollable situation and, consequently, a serious accident potential.

Takeoffs and landings in certain crosswind conditions are inadvisable or even dangerous. If the crosswind is great enough to warrant an extreme drift correction, you may well have a hazardous condition. Asways consider the takeoff or landing capabilities with respect to the reported surface wind conditions, the available landing directions and condition of the runway itself. You can tolerate far less crosswind on an icy runway than on a dry one.

Before an airplane is type certificated by the FAA, it must be flight tested to meet certain requirements. Among these is the demonstration of being satisfactorily controllable with no exceptional degree of skill or alertness on the part of the pilot in a 90-degree crosswind velocity of two-tenths of the airplane's stalling speed with power off and gear and flaps down. If stalling speed is 54 kts, then the airplane must be capable of being landed in an 11-knot 90-degree crosswind. Your airplane should have a placard containing this information.

## Factors Affecting Stalling Speed

All stalls are caused by exceeding the critical angle of attack. Knowing this particular fact does not necessarily help the pilot. It is more important for the pilot to know what factors are likely to contribute to or cause this angle of attack to be exceeded.

It is not necessary for the airplane to have a relatively low airspeed in order for it to stall (Fig. 2-15). An airplane can be stalled at any airspeed. All that is necessary is to exceed the

Fig. 2-15. The Champion Citabria (top) is a popular sport/trainer that evolved from the 7AC Champion of the forties. Inverted is the Decathlon version which has a symmetrical airfoil and is intended for advanced aerobatics (courtesy of Bellanca Aircraft Corporation).

critical angle of attack (somewhere around 18 degrees in most airplanes). This can be done at any airspeed if the pilot applies abrupt or excessive back pressure on the elevator control. A stall that occurs at a relatively high speed is referred to as an *accelerated* or *high speed stall.*

It is not necessary for an airplane to have a relatively high pitch attitude in order for it to stall. An airplane can be stalled in any attitude. Again, all that is necessary is to exceed the critical angle of attack, This can occur in any attitude by application of abrupt or excessive back pressure on the elevator control.

Weight affects stalling speed. As the weight of the airplane is increased, the stall speed increases. Due to the greater weight, a higher angle of attack must be maintained to produce the additional lift to support the additional weight in flight. Therefore, the critical angle of attack will be reached at a higher airspeed when loaded to maximum gross weight than flying solo with no baggage.

The aircraft's center of gravity (CG) location also affects stalling speed. The farther forward the center of gravity, the higher the stalling speed. The farther aft the CG, the lower the stalling speed. But this doesn't mean that the weight should be distributed to move the CG as far to the rear as possible! That could present problems with stability that far outweigh any advantage obtained by the decrease in stalling speed. Weight and balance data are contained in the Owner's Manual of every aircraft and must be religiously adhered to. It is possible to load an airplane so far outside its loading envelope that it cannot be flown. It is possible to load an airplane so badly that, although it may get off the ground, it could be close to uncontrollable, a situation that would get progressively worse as fuel was consumed. You must know how to figure weight and balance problems for any airplane of which you act as pilot in command.

### Flaps and Stalling Speed

The use of flaps reduces stalling speed. This may be readily verified by checking the color coding on any airspeed indicator. The lower airspeed limit of the white arc (power-off stalling speed with gear and flaps in the landing configuration) is less than the lower airspeed limit of the green arc (power-off stalling speed in clean configuration).

This is important to you in that, when making no-flap landings, a higher indicated airspeed (IAS) should be maintained than when landing with flaps. The manufacturer's recommendations should be adhered to regarding approach speeds in various configurations.

## Frost, Snow or Ice On the Wings

You must fully understand that a light accumulation of frost on the wings significantly increases stalling speed. Every year, a few airplanes are lost on takeoff because the pilots simply do not believe that an "insignificant" layer of frost on wings can possibly make much difference (Fig. 2-16). Obviously, it isn't the weight of the frost that poses the danger. Instead, it is the drag the frost creates. It's like having your wings' upper surfaces covered with sandpaper. Those thousands of tiny protrusions create a lot of drag. Ice or snow not only add weight, but disrupt the smooth flow of air over the wings, thereby decreasing lift. To make up for lost lift, a higher angle of attack must be used or a higher speed must be attained on the takeoff roll. The runway may not be long enough to attain the necessary speed. Even though the airplane may become airborne, it could be so close to the stall speed that it would not be possible to maintain flight once the airplane climbs above the shallow zone where ground effect prevails. A good rule-of-thumb for estimating the height of ground effect at low airspeeds is one-half the airplane's wing span.

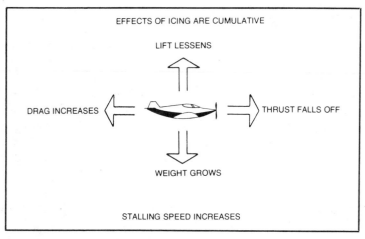

Fig. 2-16. Inflight structural icing may affect the airplane in several ways (courtesy of FAA).

## The Effect of Altitude On Airspeed

An increase in altitude has no effect on the indicated airspeed at which an airplane stalls (at altitudes normally used by general aviation aircraft). That is, for all practical purposes, the indicated stalling speed remains the same regardless of altitude. This fact is important in that the same IAS should be maintained during the landing approach regardless of the elevation or the density altitude at the airport of landing (check the aircraft's Owners Manual). If a higher than normal approach speed is used, a longer landing distance will be required. Actually, you will need extra runway anyway, because altitude *does* affect true airspeed. Since true airspeed normally increases as altitude increases (for a given indicated airspeed), then the true airspeed at which an airplane stalls generally increases with an increase in altitude. Under non-standard conditions (temperature warmer than standard), there is an additional increase in true airspeed above indicated airspeed.

The reason for this is that your airspeed indicator is a pressure instrument. It translates impact air at the pitot head into an indication of your speed through the air. Obviously, in thinner air (increases in altitude) you have to move faster through the air to get the same indicated airspeed reading that you get at a slower airspeed at a lower altitude. Since it is the volume of air over your wings that supports you at a given weight, you'll move faster to maintain that support in thinner air. But the *indicated* airspeed will remain the same.

All this is significant to you because, when landing at higher elevations or in higher density altitudes, you are operating at higher true airspeeds (and therefore higher groundspeeds) throughout the approach, touchdown and landing roll. This results in a greater distance required to clear obstacles during the approach, a longer ground roll and, consequently, the need for a longer runway. If, in addition, one should be operating under the misconception that a higher than normal indicated airspeed should be used under these conditions, the situation is further compounded due to the additional increase in groundspeed.

## Turbulence

Turbulence can cause a large increase in stalling speed. Encountering an upward vertical gust causes an abrupt change in relative wind. This results in an equally abrupt increase in angle of attack which could result in a stall. This fact is important in that, when making an approach under turbulent conditions, a higher than normal approach speed should be maintained. Also, in moderate or greater turbulence, an airplane should not be flown above maneuvering speed. At the same time, it should not be flown too far below maneuvering speed since a sudden and severe vertical gust may cause an inadvertent stall.

### Aerodynamic Loads Versus Stall Speeds

As the aerodynamic load factor increases, stalling speed increases. *Load factor* is the ratio of the load supported by the wings to actual weight of the airplane and its contents. Changes in direction cause aerodynamic loads (sometimes called "flight loads") to increase. At a load factor of two, the wings support twice the weight of the airplane; at a load factor of four, they support four times the weight of the airplane. Normal category airplanes, with a maximum gross weight of 4,000 pounds, are required to have a minimum limit load factor of 3.8. The limit load factor is the load factor an airplane can sustain without taking a permanent set in the structure. This mimimum limit load factor is attained in a constant-altitude turn at a bank of

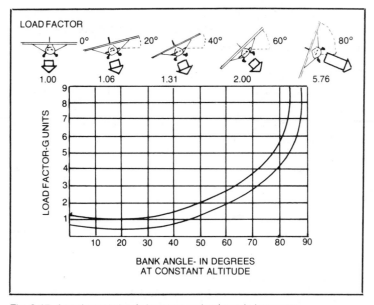

Fig. 2-17. Aerodynamic loads increase as bank angle increases.

approximately 75 degrees. The stalling speed of an airplane is doubled in a turn at this bank angle.

There are two reasons why excessively steep banks should be avoided. An airplane will stall at a much higher airspeed, and the limit load factor can be exceeded. The danger can be compounded when the nose gets down in a steep turn if the pilot attempts to raise it to the level flight attitude without shallowing the bank, since the load factor may be increased even more (Fig. 2-17). This is the situation that generally exists when, due to disorientation, the pilot enters a diving spiral (often referred to as the *graveyard spiral* and attempts to recover with elevator pressure alone.

### Maneuvers That Increase the Load Factor

Any maneuvering of the airplane that produces an increase in centrifugal force will cause an increase in load factor. Turning the airplane or pulling out of a dive are examples of maneuvering that will increase the centrifugal force and thus produce an increase in load factor. When you have a combination of turning and pulling out of a dive, such as recovering from a diving spiral, you are, in effect, placing yourself in double jeopardy. This is why you must avoid high speed diving spirals. If you accidentally get into one, be careful how you recover. Turbulence can also produce large load factors. That is why an airplane should be slowed to maneuvering speed or below when encountering moderate or greater turbulence.

### Recognizing Increased Load Factors

You can recognize an increasing load factor by the feeling of increased body weight or the feeling that you are being forced down into the seat. It is the same feeling one has when riding a roller coaster at the bottom of a dip or going around a banked curve. This feeling of increased body weight is important to the pilot because it should, if it becomes excessive, have the immediate effect of a red flag being waved in his face to warn him that the airplane will now stall at a higher airpseed or that the limit load factor can be exceeded, resulting in structural failure. The rule to remember is keep the load off your self and you will never overload the airplane.

### Airspeed and the Load Factor

Speed does not, in itself, affect the load factor. However, it has a pronounced effect on how much of an increase in load factor can be produced by strong vertical gusts, or by the pilot through abrupt or excessive application of back pressure on the elevator control. This is why airspeed should be reduced to maneuvering speed or below if moderate or greater turbulence is encountered. At maneuvering speed or below, the airplane is stressed to handle any vertical gust that normally will be encountered. Also, below this speed, the pilot can make abrupt full deflection of the elevator control and not exceed the maximum load factor for which the airplane is stressed. However, it should be understood that this is possible because the airplane will stall, thus relieving the load factor. At airspeeds above maneuvering speed, abrupt full deflection of the elevator control or strong vertical gusts can cause the limit load factor to be excceeded. As airspeed continues to increase above maneuvering speed, the limit load factor can be exceeded with less turbulence or abrupt use or deflection of the controls.

The higher the airspeed when an airplane is stalled, the greater the load factor. When an airplane stalls at a slow airspeed, the load factor will be very little more than one. When stalled at an airspeed twice as great as the normal stall speed, the limit load factor for normal category airplanes will probably be exceeded.

**3**

# The Weather Decision

It was at Oshkosh during the annual EAA Fly-In. The day's activities were over and a carload of us had gone into town for dinner. The subject of conversation at our table had turned to aviation weather after my wife Rene described, with some humor, her sensations and reactions as she crouched under a desk in a hospital hallway while an Oklahoma tornado passed over, taking certain portions of the building along with it.

We had a few more laughs as others recounted weather experiences; and then an airline captain (who is into powered hang gliding as a hobby), made an off-hand observation that later came back to us and set us to thinking. "I sometimes get the impression," he said, "that a lot of private pilots regard the study of weather as a sort of levy imposed by the FAA in return for an airman's certificate. It is something to be borne, like taxes, and they tend to give it as little thought as possible."

Of course, we agree with Captain Jeff Griffin. Like any simple truth, once someone puts it into words it becomes obvious. The paradox is that, despite the fact that at least four out of 10 major accidents in general aviation are weather-related many of us still don't take this subject very seriously.

Perhaps it is only natural; after all, weather is a complex science. Besides, pilots have long had all those nice and know-ledgeable specialists in the Flight Service Stations and the weather offices to spell out the meaning of their carefully drawn prognostic charts.

### Forecasting Limitations

Nevertheless, when flying cross-country we are sometimes reminded that there are a lot of gaps in the weather reporting system. We soon come to realize that, when we most need some exact information about a given portion of the sky (the portion we are about to enter), what we are able to get isn't all that exact. True, in ground school we sat through several hours of a very entertaining slide show designed to impart a certain understanding of the mechanics of weather. Out here on our own over strange terrain, though, we can't seem to relate whatever we recall from those colorful slides to what we see ahead of us through the windshield (Fig. 3-1).

Usually we radio the nearest FSS for an evaluation of the situation, but they can't cover all bases for us. They have no way of knowing how much judgment, experience or ability we possess, and they often have some uncertainties of their own. For example, situations that cannot be predicted with acceptable accuracy are: the time freezing rain will begin, location and occurrence of severe turbulence, location and occurrence of heavy icing, tornadoes, ceilings of 100 feet or less before they exist, thunderstorms which have not visibly begun to form, ice fog and the position of a hurricane center to nearer than 100 miles for more than 12 hours in advance.

### Accuracy Factors

In other words, the worse it is, the less the weatherman knows about it. Of the situations the weatherman can forecast usefully, here are the accuracy factors and limitations:

—A forecast of good flying weather (ceiling 3,000 feet or more and visibility three miles or greater) is usually dependable up to 12 hours in advance.

Fig. 3-1. Author Christy, with wife Rene (in white suit) and Julia Lee Downie, wife of aviation-writer Don Downie, and a Piper Turbo Lance, which is Albuquerque-bound—if the thunderstorms can be avoided.

75

Fig. 3-2. Cross-country at night in rain; hard IFR (courtesy of Beech Aircraft Corporation).

—A forecast of poor flying weather (ceiling below 1,000 feet and visibility less than one mile) is much less accurate 12 hours in advance, but is 80 percent accurate for a three to four-hour period.

—Ceiling and visibility figures should beyond be highly suspect the first two or three hours of the forecast period.

—Forecasts of poor flying conditions are most reliable when there is a distinct weather system such as a front, or trough, precipitation, etc., although there is a general tendency to forecast these on the optimistic side.

—Weather associated with fast-moving cold fronts and squall lines is the most difficult to forecast accurately.

—Surface visibility forecasts are less reliable than predicted ceilings. Snow reduces visibility forecasts to pure guesswork.

As you can see from the above FAA study, poor flying conditions are the hardest to predict. Such forecasts deteriorate rapidly. This means that every pilot should be able to do a certain amount of instant forecasting on his own. No, you don't need a degree in meteorology. Simply identify the weather hazards to flight, and learn to recognize the symptoms. Then it may be possible to resolve the "go, no-go" decision with some definite guidelines (Fig. 3-2 through 3-4).

## Fog

First, let's identify the hazards and, briefly, their causes. These are, broadly stated, *lack of visibility, turbulence, icing, hail* and *strong surface winds*. Singly, or together in storms, these are the hazards or threats to safe flight.

Lack of visibility may be caused by one of several kinds of fog, clouds, storms, snow, haze, smog and dust. Ideal atmospheric conditions for the formation of fog are high relative humidity (small spread between temperature and dew point), plenty of condensation nuclei, light surface wind and a cooling process to start the condensation. *Ground fog* actually is radiation fog and forms on clear, calm nights when the ground cools the air in contact with it to the dew point temperature. It is usually shallow, favors level ground and is usually gone by 10 a.m.

*Advection fog* is coastal fog and forms when moist air moves in over colder ground or water. *Upslope fog* is formed when moist, stable air is forced up a sloping land surface. *Steam fog* forms over water when cold air moves in over much warmer water and intense evaporation results.

## Clouds

Clouds provide you with visible evidence of what the atmosphere is doing: its movement, moisture content and stability. Looking ahead to where you will be on a cross-country flight two or three hours hence, you can anticipate developing weather if you know these three things. From the flyer's point of view,

Fig. 3-3. Cruising above 14,000 feet in an unpressurized aircraft, we are forced to don nose-bag oxygen masks (courtesy of Don Downie).

Fig. 3-4. Sunset and more showers, between Prescott, Arizona, and Needles, California (courtesy of Don Downie).

there are only two basic kinds of clouds: *cumulus* (Cu) and *stratus* (St). There are several varieties of each and many sub-species. But the lower stratus clouds and the *cumulonimbus* (Cb) or *thunderhead* will be to blame for most of your weather problems.

In stable air, stratus forms in layers with little or no vertical development. It is shapeless, fog that is above the surface. Stratus may be a few hundred feet deep or a few thousand. It may form behind slow-moving cold fronts or ahead of warm fronts, and in the latter case often produces inversions. At or above the freezing level, stratus presents a real danger of structural icing. When preceding a warm front, stratus layers may conceal imbedded thunderheads if the air mass is conditionally unstable (Fig. 3-5).

Although most cumulus clouds do not become thunderheads, all cumulonimbus clouds are born of cumulus. When the air is unstable (meaning the moisture/temperature ratio is out of balance), the sheep-type cumulus begin to take on vertical development and build into thunderheads. An individual thunderhead is rarely larger than 10 miles in diameter, and its life cycle is from about 30 to 90 minutes. However, it is common for thunderheads to develop in clusters, with individual Cbs in various stages of development. Such a system may span 100 miles and last for six to eight hours.

All thunderheads are characterized by strong updrafts during their building and mature stages which extend from near the earth's surface to several thousand feet above the visible cloud top. The greatest vertical speed occurs late in the building stage, in the upper portion of the cloud, when it may reach 3,000 fpm or more. An aircraft venturing near the base of a building or mature thunderhead can easily be carried into the cloud.

The thunderhead usually matures about 10 or 15 minutes after it has built up past the freezing level. At this point, rain and/or hail begins and downdrafts start to develop in the middle regions of the cloud. Velocities vary but may reach 2,500 fpm. Throughout the mature stage, the downdrafts continue to develop while the updrafts weaken. Finally, the entire thunderhead becomes an area of downdrafts and the dissipating stage begins. Rainfall gradually ceases. The lower level of the thunderhead often becomes stratiform in appearance, and its top develops the characteristic anvil shape (Fig. 3-6).

Fig. 3-5. Fracto-cumulus as seen from the ground at Flagstaff, Arizona (courtesy of Don Downie).

Fig. 3-6. We took this shot of a mature thunderhead from the cabin of a jetliner flying at 31,000 feet. The First Officer agreed that it was more than 50 miles away and probably topping 50,000 feet.

Thunderheads may occasionally build to 60,000 feet or more. An average thunderhead will reach 35,000 feet. Height of the tops is an indication of the violence contained within the cloud and size of the hail. Bases may be as low as a 1,000 feet or less.

*Orographic thunderstorms* develop over mountains when wind forces moist, unstable air upslope. Identification of storms from the windward side of the mountains is often difficult because stratus and stratocumulus clouds below frequently hide them from view (Fig. 3-7).

### Warm Fronts

*Warm fronts* are seldom as well defined as cold fronts. The cloud system will extend from the front's surface position to about 500 to 700 miles ahead of it. If the warm air mass is moist and stable, the sequence of cloud types as it approaches will be, first, *high cirrus*, then *cirrostratus*, followed by *altostratus* and *nimbostratus*. Precipitation will gradually increase until the frontal zone on the surface passes (Fig. 3-8).

If the warm air mass is moist and conditionally unstable, altocumulus and cumulonimbus will be imbedded in the low and middle-level stratus clouds and probably won't be visible from below. In addition to turbulence resulting from the air's instability, there's a danger of structural icing above the freezing level throughout this cloud system. Carburetor ice should be expected

Fig. 3-7. Orographic thunderstorms are formed when unstable air is pushed up a mountain and reaches an altitude where its moisture condenses.

in moist air at any temperature between 10 degrees C and 25 degrees C. Warm fronts, stable or unstable, usually present the flyer with plenty of problems, with lack of visibility and low ceilings being the main ones.

### Cold Fronts

Ordinarily, cold fronts bring a sharp change in weather and some of the most hazardous flying conditions. Here are the sequence of events with the passage of the cold front. First, the

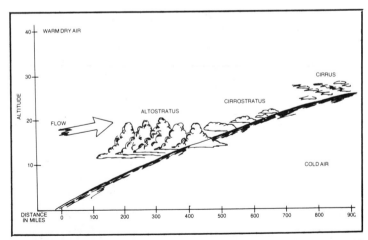

Fig. 3-8. Warm front. These systems are normally less violent than cold fronts, but bring reduced visibility to a much wider area.

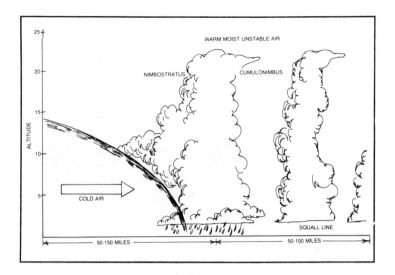

Fig. 3-9. Cold front. These weather systems usually travel 300-400 miles per day in summer and about 500 miles per day in winter.

southerly winds in the warm air ahead of the front will increase. Then altocumulus clouds appear on the horizon in the direction from which the front is approaching. Next, the clouds lower, and rain begins as the cumulonimbus move in. As the front passes, the wind will shift to a westerly or northerly direction. Rapid clearing will follow with both temperature and dew point falling (Fig. 3-9).

Cold fronts move faster in winter than in summer. A fast-moving cold front (up to 40 mph or more) will be more violent, and most of the cloudiness and precipitation will be located just ahead of it. The sky usually clears quickly after its passage, with colder temperatures and gusty, turbulent surface winds. Visibility will be good in the wake of a fast-moving cold front, but the air is often a bit bumpy.

A broad cloud pattern is produced in the warm air as it wedges upward. These clouds will extend well *behind* the surface position of a slow-moving cold front. If the warmer air being displaced is stable, these will be stratus clouds. If the warmer air is moist and conditionally unstable, these will be cumulus-type clouds, frequently developing into thunderheads.

## Squall Line Thunderstorms

Squall line thunderstorms are similar to those along a cold front though usually more violent. Cloud bases often are lower and the tops higher. The most severe conditions, such as heavy hail, destructive winds and tornadoes, generally are associated with squall line thunderstorms and are the most intense during the late afternoon and evening. Squall lines often develop about 50 to 300 miles ahead of fast-moving cold fronts. Squall lines usually form rapidly. Sometimes a series of them will precede a cold front. Frontal activity, however, isn't absolutely necessary to the formation of a squall line. A line of thunderheads may be born of, say, a low pressure trough, along strong wind shear lines, or where sea breezes converge against mountain barriers.

Obviously, the only thing to do about squall lines is to avoid them. That's not easy if you're not paying attention, because thunderheads cannot be predicted with acceptable accuracy until they have actually begun to form. So, clearly, you have to be aware of the conditions that are likely to produce them (Figs. 3-10 and 3-11).

It should be noted that weather along fronts is not always severe. Flying conditions may vary from fairly good to impossible. The severity of a front depends upon the amount of moisture available, the degree of stability of the air being lifted, speed of the frontal movement, and the amount of temperature and moisture contrast between the two air masses.

Fig. 3-10. Weather radar is now available for private aircraft. This installation is on a Cessna Skymaster.

## Turbulence

Turbulence has four main causes: vertically moving air in convective currents, air moving around or over mountains or other obstructions, wind shear and the passage of a large aircraft. You are familiar with convective currents that cause bumpiness in the lower altitudes during warm weather. They are local in nature, with both ascending and descending currents. For every rising current there must be a compensating downward current, although the descending currents may cover a broader area and possess less velocity. When sufficient moisture is present, this process will produce cumulus clouds. If the air is unstable, the cumulus will take on vertical buildup. You know what that can lead to.

Turbulence that results from air near the surface flowing over rough terrain, trees, buildings and hills may set up tricky situations for lightplanes during landing and takeoff operations. Such turbulence is of small consequence when the wind is light. In wind speeds exceeding 20 kts, though, the flow may be broken up into irregular eddies that can persist downwind to create a hazard in the landing area.

Mountain ridges can produce some especially dangerous turbulence. If the air is stable, wind blowing up the windward slope is usually fairly smooth. However, as the wind spills down the leeward side it produces downdrafts and turbulence. Allow for this when approaching mountain ridges against the wind. Winds usually blow in the direction of the passes and valleys, rather than with the general wind flow, and will be stronger and more turbulent than the general wind flow. If winds are strong, you need at least 2,000 feet between you and the ridge for a reasonably safe crossing. Climb to crossing altitude well before reaching the mountains to avoid trying to climb in a downdraft. When possible, approach the ridge at a 45-degree angle anytime you have doubts about your aircraft's ability to get across with sufficient margin. That makes it easier to turn away when the situation appears too hairy, whereas the 180-degree turn required by a direct approach could itself prove a mite too interesting. Once over the ridge, fly directly away from it.

## Standing Waves

Sometimes called "mountain waves," these waves are created when winds in excess of 50 kts blow approximately perpendicular to a mountain range. The resulting turbulence may

Fig. 3-11. Weather radar display is mounted on the center pedestal of this Skymaster.

be extreme, while the updrafts and downdrafts can extend far higher than the mountain peaks, with large waves forming on the leeward side and extending upward into the tropopause. Standing waves are found over the Rockies and Sierras and have been reported over the relatively lower Appalachians (Fig. 3-12).

Crests of standing waves are sometimes marked by stationary, lens-shaped (*lenticular*) clouds. The leeward area below the peaks may contain rotor-type clouds born of the turbulent, rolling air flow.

Within the standing wave and beneath it, there will be large variations in air pressure which will result in inaccurate altimeter readings. It is not unusual to get an altimeter reading that is more than 1,000 feet higher than is actually the case.

### Wind Shear and Wake Turbulence

Either vertical or horizontal, shear is a localized condition that occurs when a stream or mass of air moves at a relatively higher velocity and/or in a direction different than the air mass directly adjacent to it. It often is encountered when climbing or descending through a temperature inversion in which wind speed and/or wind direction markedly differ between the two dissimilar masses of air.

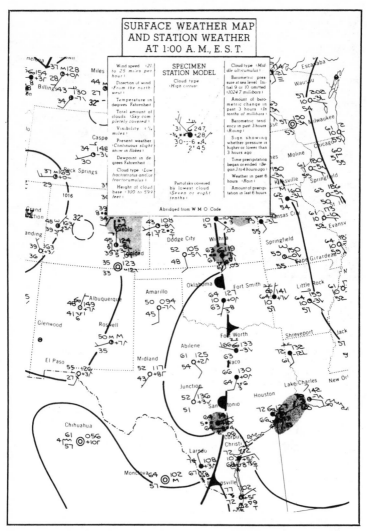

Fig. 3-12. Surface weather maps may be referenced to aid in gaining a general picture of area weather along with conditions at the destination airport (courtesy of FAA).

This condition is fairly common over the northern United States and Canada during winter where temperature inversions occur near the surface. The terrain below—usually a valley—holds cold, calm air beneath a moving layer of warmer air.

*Wake turbulence* is, in effect, a pair of tiny, twin tornadoes generated by the airfoils of large aircraft. These twisting, turbulent columns of air stream behind the big airplanes, one from each wingtip, with a downward force of about 1,500 fpm. They impose a roll-rate of up to 80 degrees per second on a light aircraft caught within one. Normally, wake turbulence is encountered only within a minute or two after the passage of a big transport airplane. However, in calm and stable air, it will not only be more severe, but may persist for five minutes or more. Wake turbulence diminishes as the general wind flow increases in velocity; but wind will also increase the distance that the turbulence may be felt (Fig. 3-13).

### Aircraft Icing

Icing is a major weather hazard to aviation. The formation of ice can dangerously distort airfoil shapes, add drag and weight, and induce structural vibration. Ice deposits of only one-half inch on the leading edge of airfoils on some aircraft reduce their lifting power as much as 50 percent, increase drag by an equal amount, and greatly increase stalling speed. One-half inch of ice can accumulate in a minute or two in some cases.

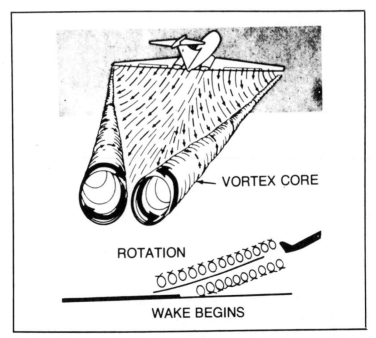

Fig. 3-13. Wake turbulence created by large aircraft can be highly dangerous to airplanes (courtesy of FAA).

An accumulation of ice on the propeller hub and blades reduces the efficiency of the propeller at best. It may create an imbalance between the blades that results in vibration severe enough to seriously threaten the engine mountings as well as the propeller itself.

Ice which forms in the engine induction system may result in power failure, as may carburetor ice. Other hazards are loss of visibility from windshield ice, impaired operation of control surfaces, brakes and landing gear, along with false indications by flight instruments due to ice in the pitot static system and loss of radio communications.

The most severe icing occurs with a free air temperature between 0 degrees Celsius and -10 degrees Celsius, though it is not uncommon at much colder temperatures. Clouds of the cumuliform type are more likely to produce serious ice formation than others, particularly if freezing rain is present. But ice can form by sublimation, so any layer of air at altitudes above the freezing level—even if clear—is a potential icing zone when its temperature-dew point spread is narrow. The accumulation rate of structural ice may vary from less than one-half inch per hour to as high as one inch per minute (for very short periods). Icing is highly unlikely at temperatures below -40 degrees Celsius.

You are concerned with three forms of ice: clear, rime and frost. Clear ice forms on structural parts of the aircraft in the shape of a blunt nose with gradual tapering toward its trailing edges. It is the most serious form because it adheres firmly and is difficult to remove.

Rime ice forms by the instantaneous freezing of small, super-cooled droplets. This traps a large amount of air, giving rime its milky, opaque appearance. It usually forms on the leading edges and protrudes forward as a sharp nose. It has little tendency to spread and is comparatively easy to remove if the aircraft is equipped with de-icing systems.

Frost can be troublesome in flight when a cold aircraft descends from a zone of subzero temperatures through a zone of warmer air with high relative humidity. Windshields are especially susceptible to frost under such conditions. Frost collecting on the upper surfaces of an aircraft parked outside overnight is, as previously mentioned, enough to render the craft unflyable.

## Go, No-Go Guidelines

What guidelines can we glean from this information that may aid in the "go, no-go" decision? The following seem to

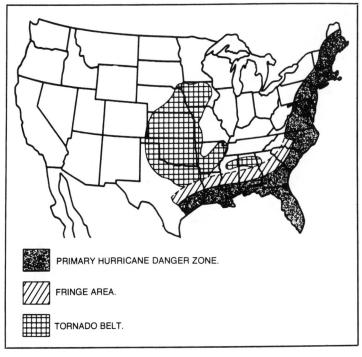

PRIMARY HURRICANE DANGER ZONE.

FRINGE AREA.

TORNADO BELT.

Fig. 3-14. Severe weather areas of the United States (courtesy of FAA).

suggest themselves. The most important thing is to honestly appraise your own abilities and limitations as a flyer. At the weather briefing, keep in mind that forecasts of poor flying weather are reasonably dependable only for the first four hours of the forecast period. The worst weather is the hardest to predict, and meteorologists tend to be optimists (Figs. 3-14 and 3-15).

Check moisture content and stability of the air mass through which you intend to fly. Temperature-dew point spreads and cloud types are indicators.

Check locations of low pressure areas, fronts and troughs. Fast-moving cold fronts usually offer quick violence, quick clearing and bumpy air. Slow-moving cold fronts may have much the same result as warm fronts, with wide frontal zones of poor visibility, precipitation, turbulence and icing above the freezing level. Not all fronts are severe, with the amount of moisture present being the primary factor.

Check winds aloft and mark the freezing level. These factors, plus visibility considerations, the altitude separation

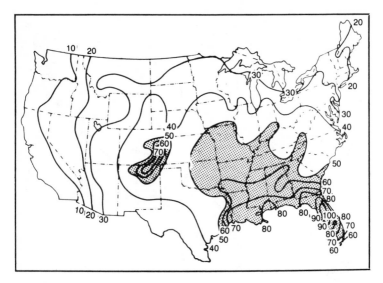

Fig. 3-15. Average number of thunderstorm days per year (courtesy of FAA).

rule and perhaps a desire to get above convective turbulence, all contribute to the selection of your cruising altitude.

When thunderstorms are present, request altitudes of bases and tops. Building thunderheads will have strong updrafts below their bases. Do not fly closer than five miles downwind of an overhanging anvil; hail sometimes is thrown from the anvil. Never fly beneath mountain thunderstorms even if the area on the other side of the mountains can be seen.

The danger of structural icing exists in a moist air mass at temperatures below freezing, particularly within cumuliform clouds. Hard glaze ice is common in cumuliform clouds. Rime ice is common in stratiform clouds.

Carburetor ice may form at temperatures as high as 25 degrees C in moist air. It is most likely when the temp and dew point approach 20 degrees C. Air intake ducts are most susceptible to icing when temperature and dew point are near 10 degrees C or lower.

Approach mountain ridges at an angle when possible, and predetermine wind direction. If clouds are present, they will usually be over the lee side. If winds are strong, climb to at least 2,000 feet above the ridge before reaching it. Winds in excess of 50 kts may create a standing wave over the lee side of high mountains. The turbulence may extend for many miles.

Table 3-1. Symbols Employed in Teletype Forecasts (courtesy of FAA).

**TERMINAL FORECASTS** contain information for specific airports on ceiling, cloud heights, cloud amounts, visibility, weather condition and surface wind. They are written in a form similar to the AVIATION WEATHER REPORT.

CEILING: Identified by the letter "C"
CLOUD HEIGHTS: In hundreds of feet above the station
CLOUD LAYERS: Stated in ascending order of height
VISIBILITY: In statute miles, but omitted if over 8 iles
SURFACE WIND: In tens of degrees and knots; omitted when less than 10.

Examples of TERMINAL FORECASTS:

C15⊕ { Ceiling,1500, broken clouds.

011/2GF   Clear, visibility one and one-half miles, ground fog

C15⊕6K { Ceiling 1500' overcast. visibility 6 miles, smoke.

C5X1/4S   Sky obscured, vertical visibility 500.' visibility one-fourth mile, moderate snow.

20⊕C70⊕3230G { Scattered clouds at 2000' ceiling 7000' overcast, surface wind 320 degrees 30 knots, gusty.

AREA FORECASTS are 12-hour forecasts of cloud and weather conditions, cloud tops, fronts, icing and turbulence for an area the size of several states. A 12-hour OUTLOOK is added. Heights of cloud tops, icing, and turbulence are above SEA LEVEL.

SIGMET advisories include weather phenomena potentially hazardous to all aircraft.

AIRMETs include weather phenomena of less severity than that covered by SIGMETs which are potentially hazardous to aircraft having limited capability due to lack of equipment or instrumentation or pilot qualifications and are at least of operational interest to all aircraft.

WINDS ALOFT FORECASTS provide a 12-hour forecast of wind conditions at selected flight levels. Temperatures will be included to all levels above 3000, except 5000 feet when this is is the lowest level forecast and 7000.

EXAMPLE:

LVL 3000 5000FT 7000 10000FT 150000FT 20000FT 25000FT
MKC 2222 2220 # 19 2220 2414 # 10 2713 # 01 2815—09 2815—17

300FT (MSL) 22012 22KT
10000FT (MSL) 240° 14KT TEMP + 10°C.

PILOTS report in-flight weather to nearest FSS. FSS.

Table 3-2. Teletype Symbols (courtesy of FAA).

*Lenticular clouds* indicate standing waves, but will not form if the air mass is dry.

Beware of wind shear associated with temperature inversions at low altitudes during landing and takeoff operations. When landing or taking off behind large aircraft, mentally picture its wake turbulence pattern and how those twin, downward-sweeping miniature tornadoes are behaving as a result of local wind conditions.

You absolutely *must* honor the obligations that go with your pilot's certificate. It often takes courage and resolve to opt for the "no-go" decision when faced with marginal and uncertain weather forecasts. Although few private pilots will take a chance with weather just for the heck of it, too many are willing to do so for what they regard as compelling reasons. These may include an important business appointment, getting home for the weekend and an obligation to passengers they can't bring themselves to disappoint (or who may think less of them for canceling). Clearly, you've got to thrust aside the *need* for going and make your decision solely on the basis of the weather conditions and the capabilities of you and your machine. Don't be suckered into the hope that you can squeeze through beneath deteriorating weather. IFR doesn't mean "I Follow Roads." See Tables 3-1 and 3-2.

**4**

# IFR Cross-Country

The following transmission (except for fictitious indentification) was received on 121.5 by Approach Control is an area of high traffic activity.

"FAA Radar, this is Skycraft 1324 at forty-five hundred on a zero six five heading. I can't locate my position. Will this heading take me to Bedrock?"

Fortunately for that pilot, this contact with radar control terminated in a safe landing—followed by suspension of his pilot's license after these additional facts emerged. Radar had observed Skycraft 1324 approaching the airport traffic area well before receiving his initial call. Approach Control had made repeated attempts to establish radio contact without success. The pilot turned on his radio only to request a vector. The pilot was directly over a metropolitan airport traffic area when two-way communications were established with Approach Control. Ceiling and visibility at the airport were 500 feet broken and one mile; PIREPS tops 12,000.

The pilot had filed no flight plane and did not hold an instrument rating. Total instrument experience was 10 hours simulated. The pilot had not checked the en route weather prior to departure. Reasons? The route was familiar, and no weather service was located on the airport of departure.

The pilot's destination was below VFR minimums at the time of his request for a heading. He did not consider the situation an emergency.

### Use and Abuse of Radar

Apart from the pilot's lack of judgment and his indifference to air traffic rules, the incident reflects a common misconception about the use of radar services. Radar is not to be considered a convenience for careless pilots who ignore the practice of careful flight planning; nor is it to be used only as a last resort for pilots who have run out of ideas.

Radar service is available to both VFR and IFR traffic. An understanding of radar functions and procedures is important to all pilots, whether instrument rated or not. Radar is used in the air traffic control system to do the following:

● Maintain surveillance of en route and terminal air traffic for more complete position information.

● Vector departing aircraft for separation and radar navigation.

● Vector en route aircraft for the most efficient use of the available airspace.

● Vector arriving aircraft for transition to final approach.

● Provide pilots with information on traffic.

● Provide radar navigation to or between established fixes.

● Provide radar navigation between airways and jet routes.

● Provide assistance to pilots of aircraft in distress.

● Provide pilots with information on storm and precipitation areas observed on the radar scopes.

● Conduct precision or surveillance approaches.

● Monitor instrument approaches.

● Coordinate the flow of VFR and IFR traffic in terminal areas.

Part 1 of the Airman's Information Manual contains general explanations of radar services. All pilots should know what to expect from radar services and what is expected of pilots by air traffic control when radar service is being provided. In other words, ground-based radar belongs to ATC and it is primarily for their use, not yours.

## ATC Clearances

If your instrument rating is still fairly new, chances are you are not yet comfortable copying an ATC clearance. Indeed, it does take time and practice.

"Flybird 22 Charlie, ATC clearance."

Don't panic. You are in no position to copy a clearance while you are busy taxiing the airplane, performing instrument checks and watching for other traffic. Simply advise the controller that you are unable to copy and will request clearance at the runup area.

The phrase "ATC clearance" normally arouses a sense of urgency, perhaps because of the way the controller announces it, at once hurried and bored. His tone of voice clearly implies that, if you are any kind of a pilot at all, you'll instantly get every word of it. Don't let him intimidate you. After all, he's being paid to serve *you*. So, don't try to copy a clearance if your hands are full at the moment; don't try to memorize what you can and then request a readback of the portions missed. Don't say you are ready to copy, that should mean at least the following:

● The aircraft is under control, preferably stopped, with parking brake set.

● You are ready with writing materials and not scrambling around a disorganized cockpit looking for your pencil, pad, etc.

● Your radios are properly tuned, with volume at a readable level.

● Appropriate route data is handy. Your requested route may not be the one specified in the clearance. If the routing is different, don't read back until you have checked it. In accepting the clearance, you also assume responsibility for compliance. Better take time to be thorough on the ground than to face confusion after takeoff.

● If you have requested a SID (Standard Instrument Departure), you have indicated to ATC that you are familiar with the SID procedure and have a copy in the cockpit.

Listed below are six actual clearances for IFR departure from the Oklahoma City area. Some are more complicated than usual, but are representative of clearances you may have to copy and execute. We reproduce them here because they will provide you with practice in your clearance shorthand if you'll have someone read them to you.

### Clearance Examples One and Two

Wiley Post Airport to Wichita Midcontinent Airport; OKC V77 ICT; departure runway 17. The following two clearances do not make use of radar which would normally be provided. "ATC clears Comanche six zero Charlie to the Wichita Midcontinent Airport via direct Tulakes Radio Beacon—the north course of the Oklahoma City localizer—Victor seventy seven. Turn left after departure; climb to intercept Victor seventy seven at five thousand or above; maintain seven thousand; report Tulakes and intercepting Victor seventy seven. Squawk 2364."

"ATC clears Comanche six zero Charlie to Wichita Midcontinent Airport via direct Oklahoma City Vortac Victor seventy seven. Turn right after departure; maintain two thousand five hundred to the Vortac on the two five eight radial. Climb in the holding pattern to five thousand before proceeding on course; maintain seven thousand. Report reaching the Oklahoma City Vortac and leaving five thousand. Departure control frequency will be one two four point six. Squawk two three six four."

## Clearance Examples Three and Four

Will Rogers Airport to Amarillo Airport; OKC V272 V140 AMA; departure runway 17. The following two clearances do not make use of radar, which would normally be provided.

"ATC clears Cessna two niner Quebec to the Amarillo Airport via direct Oklahoma City Vortac; Victor two seventy two; Victor one forty. Climb on departure heading to four thousand; turn right; cross the Oklahoma City Vortac at seven thousand or above; maintain one two thousand. Report leaving four thousand, seven thousand, and one zero thousand. Departure control frequency will be one two four point six. Squawk two three six four."

"ATC clears Cessna two niner Quebec to the Amarillo Airport via direct Oklahoma City Vortac; flight plan route. Turn right after departure; maintain five thousand or below to Oklahoma City Vortac; hold west of the Oklahoma City Vortac on the two five eight radial; climb in the holding pattern to one zero thousand before proceeding on course. Report leaving five thousand reaching one zero thousand, and passing Union Intersection. Departure control frequency will be one two four point six . . ."

## Clearance Examples Five and Six

These two flights were the from Oklahoma City's Will Rogers Airport to Tulsa Municipal Airport; OKC V14 TUL; departure runway 17. These two clearances make use of radar vectoring service.

"ATC clears Mooney two three Victor to the Tulsa Airport via Victor fourteen; maintain three thousand. Turn right after departure; heading three four zero for Vector to Victor fourteen northeast of the Oklahoma City Vortac; expect seven thousand after passing the north course of the Oklahoma City Localizer. Departure control frequency will be one two four point six . . ."

"ATC clears Mooney two three Victor to the Prague Intersection via the zero seven seven radial of the Oklahoma City Vortac; maintain three thousand. Turn left after departure; heading zero three zero for Vector to the zero seven seven radial. Departure control frequency will be one two four point six. Squawk two three six four."

Departure clearances are normally to the destination airport, but may be to a fix only a few miles from the point of departure. This short range clearance is often used to expedite departure while the flight is coordinated further by ATC. On short flights, the clearance may be to an approach fix serving the destination airport.

### VFR Operations On an Instrument Flight Plan

Some pilots seem uncertain about some aspects of VFR and "VFR Conditions on Top" while flying cross-country on an IFR clearance. The following questions and answers should clear up any doubts you may have in this regard.

Why request a "VFR Conditions on Top" clearance? In preparation for IFR flight above an overcast or in an area of generally unlimited ceilings and visibility, pilots may request VFR on Top to permit them to select an altitude, or altitudes of their choice, rather than specified ATC assigned altitudes. If during a flight "in the clear" at a specific assigned altitude turbulence or unfavorable ground speeds are encountered, or if icing in clouds ahead is expected, a "VFR Conditions on Top" clearance may allow you some choices.

When would you request a clearance *to* "VFR Conditions on Top?" Departing instrument-rated pilots who wish an IFR clearance *only to climb through* a layer of overcast or reduced visibility, and then continue flight VFR, may request ATC clearance "TO VFR Conditions on Top." This request may be made through a Flight Service Station, by telephone to ATC, or to the tower before taxiing out. The clearance, which authorizes IFR flight through the cloud layer, will contain a near-by clearance limit, routing and a request that you report reaching VFR on Top and desire to cancel the IFR portion of the flight. This type of operation can be combined with a VFR flight plan to destination (Fig. 4-1).

What restrictions apply to the pilot's choice of altitude while operating on an IFR clearance with provision to "Maintain VFR Conditions on Top?" You may fly at an altitude of your choice,

Fig. 4-1. Cessna's twin-engine pressurized Skymaster, equipped with weather radar, is an excellent IFR vehicle (courtesy of Cessna Aircraft Company).

provided that the altitude is at or above the MEA, or MOCA if appropriate, at least 1,000 feet above existing meteorological condition (cloud layer, smog, haze, etc.) if any, and is in compliance with the altitude separation rule for IFR flight, if operating 3,000 feet or more above the surface. You should be especially alert for head-on traffic when climbing or descending on the airway centerline, which is why many fly to the right of the centerline on airways.

When can a "VFR Conditions on top" request be approved by ATC? It may be approved when specifically requested by the pilot *in flight*, provided that PIREPS have not indicated that conditions are unsuitable.

What separation from other aircraft is provided to a "VFR Conditions on Top" flight? No separation is provided. However, you may expect to receive traffic information on known IFR traffic. Anytime you are in the clear, even at a specific assigned altitude, collision avoidance is the pilot's responsibility.

What is the recommended position reporting procedure for VFR on Top operation? Regardless of the altitude being flown, pilots on IFR flight plans report those fixes designated as compulsory reporting points for all altitudes, and additional position reports as requested by ATC. Operating on an IFR flight plan with an altitude assignment of "VFR Conditions on Top," you would report in the following manner.

"Skytwin four one alpha over Oklahoma City one eight; VFR Conditions on Top at eight thousand five hundred; estimating Sayre four eight; Amarillo . . ."

If your position report is made to a FSS for relay to the controlling facility (Center or Approach Control), you should state that the flight is on an IFR flight plan.

Fig. 4-2. The Piper Aztec first appeared in 1960, having evolved from the Apache (the first light twin). The Aztec has been so well received over the years that only two new models have followed the original. More than 5,000 have been produced. Pictured is the F Model, introduced in 1979 (courtesy of Piper Aircraft Corporation).

If you are on an IFR flight plan, VFR, on Top, and anticipate that you will be unable to maintain flight in VFR conditions because of reduced visibility or increasing height of the tops, what should you do? Request a specific altitude assignment and maintain flight in VFR conditions until an appropriate amended clearance is obtained (Fig. 4-2).

When may a pilot deviate from his route of flight while operating IFR with a VFR on Top clearance? Under these conditions you must comply with Instrument Flight Rules *plus* applicable Visual Flight Rules. You are expected to remain on the centerline of airways or routes described in your ATC clearance unless otherwise authorized by ATC, maneuvering as necessary to the intended flight path, or unless the exercise of emergency authority is necessary.

Why would you request a VFR climb or descent while on an IFR flight? If at the start of a flight on an IFR clearance you wish to climb in VFR conditions, or if, while flying at a specific assigned altitude, you wish to climb or descend in VFR conditions, you may request to do so (except in Positive Controlled Airspace). Sometimes such a procedure is considered a practical method of avoiding delay due to other traffic.

What are the procedures for radio communications failure during a "VFR Conditions on Top" operation? The procedures are the same as for operation at a specific assigned altitude. Pilot action in compliance with regulations is determined by existing weather conditions (VFR or IFR), as outlined in the Airman's Information Manual.

## Altimetry

Normally the effects of atmospheric pressure and temperature changes may be summarized by the adage, "Cold or low, look out below." When flying from a warm area to a cold area (assuming little or no pressure change), or when flying from a high pressure area to a low pressure area (assuming little or no temperature change), your aircraft is lower than indicated altitude, unless your altimeter has been adjusted to compensate for the change.

An *altimeter* is accurate at all altitudes only when the conditions of a "Standard Atmosphere" exist. In general, a Standard Atmosphere occurs when the sea level barometric pressure is 29.92 inches Hg., sea level free air temperature is 15 degrees C, and the temperature decreases two degrees C with each 1,000-foot increase in altitude.

This Standard Atmosphere is the arbitrary reference we use in order to describe what is happening in the atmosphere—any changes, that is, from the "standard." Since the Standard Atmosphere rarely exists, our altimeters require frequent correction.

The altimeter is a pressure measuring device. When set at 29.92, it will indicate 4,000 feet at a level where the atmospheric pressure is 25.84 inches Hg. The true altitude at which this pressure actually exists may be more or less than 4,000 feet. On a warm day the expanded air is lighter in weight per unit volume than on a standard day or a cold day. Therefore, the pressure level where the altimeter will indicate 4,000 feet is *higher* than it would be under standard conditions. On a cold day the reverse is true and the 4,000-foot pressure level will be *lower* (Fig. 4-3).

The local altimeter setting "corrects" for the difference between existing pressure and standard atmospheric pressure.

Fig. 4-3. During the early morning hours, fog blanketed the area. Now it is breaking up and burning off an hour before noon. This '68 Cessna Cardinal, which started out IFR and VFR on top, may now ammend his flight plan.

Whether local pressure is higher or lower than standard, when the aircraft altimeter is set to the local altimeter setting (assuming no setting scale error) it will indicate true altitude (MSL) at ground level. The indicated altitudes above ground level are normally not true altitudes because of nonstandard lapse rates. The point to remember is that, when all aircraft operating below 18,000 feet are using the current local altimeter setting, they have a common reference for indicated altitude.

For normal operations (except to determine true airspeed, true altitude, engine operation, etc.), you should disregard the effect of nonstandard temperatures. However, both low temperatures and low pressures should be considered when selecting altitude for terrain clearance purposes. If the local altimeter setting is lower than the setting on the *Kollsman dial*, the aircraft will be lower than its indicated altitude. A reverse situation is also true. Both pressure and temperature must be considered when determining the relation of indicated altitude to true altitude.

## ADF Procedures

Proficiency in *Automatic Direction Finder* (ADF) procedures is essential to the instrument pilot. A poor understanding of this important navigational tool can lead to critical errors under instrument conditions. An instrument pilot should be able to establish a track to a Radio Beacon (RBn) or to a Locator Outer Marker (LOM) by the use of ADF. During off-airways flying, beyond the range of VORs, the only electronic navigational aids available may be low or medium frequency homers. In an emergency the pilot may even have to use a commercial broadcast station. On flights beyond the borders of the United States, he frequently finds that ADF is still the primary radio aid to navigation (Fig. 4-4).

Before stating a discussion of ADF, a distinction should be made between the indications of the ADF and the VOR receivers. The ADF needle points to the station regardless of aircraft heading and position. The VOR receiver, with the CDI centered, indicates the magnetic bearing from the aircraft to the station or from the station to the aircraft, regardless of the aircraft heading.

## Bearing

A *bearing* is the relation (direction) of one object or point to another object or point. As applied to ADF, it is simply the

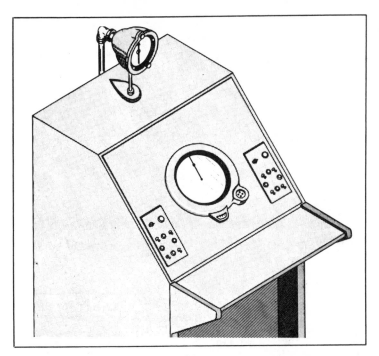

Fig. 4-4. Direction finding equipment used to provide aircraft with their location relative to the DF station (courtesy of FAA).

direction of a line from the aircraft to the station, or from the station to the aircraft.

The relative bearing of the aircraft to the station is the angular relationship between the aircraft heading and the station, measured clockwise from the nose of the aircraft. This bearing is read directly on the ADF dial, measured clockwise from zero. This is the fixed *azimuth* dial, typical of most lightplanes.

A *magnetic bearing* is the direction of an imaginary line from the aircraft to the station or from the station to the aircraft, referenced to magnetic north. To determine the magnetic bearing to the station, add the magnetic heading of the aircraft to the relative bearing shown on the ADF dial. If the sum is more than 360 degrees, subtract 360. The reciprocal of this bearing is the magnetic bearing from the station to the aircraft. Anytime the magnetic compass reads "north," the ADF needle reads the magnetic bearing *to* the station. Any time the magnetic compass reads "south," the ADF needle reads the magnetic bearing *from* the station.

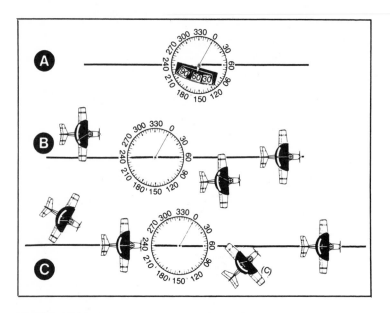

Fig. 4-5. (A) The course selector permits selection of any course. (B) The Left-Right needle shows the position of the aircraft in relation to the course selected. (C) The To-From indicator shows the position of the aircraft in relation to the station whether you are flying to or from the station tuned (courtesy of FAA).

To *find true or compass bearings,* use the same procedure described for finding magnetic bearings. Substitute true heading or compass heading for magnetic heading. A compass bearing may be changed to a magnetic bearing by applying deviation. A magnetic bearing may be changed to a true bearing by applying variation.

### ADF Homing and Tracking

ADF *homing* is flying the aircraft on any heading required to keep the ADF needle on zero until the station is reached. ADF *tracking* is the procedure of flying a straight geographical flight path inbound or outbound from a low or medium frequency facility. A heading is established that will maintain the desired track regardless of wind drift.

For *ADF tracking inbound,* turn the aircraft until it is pointed directly toward the station with an ADF relative bearing of zero. While holding a constant heading, any deflection of the ADF needle indicates a crosswind. If the needle deflects right, the crosswind is from the right and vice versa. The needle indicates the direction of the turn required to intercept the track. The turn should be made when there is a definite deflection of two to five degrees. The angle of interception will depend on the rate at which the aircraft drifted from the track, the distance from the station, and how quickly you wish to return to track (Figs. 4-5 and 4-6).

The procedure for tracking outbound from a station is basically the same as for tracking inbound. The main difference is that the ADF needle moves further away from the 180-degree position as the change of heading is made toward the desired track.

## The ATC Transponder

Written tests for the Instrument Pilot and Airline Transport Pilot ratings include questions pertaining to transponders and the operation of "secondary" radar. The FAA says that test analyses and responses to oral questions by instrument pilot examiners show that many applicants lack essential knowledge in this area.

ATCRBS is the abbreviation for *Air Traffic Control Radar Beacon System*, also known as *Secondary Surveillance Radar*. Secondary radar relies on the exchange of electronic signals between a ground radar beacon antenna (interrogator) and an aircraft transponder. A primary radar system depends on "skin paint" or echo return from the aircraft structure, on a radar scope for indentification. Secondary radar has these advantages. It reinforces the radar target, allows rapid target identification

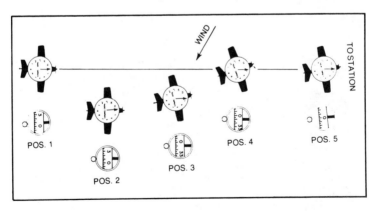

Fig. 4-6. Tracking inbound on ADF. A 20-degree correction is applied when a five-degree drift is noted (courtesy of FAA).

and extends the radar coverage area. Secondary radar is usually slaved with the primary surveillance radars, a common pedestal supporting both antennae.

The ground equipment transmits an ultra high frequency pulsed signal on 1030 MHz to the aircraft transponder which receives the signal, interprets it and replies by transmitting a coded signal on 1090 MHz to the ground reciever. This unit, in turn, decodes the signal and causes it to appear on the radar scope in a distinct pattern, normally two short parallel lines. The interrogator transmits only on 1030 MHz and the transponder replies only on 1090 MHz. Mode and code changes are made by varying the time interval between pulsed signals, not be frequency change. The transponder operates on "line of sight." Therefore, range can be increased by climbing to a higher altitude. Another factor bearing on transponder operation is the attitude of the aircraft. In a bank, part of the aircraft structure may block signals from the interrogator (Fig. 4-7).

A typical lightplane transponder will have five mode positions: OFF, SBY, ON, ALT and TST. The standby (SBY) position allows you to keep the transponder warmed up and ready for use while otherwise inoperative. When switched to the ON position, the transponder responds to the interrogating radar on mode code A/3. This is a code assocated with a non-altitude reporting type of reply. When switched to the altitude (ALT) mode position the transponder replies to the interrogating radar in mode C. This mode is reserved for use when connected to an altitude encoding altitmeter.

The test model (TST) is for a self-check of the unit. Except for the best (most expensive) 500 watt transponders, the test mode does not really perform an end-to-end test of the unit.

Fig. 4-7. DME (Distance Measuring Equipment) measures the micro-seconds required to send and receive a VHF signal to and from a given ground facility, and that time lapse is continuously translated into distance from the facility (courtesy of RCA).

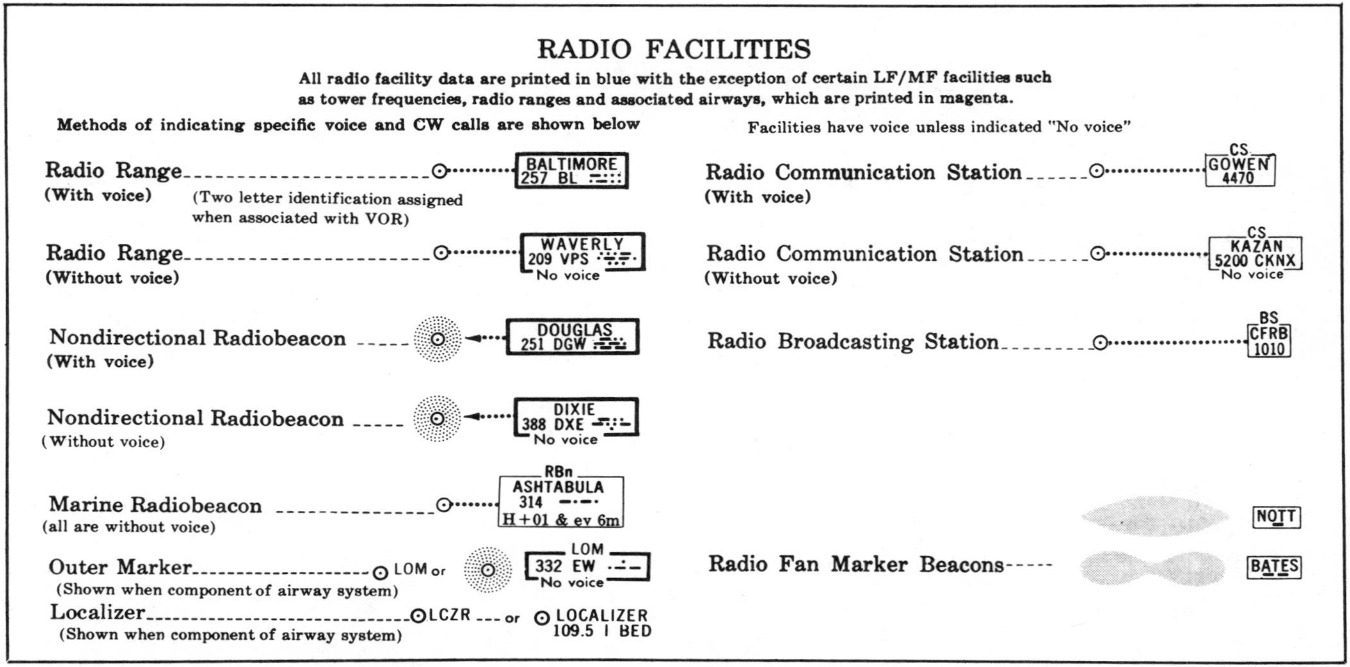

# RADIO FACILITIES

All radio facility data are printed in blue with the exception of certain LF/MF facilities such as tower frequencies, radio ranges and associated airways, which are printed in magenta.

Methods of indicating specific voice and CW calls are shown below

Facilities have voice unless indicated "No voice"

Radio Range ............. ⊙ BALTIMORE 257 BL ▄▀▄
(With voice)
(Two letter identification assigned when associated with VOR)

Radio Communication Station ............. ⊙ CS GOWEN 4470
(With voice)

Radio Range ............. ⊙ WAVERLY 209 VPS ▄▀▄
(Without voice)
No voice

Radio Communication Station ............. ⊙ CS KAZAN 5200 CKNX
(Without voice)
No voice

Nondirectional Radiobeacon ............. ⊛ DOUGLAS 251 DGW ▄▀▄
(With voice)

Radio Broadcasting Station ............. ⊙ BS CFRB 1010

Nondirectional Radiobeacon ............. ⊛ DIXIE 388 DXE ▄▀▄
(Without voice)
No voice

Marine Radiobeacon ............. ⊙ RBn ASHTABULA 314 H +01 & ev 6m
(all are without voice)

Radio Fan Marker Beacons ...... NOTT BATES

Outer Marker ............. ⊙ LOM or
(Shown when component of airway system)
⊙ LOM 332 EW ▄▀▄
No voice

Localizer ............. ⊙ LCZR ---- or ⊙ LOCALIZER 109.5 I BED
(Shown when component of airway system)

Fig. 4-8. You will become intimately familiar with the chart symbols representing the various types of navigation radio facilities (courtesy of FAA).

The best way to check your unit is to ask ATC to request that you "ident." Then press your ident button and, if your transponder is operating properly, the radar operator's display will show an ID symbol attached to your aircraft's return. A second way to check the transponder is to rotate the ident pushbutton until the reply lamp illuminates. Every time the transponder is interrogated, the light will blink.

In practice, you should turn on the transponder when entering the runway for takeoff. Turn it off after touchdown. Sometimes a controller may ask you to "stop squawk," to turn off the transponder, probably because you are close enough to the terminal to make transponder operation unnecessary.

Never operate a transponder on code 0000. This is reserved for *North American Air Defense* (NORAD). Code 7700 is the emergency code and means "Mayday" to the controller. Do not switch through 7700 when changing codes because this causes a momentary false alarm.

Today, the so-called secondary radar has become the primary system. Primary radar is essentially a back-up. To receive complete radar services, a transponder is necessary (Fig. 4-8).

# 5

# Ownership, Maintenance and Refurbishing of Private Aircraft

At the beginning of the 1980s it seems clear that general aviation will experience many changes during this decade. Inflation, the fuel crunch and more complex air traffic control system are conspiring to limit pleasure flying in production aircraft, while the demands of business must inevitably put more and more corporate-owned airplanes into the air. Increasingly, business will be pushed into private air transportation whether the businessmen like it or not (Fig. 5-1). It's a matter of economics. Time is money. Since any business machine—from the office copier to the company airplane—is subject to tax write-offs for its acquisition and use, those businesses that can profit from the employment of a company plane will buy them.

## Ownership Considerations

This is not to say that all those who fly strictly for pleasure or personal convenience will be squeezed out of the air. That will not happen—at least, not within the foreseeable future. There will be a slowdown, perhaps a decline in the number of single-engine lightplanes manufactured, especially the heavy singles (Fig. 5-2). But the homebuilts will continue to proliferate, along with the ultra-lights. A lot of old ragwings will be refurbished and their values will escalate, especially those in the 65-90 horsepower range.

It is possible that the "Rutan Revolution" will develop and that these designs will offer improvements in safety, performance and fuel efficiency that could significantly affect the aviation scene. However, American lightplane makers have been building essentially the same airplanes—powered with the same engines—for more than 30 years. We probably shouldn't expect them to suddenly find the boldness or the vision to leave the beaten track. Like the major American automakers, they will

Fig. 5-1. Businessmen in increasing numbers are discovering the profit potential in the company-owned airplane (courtesy of Beech Aircraft Corporation).

have to be backed against the wall of economic disaster before recognizing that they have promoted the technology of the 1940s beyond its marketable life.

Meanwhile, those of us who must look for ways to compromise with the sharply rising costs in order to continue to justify our flying, and who aren't exactly ecstatic over the idea of building our own Rutan design, may take a less dramatic approach by performing much of our own aircraft maintenance. Part 43 of the FARs states that "the holder of a pilot certificate issued under FAR, Part 61 may perform preventative maintenance on any aircraft owned or operated by him that is not used in air carrier service." This preventative maintenance is spelled out in Appendix A of Part 43, with 25 specific operations listed. However, there is almost no limit to the repair/refurbishing work you can do on your airplane if your work is monitored by a qualified aircraft mechanic and is "sighted-off" by a mechanic with an inspector's rating.

### Pilot/Owner Maintenance

Following are the 25 maintenance operations a pilot/owner may legally perform, unsupervised, on his aircraft (Fig. 5-3):

- Removal, installation and repair of landing gear tires.
- Replacing elastic shock absorber cords on landing gear.
- Servicing landing gear shock struts by adding oil, air or both.

110

● Servicing landing gear wheel bearings, such as cleaning and greasing.

● Replacing defective safety wiring or cotter keys.

● Lubrication not requiring disassembly other than removal of nonstructural items such as cover plates, cowlings and fairings.

● Making simple fabric patches not requiring rib stitching or the removal of structural parts or control surfaces.

● Replenishing hydraulic fluid in the hydraulic reservoir.

● Refinishing decorative coating of fuselage, wings, tail group surfaces (excluding balanced control surfaces), fairings, cowlings, landing gear, cabin or cockpit interior when removal or disassembly of any primary structure or operating system is not required.

● Applying preservative or protective material to components where no disassembly of any primary structure or operating system is involved and where such coating is not prohibited or is not contrary to good practices.

● Repairing upholstery and decorative furnishings of the cabin or cockpit interior when repairing does not require disassembly of any primary structure or operating system, interfere with an operating system or affect the primary structure of the aircraft.

Fig. 5-2. The relatively high first cost of light aircraft is primarily due to the fact that airplanes are mostly hand-built. Every rivet represents several individual operations.

Fig. 5-3. Pilot/owner maintenance can significantly reduce the cost of light-plane ownership.

● Making small, simple repairs to fairings, nonstructural cover plates, cowlings, and small patches and reinforcements not changing the contour so as to interfere with proper airflow (Fig. 5-4).

● Replacing side windows where that work does not interfere with the structure or any operating system such as controls, operating equipment or electrical systems.

● Replacing safety belts.

● Replacing seats or seat parts with replacement parts approved for the aircraft, not involving disassembly of any primary structure or operating system.

● Troubleshooting and repairing broken circuits in landing light wiring circuits.

● Replacing bulbs, reflectors and lenses of position and landing lights.

● Replacing wheels or skis where no weight and balance computation is involved.

● Replacing any cowling not requiring the removal of the propeller or disconnection of flight controls.

● Replacing or cleaning of spark plugs and setting of spark plug cap clearance.

● Replacing any hose connection except hydraulic connections.

● Replacing fabricated fuel lines.

● Cleaning fuel and oil strainers.

● Replacing batteries and checking the fluid level and specific gravity.

● Removing and installing glider wings and tail surfaces that are specifically designed for quick removal and installation, when such removal and installation can be accomplished by the pilot.

As previously stated, none of the above operations need be monitored by a licensed AP (Airframe and Powerplant mechanic). If you want to perform other repair jobs on your airplane that must be supervised by an aircraft mechanic, you should know that FAR, Part 65.81, requires that even a licensed mechanic must have previous experience concerning that particular operation in order to be entirely legal. Only an AI (mechanic with an inspector's rating) can return an aircraft to service following major repairs. A licensed AP must have certain

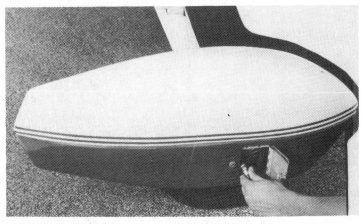

Fig. 5-4. Tires enclosed by speed fairings are often neglected. Purchase your own gauge; gauges borrowed from line boys are usually inaccurate as a result of internal dirt.

specified experience and must pass a special test in order to become an AI.

## Fabric Installation

Working under the supervision of an aircraft mechanic who has had fabric experience, you may completely re-cover and finish any fabric-covered airplane. A lot of Pipers, Taylorcrafts, Stinsons and Aeroncas were produced during the 1940s and 1950s (with engines that burn 3½ to 5 gallons of fuel per hour) that are fabric-covered, and the early Cessna 120/140 and 170 models have fabric-covered wings. Since the cheapest re-cover job around is going to cost at least $3,000, you can appreciate the opportunity this offers to the pilot who is willing to tackle the job himself. Total cost of the materials, the best available, will not exceed $750. A very good job—one that will last up to 15 years—may be done somewhat cheaper; no special skills are needed.

A lot of veteran aircraft mechanics will try to tout you to aircraft grade cotton fabric finished out with aircraft *butyrate dopes*. This is because they are experienced with these materials and can turn out first class work using them, and for years after the synthetic fabrics became available for aircraft covering, no finishes were available that would adhere well to them. A lot of the old-timers are still suspicious of the Dacron fabrics approved for aircraft covering. They are generally not inclined to take a chance with a fabric/finish system with which they are not familiar.

Nevertheless, you should consider nothing but Dacron. It costs less than aircraft grade cotton, is much stronger and lasts twice as long. Since your aircraft fabric experience is zero, you will have no more to learn using Dacron than using cotton. Finishing systems have long since been developed to solve the paint adhesion problem. Another consideration is that your airplane is going to be more attractive in the used market several years from now if it is covered with Dacron (Fig. 5-5).

Currently, there are three aircraft Dacron covering/finishing systems approved by the FAA. One of these systems must be used when re-covering a production airplane. (You can cover a homebuilt aircraft with your own system if the FAA inspector will allow it). A covering system consists of the fabric, tapes, rib-stitch cord, cement, thinners, undercoats and finish coats. You must use (which is to say you must in order to be

Fig. 5-5. The Bellanca Viking has been built in relatively small number but possesses a loyal group of owners. It is the only high performance lightplane with fabric (Dacron) covering.

legal) all the products of a given system, without mixing or substituting. In other words, you are not supposed to use, say, *Stits fabric* and *Eonnex finishes*.

The three systems are: *Stits Poly-Fiber*, *Ceconite* and *Eonnex*. The Stits process is probably the best and most expensive. Ceconite is very popular, perhaps because it employs the familiar butyrate dopes. Eonnex is the least expensive, requires less labor and is lightest in weight when finished out. The Eonnex process uses but three finishing coats (the fabric is pretreated), and these coats are a water-soluble emulsion paint.

Full particulars on each system, including application techniques, are available from the manufacturers: Stits Aircraft Coatings, P.O. Box 3084, Riverside, CA 92509; Ceconite, Inc., 4677 Worth St., Los Angles, CA 90063; and Eonair, Inc., 417 Watts Drive, Bakersfield, CA 93307.

The application of Dacron to an airframe is very much the same as with cotton fabric. The primary difference in working the two is that cotton is tautened with distilled water after the airframe is covered, while Dacron is tautened by applying heat, usually with a household electric iron.

The covering process may be greatly simplified at very little extra cost by ordering pre-sewn "envelopes" or "slip covers" that are cut and sewn to fit your airplane. *Stits, Ceconite* and *Eonnex* can tell you the sources of envelopes for their respective systems.

### Refinishing Metal Aircraft

It currently costs a minimum of $1,200 to have a two-place all-metal airplane stripped of its old paint and completely refinished. At least 80 percent of this cost is chargeable to labor.

The best materials (the most expensive) will add little to the total cost.

It is not easy to find a shop that will do the job right. The secret of a really good paint job is in proper preparation of the airframe before any paint goes on. The primary purpose of paint on an all-metal airplane is to protect the plane from corrosion.

The aluminum alloy used to cover airplanes corrodes easily. This metal is plated with a thin coating of pure aluminum to inhibit the formation of corrosion salts, but such a surface offers a poor foundation for paint. Therefore, the skin must be thoroughly cleaned and then treated with a mild acid etch, followed by a primer coating which not only bonds well to the metal but contains chromates for corrosion protection. Another important property of the primer is that it must provide a good adhesive base for the finish coatings.

Other important factors include the necessity that all materials used are chemically compatible. The use of a different brand of thinner or retarder (retarder is often employed to slow the drying process when atmospheric conditions require it) can spoil an otherwise good paint job. Different brands of paint and primers contain different kinds of thinners in their formulas, and to intermix them is to invite disaster.

A totally clean surface—and we do mean *clean* of everything including fingerprints—is a critical first step in the refinishing process. A phosphoric acid etch then provides a firm and lasting primer bond. The primer that follows will be a two-part epoxy with a high zinc chromate content (in a really first class job). The final finish coats that go over the primer will be a top quality two-part polyurethane enamel such as Stits *Aluma-Thane*, DuPont *Imron* or Grow Chemical's *Alumigrip*. We like Stits *Aluma-Thane* because we're convinced that Stits has the best primer, and it isn't wise to mix a paint system.

Sometimes—perhaps more often than not—the mixing of paint systems, substitution of materials, or other mistakes or omissions during the painting process do not show up for months, or even a year or more. When your expensive paint job (currently about $1,800 on a single-engine four-placer) begins to blister, crack or peel, it's a bit late to question why. A properly applied polyurethane finish should last for at least 10 years.

Cessna switched from acrylic lacquer to polyurethane (*Imron*) in June, 1977. Beechcrafts are finished in Alumigrip. Piper says it is now using a "modified" polyurethane.

## Alternative Finishes

In the past, a lot of airplanes have been finished with acrylic lacquer and synthetic enamel. Airframe makers liked acrylic lacquer because it was fast and kept a production line moving. However, lacquer must be applied under carefully controlled conditions. Few shops in the field are set up to properly apply this finish. In any case, this old automotive finish is not especially durable and is quite vulnerable to 100 octane low-lead aviation fuel, which was Cessna's main reason for discontinuing its use.

The synthetic enamels, such as DuPont Dulux, are also automotive paints that have been extensively used on airplanes. Some owners, not wanting to invest in a complete refinishing job, may opt to have their airplanes sanded and then refinished with synthetic enamel. If the old finish is merely soft and faded, this method may be obtained for as little as $400—less if the plane owner is willing to do the sanding himself. Don't expect the high gloss and the rock-hard durability of a urethane finish, however (Fig. 5-6).

Fig. 5-6. The Bellanca wing is all-wood. Lighter, more resilient and at least as strong as metal, it is resin-dipped to seal out moisture (courtesy of Bellanca Aircraft Corporation).

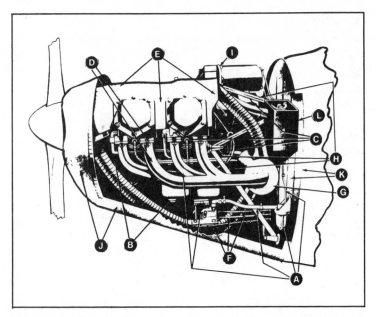

Fig. 5-7. (A) Check fuel lines for leaks and security of attachment; clean gascolater; assure that carburetor-heat doors operate freely. (B) Inspect oil sump and oil lines. When changing oil, strain old oil through a strainer and check for metal particles that tip-off internal engine damage. (C) Check magneto hold-down nuts and ignition wiring. (D) Inspect exhause manifold. (E) Make sure engine baffles are secure and that no air leaks allow cooling air pressure to deteriorate. (F) Examine throttle, mixture and carburetor heat controls . (G) Check heater shroud for leaks and security of attachment. (H) Examine engine mounting for cracks with a magnifying glass, especially welded joints and the tubing near the welds. (I) Check accessory mountings. (J) Check cowling fasteners and examine inside surfaces of cowling for sign of chafing. (K) Check firewall insulation for oil saturation (L) Inspect battery connections and electrolyte level (courtesy of FAA).

You may, of course, repaint your airplane yourself and save at least 80 percent of the normal cost. Finding a proper place to work is probably the hardest part of a do-it-yourself aircraft painting project. If you do consider performing this operation, we recommend that you read *Refinishing Metal Aircraft* (TAB book No. 2291) which details all procedures, including use of the spray gun.

## Engine Maintenance/Overhaul

Civilian aircraft mechanics generally earn no more, and often less, than automobile mechanics despite the fact that the aircraft mechanic must have formal training and a license issued by the FAA after passing a rigid examination. The mechanics are thereafter responsible for the work they perform, with the threat of a whole range of federal penalties possible for any significant lapse in the performance of their duties. As a result, many disappear into auto repair shops every year for better pay and where there are no standards and practically no responsibility. This is why there is an estimated shortage of 30,000 aviation mechanics in the United States today. The situation will get worse before it gets better.

You may be fortunate enough to be acquainted with an aircraft repair station that employs some experienced, top mechanics. Such an operation will usually display a sign identifying it as officially approved by the FAA. It's a good "sign," because a shop has to meet certain standards in order to earn it.

All this becomes especially relevant to you when engine overhaul time comes around. A major engine overhaul is costly, even on the smallest aircraft engine, and you want the best job you can get for the money. How do you ensure this? First, understand that there is more than one kind of overhaul.

Aircraft engine service manuals list two different sets of tolerances or limits allowed between the mating parts, *new* limits and *service* limits. For example, the clearance allowed between the crankshaft and main bearings may be listed as

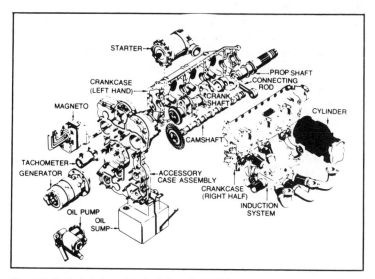

Fig. 5-8. Exploded view of typical six-cylinder light aircraft engine (courtesy of FAA).

119

.0005-inch minimum *new* limit and .0025-inch maximum *new* limit. The *service* limit may be .005-inch.

A major overhaul in the field will return the engine's mating parts to the prescribed *service* limits (if the job is done right). The engine should then be good for another 1,200 to 2,000 hours or whatever the manufacturer recommends as the normal time between overhaul (TBO) assuming, of course, the engine is properly maintained and not abused (Fig. 5-7).

There is another way to go and you should give it careful consideration, especially if your engine has already been majored a couple of times. Exchange your engine for are manufactured engine from Lycoming or Continental. The remanufactured engine will cost about one-third more than a major overhaul performed in the field. However, the remanufactured Lycoming or Continental will have all its mating parts set up to *new* limits. Major components such as crankshaft or cylinders will meet these standards. The remanufactured engine will have a new serial number, new engine log and new engine warranty. It may be obtained with prior arrangement through any Lycoming or Continental approved repair station. We say "prior arrangement" because that way you can reduce your down-time to just a day or two. You need not take your airplane out of service until the engine arrives from the factory. All the mechanics have to do is install the new one and ship yours back to the factory. The run-out you exchange must be intact.

Escalating maintenance costs in the field and the aircraft mechanic shortage (this latter factor often translating into extended down-time) may markedly influence your decision when choosing between a major overhaul in the field and a factory remanufactured engine (Fig. 5-8).

# Aviation Today

General aviation is now one of the world's largest passenger carriers, boarding nearly 100 million people annually. It represents thousands of jobs, millions of dollars in revenues, and the growth of thousands of cities, businesses, services and manufacturing facilities thoroughly the United States. General aviation (all civil flying except the airlines) is now the largest and in many ways the most significant segment of this country's air transportation system.

As major partners in this system, general aviation and the airlines together make up the nation's balanced air transport network—the safest, most responsive and most efficient in the world. The airlines serve approximately 500 of the nation's 13,000 airports, carrying more than 200 million passengers annually. General aviation also serves those 500 airports, along with the other 12,500.

Thirty of the 500 airports served by the airlines generate 70 percent of their total passenger traffic, and 150 of these airports board 96 percent of the traffic. In other words, more than 13,000 airports, and the communities they serve, rely at least partially, and in most cases entirely, on general aviation for air transportation.

Within the diverse and varied categories of general aviation, there are many reasons why people fly. For example, more than 70 percent of all general aviation operations are for business or commercial purposes. About 20 percent is for personal transportation, and a little over five percent is for sport (Fig. 6-1).

As an ecological sidenote, general aviation is a very clean form of transportation, because aviation safety requires an engine that is well maintained and periodically inspected by qualified examiners. In addition, 90 percent of the fuel used is burned at levels that will not affect the air we breathe.

Fig. 6-1. Actor George Kennedy flies his Bonanza partly for business and partly for pleasure. Many actors, entertainers and sports personalities own and fly airplanes.

## Industry

Thirty years ago, more than half of America's manufacturing plants were located in cities with populations of at least 100,000. By 1956, however, one-third of all new factories were going up in smaller towns and cities. And today industrial decentralization continues away from major population centers to smaller communities that have something in common—a general aviation airport.

From the strictly business viewpoint of an expanding industrial firm, these communities and their airports mean proximity to raw materials, lower land and capital investment costs, a less competitive labor force, and better living conditions for their employees. It also means that accessibility, both in and out, is assured by the airport.

To run a successful industrial operation in areas that used to be referred to as the "the sticks," it is necessary to have a

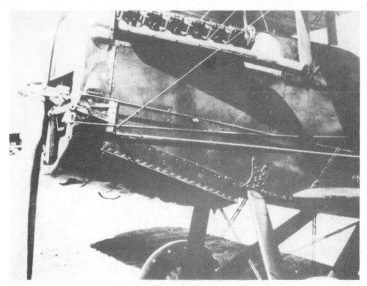

Fig. 6-2. What else is new? The U.S. Army Air Service was experimenting with controllable-pitch propellers in the early 1920s.

community airport. Surveys of major American corporations have shown that most of them are reluctant to locate plants and offices in an area that lacks adequate airport facilities.

Time and again it has been proven that a town without an adequate airport stands a good chance of becoming a ghost town (Fig. 6-2). At best, it certainly will not do much growing. On the

Fig. 6-3. Propeller of the future? Lockheed engineer Charles Miller says, "Using the prop-fan, we could fly propeller-driven aircraft at the same speeds the turbo-fans are flying today, and we can save a tremendous amount of fuel doing it." These very thin blades are also said to be extremely quiet (courtesy of Lockheed-Georgia Company).

Fig. 6-4. Ranchers and farmers were among the first businessmen to put the airplane to work earning its keep.

other hand, every time general aviation brings in new industry, it simultaneously creates new benefits for the community. For every 100 new industrial jobs, there is an economic fallout—a million more dollars in personal income, more than a half-million dollars in additional retail sales, four new retail stores and 68 new employees. The very map of American industrialization is changing perceptibly, and general aviation is one of the reasons why.

## Business Flying

Business flying represents the largest category of general aviation. In addition to over 140,000 personally owned aircraft, many of which are used for business purposes, there are 45,000

Fig. 6-5. Dedicated Bonanza owners, wishing for more cabin space, were rewarded by the appearance of the Model 36 Bonanza in 1968. The fuselage was moved 10 inches forward over the wing and the aft bulkhead moved 19 inches aft to gain an additional six cubic feet in the cabin—with no penalty on performance (courtesy of Beech Aircraft Corporation).

Fig. 6-6. About 5,000 Beechcraft Barons (Model 55) have been built in five versions with engine ranging from 260 to 310 hp. The Baron is the true "Twin Bonanza," although the big Model 50, long out of production, officially had that name (courtesy of Beech Aircraft Corporation).

business-owned aircraft that are used solely for this purpose. These thousands of airplanes make more than six million flights per year—almost as many as all the airlines put together.

Why are business aircraft employed so extensively? And why is the number of business aircraft constantly growing?

The answer is simple—good economics and high efficiency. Businessmen use general aviation aircraft to save time transporting their people and their products and, equally important, their supplies and parts to keep production lines moving.

Nearly one-third of all business flights into major metropolitan airports each year connect with a scheduled airline flight. The vast majority of general aviation business flights, however, are between communities that lack adequate airline service.

Fig. 6-7. If you ever doubted what your ground instructor told you about spiraling propeller wash, here is unmistakable proof. The prop tips on this Lockheed L-100 (Hercules variant) are condensing the moisture in the air and perfectly tracing the prop wash of each (courtesy of Lockheed-Georgia Company).

Fig. 6-8. The Cessna 402 may be configured for cargo or office space aloft. Engines are Continental TSIO-520-E rated at 300 hp, which give the 6,300-pound 402 a 660-mile range at a speed of 188 kts (courtesy of Cessna Aircraft Company).

Business flying in general aviation has the flexibility to be at the right place at the right time, and the exceptional utility to perform where others can't (Fig. 6-3).

For example, to fly from Akron, Ohio, to Huntsville, Alabama, using only scheduled airlines, would take 7½ hours, with two connections. The same trip via a business aircraft would take less than three hours and would be a direct, non-stop flight. This is typical of the economy and utility of business flying. It is indicative of why many business flights would be difficult, if not impossible, without general aviation.

Fig. 6-9. New in 1980 was Cessna's Corsair propjet, a six to eight place pressurized craft in the 300 mph and $825,000 class (courtesy of Cessna Aircraft Company).

There is also a direct correlation between the use of a business aircraft and the financial well-being of the firms that employ them. In a survey of the top 1,000 industrial companies, conducted by Aviation Data Services, it was found that almost half, or 432 of them, operate their own aircraft. These 432 companies grossed nearly 80 percent of the total sales for the entire group, and earned 84 percent of the profits.

There is another aspect to business flying. Only 10 percent of the entire business fleet are turbo-prop or jet aircraft. The remaining 90 percent are piston-engine aircraft, operated mainly by smaller companies around the country to increase their productivity and their power to compete in the marketplace. The effective use of a business plane, as a key tool in a firm's operations, is really what business flying is all about (Figs. 6-4 through 6-9).

# Air Traffic
# Control System Glossary

The primary value of this section is to promote a common understanding of the terms used by pilots, air traffic controllers and the flight specialists who man the FSS facilities. Serious aircraft accidents have resulted from misunderstandings between pilots and ATC personnel. Recently, a Cessna 421 crashed in mountainous terrain about 21 nautical miles north of Nogales, Arizona. The pilot had received an instrument flight rules (IFR) clearance to depart Nogales and proceed to Tucson, Arizona, before proceeding west toward his destination of Fresno, California. Although the pilot initially requested a routing via a navigational fix to the northwest of the Nogales Airport, he accepted the direct clearance and proceeded to the north on a straight line course to Tucson with an assigned altitude which did not provide adequate terrain clearance.

The Flight Service Station specialist who relayed the IFR clearance to N999MB stated that he had expected the pilot to "fly west." He advised the pilot to expect radar vectors after takeoff. The departure controller at Davis-Monthan RAPCON indicated that he was generally aware of a published departure procedure at Nogales (which included a northwesterly climb from the airport). However, he did not know if the pilot would fly the published departure route and, based on the IFR flight plan, believed the pilot might possibly proceed on a direct route from Nogales to Tucson. An assistant chief at the RAPCON, who had formulated the IFR clearance, stated that he expected the pilot to comply with the published departure procedure even if it was not included in the clearance, and even though it diverged from the direct route by about 12 nmi.

A number of other such misunderstandings may be gleaned from NTSB accident reports. There is no way to determine how many other air traffic glitches go unreported because of happier endings. In many cases, both parties clearly understand what is said, but simply attach different meanings to a given term or phrase. Many simple terms have special meanings in the ATC controller's lexicon. Every pilot should know each of the following terms and the full meaning of each as it applies to the operation of his aircraft.

Fig. G-1. The workhorse Cessna 185 has changed little over the years. Pictured is a 1968 model. Cessna clearly doesn't believe in tampering with success (courtesy of Cessna Aircraft Company).

**abbreviated IFR flight plane:** An authorization by ATC requiring pilots to submit only that information needed for the purpose of ATC. It includes only a small portion of the usual IFR flight plan information. Other information may be requested if needed by air traffic control for separation or control purposes. It is frequently used by aircraft which are airborne and desire an instrument approach, or by aircraft on the ground which desire a climb to VFR on top.

**abeam:** An aircraft is "abeam" a fix, point or object when that fix, point or object is approximately 90 degrees to the right or left of the aircraft track. Abeam indicates a general position rather than a precise point (Fig. G-1).

**abort:** To terminate a preplanned aircraft maneuver; e.g., an aborted takeoff.

**acknowledge:** To let one know that you have received and understood his message.

**aerobatic flight:** An intentional maneuver involving an abrupt change in an aircraft's attitude, an abnormal attitude or abnormal acceleration, not necessary for normal flight. (Refer to FAR Part 91).

**additional services:** Advisory information provided by ATC which includes but is not limited to the following: traffic advisories; vectors, when requested by the pilot, to assist aircraft receiving traffic advisories to avoid observed traffic; altitude deviation information of 300 feet or more from an assigned altitude as observed on a verified (reading correctly) automatic altitude readout (Mode C); advisories that traffic is no longer a factor; weather and chaff information; weather assistance; bird activity information and holding pattern surveillance.

Additional services are provided to the extent possible contingent only upon the controller's capability to fit them into the performance of higher priority duties and on the basis of limitations of the radar, volume of traffic, frequency of congestion and controller workload. The controller has complete discretion for determining if he is able to provide or continue to provide a service in a particular case. The controller's reason not to provide or continue to provide a service is not subject to question by the pilot and need not be made known to him.

**administrator**: The Federal Aviation Administrator or any person to whom he has delegated his authority.

**advise intentions**: Tell me what you plan to do.

**advisory**: Advice and information provided to assist a pilot in the safe conduct of flight and aircraft movement.

**advisory frequency**: The appropriate frequency to be used for Airport Advisory Service.

**advisory service**: Advice and information provided by a facility to assist pilots in the safe conduct of flight and aircraft movement.

**arial refueling/inflight refueling**: A procedure used by the military to transfer fuel from one aircraft to another during flight.

**aerodrome**: A defined area on land or water (including any buildings, installations and equipment) intended to be used either wholly or in part for the arrival, departure and movement of aircraft.

**aeronautical beacon**: A visual navigation aid displaying flashes of white and/or colored light to indicate the location of an airport, a heliport, a landmark, a certain point of a Federal Airway in mountainous terrain or a hazard.

**aeronautical chart**: A map used in air navigation containing all or part of the following. Topographic information features the portrayal of relief, and a judicious selection of visual check points for VFR flight: hazards and obstructions, navigation aids, navigation routes, designated airspace and airports. Commonly used aeronautical charts include the following.

*Sectional charts* —1:500,000—are designed for visual navigation of slow or medium speed aircraft. Topographic information on these charts features surface elevation. Aeronautical information includes visual and radio aids, airports, controlled airspace, restricted areas, obstructions and related data.

*VFR terminal area charts* —1:250,000—depict Terminal Control Area (TCA) airspace which provides for the control or segregation of all the aircraft within the TCA. The chart depicts topographic information and aeronautical information which includes visual and radio aids to navigation, airports, controlled airspace, restricted areas, obstructions and related data.

*World Aeronautical Charts* (WAC)—1:1,000,000—provide a standard series of aeronautical charts covering land areas of the world, at a size and scale convenient for navigation by moderate speed aircraft. Topographic information includes cities and towns, principal roads, railroads, distinctive landmarks, drainage and relief. Aeronautical information includes visual and radio aids to navigation, airports, airways, restricted areas, obstructions and other pertinent data.

*En route low altitude charts* provide aeronautical information for the en route instrument navigation (IFR) in the low altitude stratum.

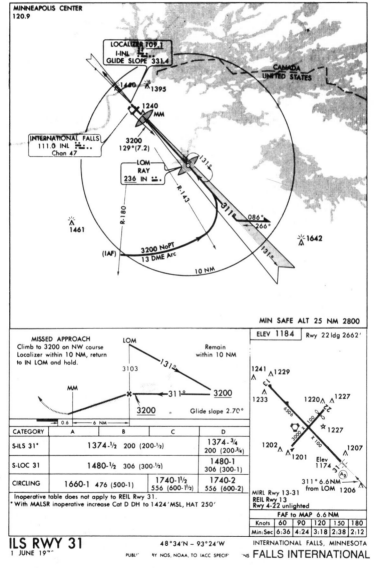

Fig. G-2. Typical instrument approach plate.

Information includes the portrayal of airways, limits of controlled airspace, position identification and frequencies of radio aids, selected airports, minimum en route and minimum obstruction clearance altitudes, airway distances, reporting points, restricted areas and related data. Area charts which are a part of this series furnish terminal data at a large scale in congested areas.

*En route high altitude charts* provide aeronautical information for en route instrument navigation (IFR) in the high altitude stratum. Information includes the portrayal of jet routes, identification and frequencies of radio aids, selected airports, distances, time zones, special use airspace and related information.

*Area navigation (RNAV) high altitude charts* provide aeronautical information for en route IFR navigation for high altitude air routes established for aircraft equipped with RNAV system. Information includes portrayal of RNAV routes, waypoints, track angles, changeover points, distances, selected navigational aids and airports, special use airspace, oceanic routes and transitional information.

*Instrument Approach Procedures (IAP) charts* portray the aeronautical data which is required to execute an instrument approach to an airport. These charts depict the procedures, including all related data, and the airport diagram. Each procedure is designated for use with a specific type of electronic navigation system including NDB, TACAN, VOR, ILS and RNAV. These charts are identified by the type of navigational aids which provide final approach guidance (Fig. G-2).

*Standard Instrument Departure* (SID) *charts* are designed to expedite clearance delivery and to facilitate transition between takeoff and en route operations. Each SID procedure is presented as a separate chart and may serve a single airport or more than one airport in a given geographical location.

*Standard Terminal Arrival (STAR) charts* are designated to expedite air traffic control arrival route procedures and to facilitate transition between en route and instrument approach operations. Each STAR procedure is presented as a separate chart and may serve a single airport or more than one airport in a given geographical location.

*Airport and taxi charts* are designed to expedite the efficient and safe flow of ground traffic at an airport. These charts are identified by the local airport name.

**affirmative**: Yes.

**air carrier district office** (ACDO): An FAA field office serving an assigned geographical area, staffed with Flight Standards personnel serving the aviation industry and the general public, on matters related to the certification and operation of scheduled air carriers and other large aircraft operations.

**aircraft**: A device that is used or intended to be used for flight in the air and when used in air traffic control terminology may include the flight crew.

**aircraft approach category**: A grouping of aircraft based on a speed of 1.3 $V_{so}$ (at maximum certificated landing weight), or on maximum certificated landing weight. $V_{so}$ and the maximum certificated landing weight are those values as established for the aircraft by the certificating authority of the country of registry. If an aircraft falls into two categories, it is placed in the higher of the two. The categories are as follows: Category A, speed less than 91 knots; weight less than 30,001 lbs.; Category B, speed 91 knots or more but less than 121 knots, weight 30,001 pounds (lbs.) or more but less than 60,001 lbs; Category C, speed 121 knots or more but less than 141 knots, weight 60,001 lbs. or more but less than 150,001 lbs,; Category D, speed 141 knots or more but less than 166 knots, weight 150,001 lbs. or more; Category E, speed 166 knots or more, any weight.

**aircraft classes**: For the purposes of wake turbulence separation minima, ATC classifies aircraft as *heavy, large* and *small*. Heavy aircraft are capable of takeoff weights of 300,000 lbs. or more whether or not they are operating at this weight during a particular phase of flight. Large aircraft are more than 12,500 lbs. with a maximum certificated takeoff weight up to 300,000 lbs. Small aircraft are 12,500 lbs. or less, maximum certificated takeoff weight.

**air defense emergency**: A military emergency condition declared by a designated authority. This condition exists when an attack upon the continental United States, Alaska, Canada or American installations in Greenland by hostile aircraft or missiles is considered probable, imminent or is taking place.

**air defense identification zone** (ADIZ): The area of airspace over land or water, extending upward from the surface, within which the ready identification, the location, and the control of aircraft are required in the interest of national security. A domestic air defense identification zone is an ADIZ within the United States along an international boundary of the United States. A coastal air defense identification zone is an ADIZ over the coastal waters of the United States. A distant early warning identification zone (DEWIZ) is an ADIZ over the coastal waters of Alaska.

**airman's information manual (AIM)**: A publication containing basic flight information and ATC procedures designed primarily as a pilot's instructional manual for the use in the national airspace system.

**Airman's Meteorological Information (AIRMET)**: Inflight weather advisories which cover moderate icing, moderate turbulence, sustained winds of 30 knots or more within 2,000 feet of the surface, and the initial onset of phenomena producing extensive areas of visibilities below three miles or ceilings less than 1,000 feet. AIRMET concerns weather phenomena which are of operational interest to all aircraft and potentially hazardous to aircraft having limited capability because of lack of equipment, instrumentation or pilot qualifications. It concerns weather of less severity than SIGMETs.

**air navigation facility**: Any facility used in, available for use in, or designed for use in aid of air navigation, including landing areas, lights, any apparatus or equipment for disseminating weather information, for signaling, for radio-directional finding, or for radio or other electrical communication, and for any other structure or mechanism having a similar purpose for guiding or controlling flight in the air or the landing and takeoff of aircraft.

**airport**: An area of land or water that is used for, or intended to be used for, the landing and takeoff of aircraft, including buildings and facilities, if any.

**airport advisory area**: The area within five statute miles of an airport not served by a control tower, i.e., there is no tower or the tower is not in operation, on which is located a Flight Service Station.

**Airport Advisory Service** (AAS): A service provided by Flight Service Stations at airports not served by a control tower. This service provides information to arriving and departing aircraft concerning wind direction and speed, favored runway, altimeter setting, pertinent known traffic and field conditions, airport taxi routes and traffic patterns, and authorized instrument approach procedures. This information is advisory in nature and does not constitute an ATC clearance.

**airport elevation/field elevation**: The highest point of an airport's usable runways measured in feet from MSL (Fig. G-3).

Fig. G-3. Los Angeles International (LAX) on a rare clear day. Notice parallel runways with satellite parking areas. This was one of the first TCAs established in the airways system (courtesy of Don Downie).

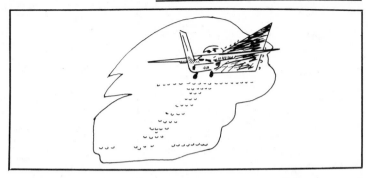

Fig. G-4. Approach lights allow the pilot to make a transition from an instrument to a visual approach.

**airport/facility directory**: A publication designed primarily as a pilot's operational manual containing all airports, seaplane bases and heliports open to the public. It includes communications data, navigational facilities and certain special notices and procedures. This publication is issued in seven volumes according to geographical area.

**airport information desk/aid**: An airport unmanned facility designed for pilot self-service briefing, flight planning and filing of flight plans.

**airport lighting**: Various lighting aids that may be installed on an airport. Types of airport lighting include Approach Light System (ALS), which is an airport lighting facility which provides visual guidance to landing aircraft by radiating light beams in a directional pattern by which the pilot aligns the aircraft with the extended centerline of the runway on his final approach for landing. Condenser-Discharge Sequential Flashing Lights/Sequenced Flashing Lights may be installed in conjunction with the ALS at some airports. Types of approach light systems are: ALSF-I, Approach Light System (Fig. G-4) with sequenced flashing lights in ILS Cat-I configuration; ALSF-II, Approach Light System with sequenced flashing lights in ILS Cat-II configuration; SSALF, Simplified Short Approach Light System with sequenced flashing lights; SSALR, Simplified Short Approach Light System with runway alignment indicator lights; MALSF, Medium Intensity Approach Light System with sequenced flashing lights; MALSR, Medium Intensity Approach Light System with runway alignment indicator lights; LDIN, Sequenced Flashing Lead-in Lights; and RAIL, Runway Alignment Indicator Lights (sequenced flashing lights which are installed only in combination with other light systems).

Runway lights/runway edge lights have a prescribed angle of emission used to define the lateral limits of a runway. Runway lights are uniformly spaced at intervals of approximately 200 feet, and the intensity may be controlled or preset.

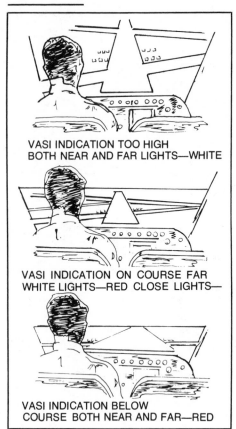

VASI INDICATION TOO HIGH
BOTH NEAR AND FAR LIGHTS—WHITE

VASI INDICATION ON COURSE FAR
WHITE LIGHTS—RED CLOSE LIGHTS—

VASI INDICATION BELOW
COURSE BOTH NEAR AND FAR—RED

Fig. G-5. Visual Approach
Indicator (VASI) system.

*Touchdown zone lighting* consists of two rows of transverse light bars located symmetrically about the runway centerline normally at 100-foot intervals. The basic system extends 3,000 feet along the runway.

*Runway centerline lighting* is flush-mounted centerline lights spaced at 50-foot intervals beginning 75 feet from the landing threshold and extending to within 75 feet of the opposite end of the runway.

Threshold lights are fixed green lights arranged symmetrically left and right of the runway centerline, identifying the runway threshold.

Runway End Identifier Lights (REIL) are two synchronized flashing lights, one on each side of the runway threshold, which provide rapid and positive identification of the approach end of a particular runway.

Visual Approach Slope Indicator (VASI) is an airport lighting facility providing vertical visual approach slope guidance to aircraft during approach to landing. It radiates a directional pattern of high intensity red and white focused light beams which indicate to the pilot that he is "above path" if white/white, and that he is below path if red/red. Red/white indicates that he is on path. Some airports serving large aircraft have three-bar VASIs which provide two visual glide paths to the same runway (Fig. G-5).

Boundary Lights define the perimeter of an airport or landing area.

**airport rotating beacon/rotation beacon:** A visual navigation aid operated at many airports. At civil airports, alternating white and green flashes indicate the location of the airport. The total number of flashes are 12 to 15 per minute. At military airports, the beacons flash alternately white and green, but are differentiated from civil airports by dualpeaked (two quick) white flashes between the green flashes. Normally, operation of an airport rotating beacon during the hours of daylight means that the reported ground visibility at the airport is less than three miles and/or the reported ceiling is less than 1,000 feet. Therefore, an ATC clearance is required for landing or takeoff.

**Airport Surface Detection Equipment (ASDE):** Radar equipment specifically designed to detect all principal features on the surface of an airport, including aircraft and vehicular traffic, and to present the entire image on a radar indicator console in the control tower. The equipment is used to augment visual observation by tower personnel of aircraft and/or vehicular movements on runways and taxiways.

**Airport Surveillance Radar (ASR):** Approach control radar used to detect and display an aircraft's position in the terminal area. ASR provides range and azimuth information but does not provide elevation data. Coverage of the ASR can extend up to 60 miles.

**airport traffic area:** Unless otherwise specifically designated in FAR Part 93, that airspace within a horizontal radius of five (5) statute miles from the geographical center of any airport at which a control tower is operating, extending from the surface up to, but not including, an altitude of 3,000 feet above the elevation of the airport. Unless otherwise authorized or required by ATC, no person may operate an aircraft within an airport traffic area except for the purpose of landing at, or taking off from, an airport within that area. ATC authorization may be given as individual approval of specific operations or may be contained in written agreements between airport users and the tower concerned.

**airport traffic control service:** A service provided by a control tower for aircraft operating on the movement area and in the vicinity of an airport.

**Air Route Surveillance Radar (ARSR):** Air Route Traffic Control Center (ARTCC) radar used primarily to detect and display an aircraft's position while en route between terminal areas. The ARSR enables controllers to provide radar air traffic control service when aircraft are within the ARSR coverage. In some instances, ARSR may enable an

ARTCC to provide terminal radar services similar to, but usually more limited, than those provided by a radar approach control.

**Air Route Traffic Control Center (ARTCC):** A facility established to provide air traffic control service to aircraft operating on IFR flight plans within controlled airspace and principally during the en route phase of the flight. When equipment capabilities and controller workload permit, certain advisory/assistance services may be provided to VFR aircraft.

**airspeed:** The speed of an aircraft relative to its surrounding air mass. The unqualified term "airspeed" may mean *indicated airspeed*, the speed shown on the aircraft airspeed indicator. This is the speed used in pilot/controller communications under the general term "airspeed." True airspeed is the airspeed of an aircraft relative to undisturbed air. It is used primarily in flight planning and the en route portion of flight. When used in pilot/controller communications, it is referred to as "true airspeed" and not shortened to "airspeed."

**airstart:** The starting of an aircraft engine while the aircraft is airborne, preceded by engine shutdown during training flights or by actual engine failure.

**air traffic:** Aircraft operating in the air or on an airport surface, exclusive of loading ramps and parking areas.

**air traffic clearance/ATC clearance:** An authorization by Air Traffic Control, for the purpose of preventing collision between known aircraft, for an aircraft to proceed under specified traffic conditions within controlled airspace.

**air traffic control (ATC):** A service operated by appropriate authority to promote the safe, orderly and expeditious flow of air traffic.

**air traffic control specialist/controller:** A person authorized to provide air traffic control service. This term refers to en route and terminal control personnel. Flight Service personnel are referred to as Flight Service Specialists.

**Air Traffic Control Systems Command Center (ATCSCC):** An air traffic service facility consisting of four operational units, and located in FAA Headquarters. *Central Flow Control Function* (CFCF) is responsible for coordination and approval of all major inter-center flow control restrictions on a system basis in order to obtain maximum utilization of the airspace. *Central Altitude Reservation Function* (CARF) is responsible for coordinating, planning and approving special user requirements under the *Altitude Reservation* (ALTRV) concept. Airport Reservation Office (ARO) is responsible for approving IFR flights at designated high density traffic airports during specified hours. The ATC contingency command post is a facility which enables the FAA to manage the ACT system when significant portions of the system's capabilities have been lost or threatened.

**airway beacon**: Used to mark airway segments in remote mountain areas. The light flashes Morse Code to identify the beacon site.

**airway/federal airway**: A control area or portion thereof established in the form of a corridor, the centerline of which is defined by radio navigational aids.

**alert area**: See *special use airspace*.

**Alert Notice (ALNOT)**: A message sent by a Flight Service Station (FSS) that requests an extensive communications search for overdue, unreported or missing aircraft.

**all weather low altitude training route**: See *olive branch routes*.

**alpha-numeric display/data block**: Letters and numerals used to show identification, altitude, beacon code and other information concerning a target on a radar display.

**alternate airport**: An airport at which an aircraft may land if a landing at the intended airport becomes inadvisable.

**altimeter setting**: The barometric pressure reading used to adjust a pressure altimeter for variations in existing atmospheric pressure or to the standard altimeter setting of 29.92 Hg (Fig. G-6).

**altitude**: The height of a level, point or object measured in feet (or meters) above ground level (AGL) or from mean sea level (MSL). MSL altitude is expressed in feet or meters, from mean sea level. AGL altitude is expressed in feet or meters, measured above ground level. Indicated altitude is the altitude as shown by an altimeter. On a pressure or barometric altimeter it is altitude as shown uncorrected for

Fig. G-6. Barometric pressure is dialed into the "Kollsman" window (K) in face of the altimeter.

instrument error and uncompensated for variation from standard atmospheric conditions.

**altitude readout/automatic altitude report**: An aircraft's altitude, transmitted via the Mode C transponder feature, that is visually displayed in 100-foot increments on a radar scope having that readout capability.

**altitude reservation (ALTRV)**: Airspace utilization under prescribed conditions normally employed for the mass movement of aircraft or other special user requirements which cannot otherwise be accomplished. ALTRVs are approved by the appropriate FAA facility.

**altitude restriction**: An altitude or altitudes stated in the order flown, which are to be maintained until reaching a specific point or time. Altitude restrictions may be issued by ATC due to traffic, terrain or other airspace considerations.

**altitude restrictions are cancelled**: Adherence to previously imposed altitude restriction is no longer required during a climb or descent.

**approach clearance**: Authorization by ATC for a pilot to conduct an instrument approach. The type of instrument approach for which cleared and other pertinent information is provided in the approach clearance when required.

**approach control**: A terminal air traffic control facility providing approach control service.

**approach control service**: Air traffic control service for arriving and departing VFR/IFR aircraft and, on occasion, en route aircraft. At some airports not served by an approach control facility, the ARTCC provides limited approach control service.

**approach gate**: The point on the final approach course which is one mile from the final approach fix on the side away from the airport or five miles from landing threshold, whichever is farther from the landing threshold. This is an imaginary point used within ATC as a basis for final approach course interception for aircraft being vectored to the final approach course.

**approach light system**: See *airport lighting*.

**approach sequence**: The order in which aircraft are positioned while on approach or awaiting approach clearance.

**approach speed**: The recommended speed contained in aircraft manuals used by pilots when making an approach to landing. This speed will vary for different segments of an approach as well as for aircraft weight and configuration.

**apron/ramp**: A defined area, on a land airport, intended to accommodate aircraft for purposes of loading or unloading passengers or cargo, refueling, parking or maintenance. With regard to seaplanes, a ramp is used for access to the apron from the water.

**arc**: The track over the ground of an aircraft flying at a constant distance from a navigational aid by reference to distance measuring equipment (DME).

**area navigation (RNAV):** A method of navigation that permits aircraft operations on any desired course within the coverage of station-reference navigation signals or within the limits of self-contained system capability. *Area navigation low route* is within the airspace extending upward from 1,200 feet above the surface to, but not including, 18,000 feet MSL. *Area navigation high route* is within the airspace extending upward from and including 18,000 feet MSL to flight level 450. *Random area navigation routes* are direct routes, based on area navigation capability, between waypoints defined in terms of degree/distance fixes or offset from published or established routes/airways at specified distance and direction. RNAV waypoint (W/P) is a predetermined geographical position used for route or instrument approach definition or progress reporting purposes that is defined relative to a VORTAC station position.

**army aviation flight information bulletin (USAFIB):** A bulletin that provides air operation data covering Army, National Guard and Army Reserve aviation activities.

**Army Radar Approach Control (ARAC):** An air traffic control facility located at a U.S. Army airport utilizing surveillance and normally precision approach radar and air/ground communications equipment to provide approach control services to aircraft, departing or transiting the airspace controlled by the facility. Service may be provided to both civil and military airports. Similar to TRACON (FAA), RAPCON (USAF) and RATCF (Navy).

**arresting system:** A safety device consisting of two major components, namely, engaging or catching devices, and energy absorption devices for the purpose of arresting both tail hook and/or non-tail hook equipped aircraft. It is used to prevent aircraft from overrunning runways when the aircraft cannot be stopped after landing or during aborted takeoff. Arresting systems have various names, e.g., arresting gear, hook, device, wire, barrier cable.

**arrival time:** The time an aircraft touches down on arrival.

**ARTCC:** See *Air Route Traffic Control Center*.

**ASR approach:** See *Surveillance approach*.

**ATC advises:** Used to prefix a message of noncontrol information when it is relayed to an aircraft by other than an air traffic controller.

**ATC assigned airspace (ATCAA):** Airspace of defined vertical/lateral limits, assigned by ATC, for the purpose of providing air traffic segregation between the specified activities being conducted within the assigned airspace and other IFR air traffic.

**ATC clearance:** see *Air Traffic Clearance*.

**ATC clears:** Used to prefix an ATC clearance when it is relayed to an aircraft by other than an air traffic controller.

Fig. G-7. Cessna Skylane with retractable gear cruises at 156 kts with a useful load of 1,360 pounds. Also available with turbocharging (courtesy of Cessna Aircraft Company).

**ATC instruction:** Directive used by air traffic control for the purpose of requiring a pilot to take specific actions; e.g., "Turn left heading two five zero," "Go around," "Clear the runway."

**ATCRBS:** See *Radar*.

**ATC requests:** Used to prefix an ATC request when it is relayed to an aircraft by other than an air traffic controller (Fig. G-7).

**Automated Radar Terminal Systems (ARTS):** The generic term for the ultimate in functional capability afforded by several automation systems. Each differs in functional capabilities and equipment. ARTS plus a suffix Roman numeral denotes a specific system. A following letter denotes a major modification to that system. In general, an ARTS displays for the terminal controller aircraft identification, flight plane data, other flight associated data, e.g., altitude and speed, and aircraft position symbols in conjunction with his radar presentation. Normal radar co-exists with the alpha-numeric display. In addition to enhancing visualization of the air traffic situation, ARTS facilitate intra/inter-facility transfer and coordination of flight information. These capabilities are enabled by specially designed computers and subsystems tailored to the radar and communications equipments and operational requirements of each automated facility. Modular design permits adoption of improvements in computer software and electronic technologies as they become available, while retaining the characteristics unique to each system.

ARTS IA are the functional capabilities and equipment of the New York Common IFR Room Terminal Automation System. It tracks primary as well as secondary targets derived from two radar sources. The aircraft targets are displayed on a radar type console by means of an alpha-numeric generator. Aircraft identity is depicted in association with the appropriate aircraft target. When the aircraft is equipped with an encoded altimeter (Mode C), its altitude is also displayed. The system can exchange flight plan information with the ARTCC.

ARTS II is a programmable non-racking computer-aided display susbsystem capable of modular expansion. ARTS II systems provide a level of automated air traffic control capability at terminals having low to medium activity. Flight identification and altitude may be associated with the display of secondary radar targets. Also, flight plan information may be exchanged between the terminal and ARTCC.

ARTS III is the Beacon Tracking Level (BTL) of the modular programmable automated radar terminal system in use at medium to high activity terminals. ARTS III detects, tracks and predicts secondary radar-derived aircraft targets. These are displayed by means of computer-generated symbols and alphanumeric characters depicting flight identification, aircraft altitude, ground speed and flight plan data. Although primary targets are not tracked, they are displayed coincident with the secondary radar as well as the symbols and alphanumerics. The system has the capability of communicating with ARTCCs and other ARTS III facilities.

ARTS IIIA is the Radar Tracking and Beacon Tracking Level (RT&BTL) of the modular, programmable automated radar terminal system. ARTS IIIA detects, tracks and predicts primary as well as secondary radar-derived aircraft targets. An enhancement of the ARTS

Fig. G-8. ADF pointer ("A" at left) and NDB selector ("A" at right), as installed in a Cessna Turbo Skymaster (courtesy of Cessna Aircraft Company).

143

III, this more sophisticated computer-driven system will eventually replace the ARTS IA system and upgrade about half of the existing ARTS III systems. The enhanced system will provide improved tracking, continuous data recording and fail-safe capabilities.

**automatic altitude reporting**: That function of a transponder which responds to Mode C interrogations by transmitting the aircraft's altitude in 100-foot increments.

**Automatic Carrier Landing System (ACLS)**: U.S. Navy final approach equipment consisting of precision tracking radar coupled to a computer data link to provide continuous information to the aircraft, monitoring capability to the pilot and a backup approach system.

**Automatic Direction Finder (ADF)**: An aircraft radio navigation system which senses and indicates the direction to a L/MF nondirectional radio beacon (NDB) ground transmitter (Fig. G-8). Direction is indicated to the pilot as magnetic bearing or as a relative bearing to the longitudinal axis of the aircraft depending on the type of indicator installed in the aircraft. In certain applications, such as military, ADF operations may be based on airborne and ground transmitters in the VHF/UHF frequency spectrum (Fig. G-9).

**Automatic Terminal Information Service (ATIS)**: The continuous broadcast of recorded noncontrol information in selected terminal areas. Its purpose is to improve controller effectiveness and to relieve frequency congestion by automating the repetitive transmission of essential but routine information, e.g., "Los Angles Information Alpha. 1300 Greenwich Weather, measured ceiling 2000 overcast, visibility three, haze, smoke, temperature seven one, wind two five zero at five; altimeter two niner niner six. ILS runway two five left approach in use, runway two five right closed, advise you have Alpha."

**autorotation**: A rotor flight condition in which the lifting rotor is driven entirely by action of the air when the rotorcraft is in motion. Autorotative landing touchdown is used by a pilot to indicate that he will be landing without applying power to the rotor. Low level autorotation

Fig. G-9. Cessna 300A Nav-O-Matic Autopilot.

commences at an altitude well below the traffic pattern, usually below 100 feet AGL, and is used primarily for tactical military training. 180 degrees autorotation is initiated from a downwind heading and is begun well inside the normal traffic pattern. A "go-around" may not be possible during the latter part of this maneuver.

**aviation weather service**: A service provided by the National Weather Service (NWS) and FAA which collects and disseminates pertinent weather information for pilots, aircraft operators and ATC. Available aviation weather reports and forecasts are displayed at each NWS office and FAA FSS.

**base leg**: See *traffic pattern*.

**beacon**: See *radar, non directional beacon, marker beacon, airport rotating beacon, aeronautical beacon*, and *airway beacon*.

**bearing**: The horizontal direction to or from any point, usually measured clockwise from true north, magnetic north or some other reference point, through 360 degrees.

**below minimums**: Weather conditions below the minimums prescribed by regulation for the particular action involved: e.g., landing minimums and takeoff minimums.

**blast fence**: A barrier that is used to divert or dissipate jet or propeller blast.

**blind speed**: The rate of departure or closing of target relative to the radar antenna at which cancellation of the primary radar target by moving target indicator (MTI) circuits in the radar equipment causes a reduction or complete loss of signal.

**blind spot/blind zone**: An area from which radio transmissions and/or radar echoes cannot be received. The term is also used to describe portions of the airport not visible from the control tower.

**boundary lights**: See *airport lighting*.

**braking action (good, medium, fair, poor, nil)**: A report of conditions on the airport movement area providing a pilot with a degree/quality of braking that he may expect.

**broadcast**: Transmission of information via radio for which an acknowledgment is not expected.

**call-up**: Initial voice contact between a facility and an aircraft, using the identification of the unit being called and the unit initiating the call.

**cardinal altitudes or flight levels**: See *altitude, flight levels*.

**ceiling**: The heights above the earth's surface of the lowest layer of clouds or obscuring phenomena that is reported as "broken," "overcast," or "obscuration," and not classified as "thin" or "partial."

**celestial navigation**: The determination of geographical position by reference to celestial bodies. Normally used in aviation as a secondary means of position determination.

**center**: See *Air Route Traffic Control Center* (ARTCC).

**center's area**: The specified airspace within which an air route traffic control center (ARTCC) provides air traffic control and advisory services.

**chaff**: Thin, narrow metallic reflectors of various lengths and frequency responses, used to reflect radar energy. These reflectors when dropped from aircraft and allowed to drift downward result in large targets on the radar display.

**chase aircraft**: An aircraft flown in proximity to another aircraft normally to observe its performance during training or testing.

**circle to land/circling maneuver**: A maneuver initiated by the pilot to align the aircraft with a runway for landing when a straight-in landing from an instrument approach is not possible or is not desirable. This maneuver is made only after ATC authorization has been obtained and the pilot has established required visual reference to the airport.

**circle to runway (runway number)**: Used by ATC to inform the pilot that he must circle to land because the runway in use is other than the runway aligned with the instrument approach procedure. When the direction of the circling maneuver in relation to the airport/runways is required, the controller will state the direction (eight cardinal compass points) and specify a left or right downwind or base leg as appropriate, e.g., "Cleared VOR Runway 36 approach circle to runway 22" or "Circle northwest of the airport for a right downwind to Runway 22."

**circling minima**: See *landing minimums*.

**Clear Air Turbulence (CAT)**: Turbulence encountered in air where no clouds are present. This term is commonly applied to high-level turbulence associated with wind shear. CAT is often encountered in the vicinity of the jet stream.

**clearance**: See *Air Traffic Clearance*.

**clearance limit**: The fix, point or location which an aircraft is cleared when issued an air traffic clearance.

**clearance void if not of by (time)**: Used by ATC to advise an aircraft that the departure clearance is automatically canceled if takeoff is not made prior to a specified time. The pilot must obtain a new clearance or cancel his IFR flight plan if not off by the specified time.

**cleared as filed**: Means the aircraft is cleared to proceed in accordance with the route of flight in the flight plan. This clearance does not include the altitude, SID or SID transition.

**cleared for (type of) approach**: ATC authorization for an aircraft to execute a specific instrument approach procedure to an airport; e.g., "Cleared for ILS runway 36 approach." (See instrument *approach procedure, approach clearance*).

**cleared for approach**: ATC authorization for an aircraft to execute any standard or special instrument approach procedure for that airport.

Fig. G-10. The 1931 Great Lakes biplane sport/trainer was powered with a 90-hp Cirrus engine of questionable reliability. Restored Great Lakes flying today are usually fitted with Warner radials. New Great Lakes, with essentially the same airframe, are powered with Lycoming O-320 or IO-360 engines.

Normally, an aircraft will be cleared for a specific instrument approach procedure (Fig. G-10).

**cleared for takeoff**: ATC authorization for an aircraft to depart. It is predicated on known traffic and known physical airport conditions.

**cleared for the option**: ATC authorization for an aircraft to make a touch-and-go, low approach, missed approach, stop and go, or full stop landing at the discretion of the pilot. It is normally used in training so that an instructor can evaluate a student's performance under changing situations.

**cleared through**: ATC authorization for an aircraft to make intermediate stops at specified airports without refiling a flight plan while en route to the clearance limit.

**cleared to land**: ATC authorization for an aircraft to land. It is predicated on known traffic and physical airport conditions.

**clear of traffic**: Previously issued traffic is no longer a factor.

**climbout**: That portion of flight operation between takeoff and the initial cruising altitude.

**climb to VFR**: ATC authorization for an aircraft to climb to VFR conditions within a control zone when the only weather limitation is restricted visibility. The aircraft must remain clear of clouds while climbing to VFR (See special VFR).

147

**closed runway:** A runway that is unusable for aircraft operations. Only the airport management/military operations office can close a runway.

**closed traffic:** Successive operations involving takeoffs and landings or low approaches where the aircraft does not exit the traffic pattern.

**clutter:** In radar operations, clutter refers to the reception and visual display of radar returns caused by precipitation, chaff, terrain, numerous aircraft targets or other phenomena. Such returns may limit or preclude ATC from providing services based on radar.

**coastal fix:** A navigation aid or intersection where an aircraft transitions between the domestic route structure and the oceanic route structure.

**codes/transponder codes:** The number assigned to a particular multiple-pulse reply signal transmitted by a transponder.

**combined station/tower:** An air traffic control facility which combines the functions of a Flight Service Station and an airport traffic control tower.

**common route/common portion:** That segment of a North American route between the inland navigation facility and the coastal fix.

**compass locator:** A low power, low or medium frequency (L/MF) radio beacon installed at the site of the outer or middle marker of an instrument landing system (ILS). It can be used for navigation at distances of approximately 15 miles or as authorized in the approach procedure. An *Outer Compass Locator* (LOM) is installed at the site of the outer marker of an ILS. A *Middle Compass Locator* (LMM) is installed at the site of the middle marker of an ILS.

**compass rose:** A circle graduated in degrees, printed on some charts or marked on the ground at an airport. It is used as a reference to either true or magnetic direction.

**composite flight plan:** A flight plan which specifies VFR operation for one portion of flight and IFR for another portion. It is primarily used in military operations.

**composite route system:** An organized oceanic route structure, incorporating reduced lateral spacing between routes, in which composite separation is authorized.

**composite separation:** A method of separating aircraft in a composite route system where, by management of route and altitude assignments, a combination of half the lateral minimum specified for the area concerned and half the vertical minimum is applied.

**compulsory reporting points:** When passing over such a point, aircraft position must be reported to ATC. The points are designated on aeronautical charts by solid triangles or are filed in a flight plan as fixes selected to define direct routes. These points are geographical locations which are defined by navigation aids/fixes. Pilots should discontinue position reporting over compulsory reporting points when informed by ATC that their aircraft is in radar contact (Fig. G-11).

Fig. G-11. The Cessna Ag Truck is powered with a Continental IO-520-D engine of 285-hp and has a hopper capacity of 280 gallons (courtesy of Cessna Aircraft Company).

**consolan**: A low frequency, long-distance Navaid used principally for transoceanic navigation.

**contact**: To establish communications with (followed by the name of the facility and, if appropriate, the frequency to be used). A flight condition wherein the pilot ascertains the attitude of his aircraft and navigates by visual reference to the surface.

**contact approach**: An approach wherein an aircraft on an IFR flight plan, operating clear of clouds with at least one mile flight visibility and having an ATC authorization, may deviate from the instrument approach procedure and proceed to the airport of destination by visual reference to the surface. This approach will only be authorized when requested by the pilot and the reported ground visibility at the destination is at least one statute mile.

**conterminous United States**: The 48 adjoining states and the District of Columbia.

**continental control area**: See *controlled airspace*.

**continental United States**: The 49 states located on the continent of North America and the District of Columbia.

**control area**: See *controlled airspace*.

**controlled airspace**: Airspace, designated as a continental control area or transition area, within which some or all aircraft may be subject to air traffic control. (Refer to the Airman's Information Manual and FAR Part 71). Following are types of U.S. controlled airspace.

*Continental control area* is the airspace of the 48 contiguous states, the District of Columbia and Alaska, excluding the Alaskan Peninsula west of 160 degrees W. longitude, at and above 14,500 feet MSL. It does not include the airspace less than 1,500 feet above the surface of the earth or prohibited and restricted areas, other than the restricted areas listed in FAR Part 71.

*Control area* is airspace designated as colored Federal Airways, VOR Federal Airways, Terminal Control Areas, additional control areas and control area extensions, but not including the continental control area. Unless otherwise designated, control areas also include the airspace between a segment of a main VOR airway and its associated alternate segments. The vertical extent of the various categories of airspace contained in control areas are defined in Federal Aviation Regulations (FAR) Part 71.

*Control zone* is controlled airspace which extends upward from the surface and terminates at the base of the continental control area. Control zones that do not underlie the continental control area have no upper limit. A control zone may include one or more airports. It is normally a circular area within a radius of five statute miles and any extensions necessary to include instrument approach and departure paths.

*Terminal Control Area (TCA)* is controlled airspace extending upward from the surface, or higher to specified altitudes, within which all aircraft are subject to operating rules and pilot and equipment requirements specified in FAR Part 91. TCAs are depicted on sectional, World Aeronautical, en route low altitude DOD FLIP and TCA charts.

*Transition area* is controlled airspace extending upward from 700 feet or more above the surface of the earth when designated in conjunction with an airport for which an approved instrument approach procedure has been prescribed, or from 1,200 feet or more above the surface of the earth when designated in conjunction with airway route structures or segments. Unless otherwise limited, transition areas terminate at the base of the overlying controlled airspace. Transition areas are designed to contain IFR operations in controlled airspace during portions of the terminal operation, and while transiting between the terminal and en route environment.

**controller**: See *Air Traffic Control Specialist*.

**control sector**: An airspace area of defined horizontal and vertical dimensions for which a controller, or group of controllers, has air traffic control responsibility, normally within an air route traffic control center or an approach control facility. Sectors are established based on predominant traffic flows, altitude strata and controller workload. Pilot communications during operations within a sector are normally maintained on discrete frequencies assigned to the sector (Fig. G-12).

**control slash**: A radar beacon slash representing the actual position of the associated aircraft. Normally, the control slash is the one closest to the interrogating radar beacon site. When ARTCC radar is operating in narrowband (digitized) mode, the control slash is converted to a target symbol.

**control zone**: See *controlled airspace*.

**coordinates**: The intersection of lines of reference, usually expressed in degrees, minutes, and seconds of latitude and longitude, used to determine position or location.

Fig. G-12. The 1962 Beechcraft Debonair (Model 33) was actually a straight-tailed Bonanza with 225 hp. The Debonair was officially renamed "Bonanza" in 1968.

**coordination fix:** The fix in relation to which facilities will hand-off, transfer control of an aircraft, or coordinate flight progress data. For terminal facilities it may also serve as a clearance for arriving aircraft.

**correction:** An error has been made in the transmission and the correct version follows.

**course:** The intended direction of flight in the horizontal plane measure in degrees from north. The ILS localizer signal pattern usually specified as front course or back course.

**critical engine:** The engine which, upon failure, would most adversely affect the performance or handling qualities of an aircraft.

**cross (fix) at (altitude):** Used by ATC when an altitude restriction at a specified fix is required.

**cross (fix) at or above (altitude):** Used by ATC when an altitude restriction at a specified fix is required. It does not prohibit the aircraft from crossing the fix at a higher altitude than specified; however, the higher altitude may not be one that will violate a succeeding altitude restriction or altitude assignment.

**cross (fix) at or below (altitude):** Used by ATC when a maximum crossing altitude at a specific fix is required. It does not prohibit the aircraft from crossing the fix at a lower altitude; however, it must be at or above the minimum IFR altitude.

**crosswind:** When used concerning the traffic pattern, the word means "crosswind leg." When used concerning wind conditions, the word means a wind not parallel to the runway or the path of an aircraft.

**crosswind component:** The wind component measured in knots at 90 degrees to the longitudinal axis of the runway.

**cruise:** Used in an ATC clearance to authorize a pilot to conduct flight at any altitude from the minimum IFR altitude up to and including the altitude specified in the clearance. The pilot may level-off at any intermediate altitude within his block of airspace. Climb/descent within the block is to be made at the discretion of the pilot. However, once the pilot starts descent and reports leaving an altitude in the block, he may not return to that altitude without additional ATC clearance. Further, cruise is approval for the pilot to proceed to and make an approach at destination airport and can be used in conjunction with an airport clearance limit at locations with a standard/special instrument approach procedure. The FARs require that if an instrument letdown to an airport is necessary, the pilot shall make the letdown in accordance with a standard/special instrument approach procedure for that airport. Cruise can also be used with an airport clearance limit at locations that are within/below/outside controlled airspace and without a standard/special instrument appraoch procedure. Such a clearance is *not authorization* for the pilot to descend under IFR conditions below the applicable minimum IFR altitude. Nor does it imply that ATC is exercising control over aircraft in uncontrolled airspace. However, it provides a means for the aircraft to proceed to destination airport, descend and land in accordance with applicable FARs governing VFR flight operations. Also, this provides search and rescue protection until such time as the IFR flight plan is closed.

**cruising altitude/level:** An altitude or flight level maintained during an en route level flight. This is a constant altitude and should not be confused with a cruise clearance.

**Decision Height (DH):** With respect to the operation of aircraft, it means the height at which a decision must be made during an ILS or PAR instrument approach, to either continue the approach or execute a missed approach.

**decoder:** The device used to decipher signals received from ATCRBS and SIF transponders to effect their display as select codes.

**Defense Visual Flight Rules (DVR):** Rules applicable to flights within an ADIZ conducted under the visual flight rules in FAR Part 91.

**delay indefinite (reason if known) expect approach/further clearance (time):** Used by ATC to inform a pilot when an accurate estimate of the delay time and the reason for the delay cannot immediately be determined; e.g., a disabled aircraft on the runway, terminal or area saturation, weather below landing minimums.

**departure control:** A function of an approach control facility providing air traffic control service for departing IFR and, under certain conditions, VFR aircraft.

**departure time:** The time an aircraft becomes airborne.

**deviations:** A departure from a current clearance, such as an off-course maneuver to avoid weather or turbulence. Where specially authorized in the FARs and requested by the pilot ATC may permit pilots to deviate from certain regulations.

**DF approach procedure**: Used under emergency conditions where another instrument approach procedure cannot be executed. DF guidance for an instrument approach is given by ATC facilities with DF capability.

**DF fix**: The geographical location of an aircraft obtained by one or more direction finders.

**DF guidance steer**: Headings provided to aircraft by facilities equipped with direction finding equipment. These headings, if followed, will lead the aircraft to a predetermined point such as the DF station or an airport. DF guidance is given to aircraft in distress or to other aircraft which request the service. Practice DF guidance is provided when workload permits (Fig. G-13).

**direct**: Straight line flight between two navigational aids, fixes, points or any combination thereof. When used by pilots in describing off-airway routes, points defining direct route segments become compulsory reporting points unless the aircraft is under radar contact.

**Direction Finder (DF/UDF/VDF/UVDF)**: A radio receiver equipped with a direction-sensing antenna used to take bearings on a radio transmitter. Specialized radio direction finders are used in aircraft as navigation aids. Others are ground-based primarily to obtain a "fix" on a pilot requesting orientation assistance or to locate downed aircraft. A location "fix" is established by the intersection of two or more bearing lines plotted on a navigational chart using either two separately located direciton finders, or by the pilot plotting the bearing indications of his DF on two separately located ground based transmitters. Both transmitters can be identified on his chart. UDFs receive signals in the ultra high frequency radio broadcast band, VDFs in the very high frequency band and UVDFs in both bands. ATC provides DF service at those air traffic control towers and Flight Service Stations listed in the Airport/Facility Directory, and DOD FLIP IFR En Route Supplement.

**discrete code/discrete beacon code**: As used in the air traffic control radar beacon system (ATCRBS), any one of the 4096 selectable Mode

Fig. G-13. The Piper Archer II evolved from the Cherokee 180. (courtesy of Piper Aircraft Corporation).

3/A aircraft transponder codes except those ending in zero zero. Discrete codes are 0010, 1201, 2317 and 7777. Non-discrete codes are 0100, 1200 and 7700. Non-discrete codes are normally reserved for radar facilities that are not equipped with discrete code capability and for other purposes such as emergencies (7700), VFR aircraft (1200), etc.

**discrete frequency**: A separate radio frequency for use in direct pilot-controller communications in air traffic control. It reduces frequency congestion by controlling the number of aircraft operating on a particular frequency at one time. Discrete frequencies are normally designated for each control sector in en route/terminal ATC facilities. Discrete frequencies are listed in the Airport/Facility Directory, and DOD FLIP IFR En Route Supplement.

**displaced threshold**: A threshold that is located at a point on the runway other than the designated beginning of the runway.

**Distance Measuring Equipment (DME)**: Equipment (airborne and ground) used to measure, in nautical miles, the slant range distance of an aircraft from the DME navigational aid.

**DME fix**: A geographical position determined by reference to a navigational aid which provides distance and azimuth information. It is defined by a specific distance in nautical miles and a radial or course (i.e., localizer) in degrees magnetic from that aid.

**DME separation**: Spacing of aircraft in terms of distances (nautical miles) determined by reference to DME equipment.

**DOD FLIP**: Department of Defense Flight Information Publications used for flight planning, en route and terminal operations. FLIP is produced by the Defense Mapping Agency for worldwide use. United States Government Flight Information Publications (en route charts and instrument approach procedure charts) are incorporated in DOD FLIP for use in the National Airspace System (NAS).

**downwind leg**: See *traffic pattern*.

**drag chute**: A parachute device installed on certain aircraft which is deployed on landing roll to assist in deceleration of the aircraft.

**duty priority**: The order of providing various services by air traffic controllers and flight service specialists.

Air Traffic Controllers give first priority to separation of aircraft as required in the *Controllers' Handbook* and to the issuance of safety advisories. Give second priority to other services that are required but do not involve separation of aircraft. Give third priority to additional service to the extent possible. Priority for the handling of emergencies cannot be prescribed because of the infinite variety of possible situations which may occur.

Flight Service Specialist duty priorities include emergency or urgent actions when life or property is in immediate danger, actions required by indications of NAVAID malfunctioning, services to airborne aircraft, weather observations and PIREPs, preflight pilot briefings, unscheduled broadcasts, teletypewriter duties, transcribed weather broadcasts and pilot automatic telephone weather answering service and scheduled broadcasts.

**Emergency Locator Transmitter (ELT):** A radio transmitter attached to the aircraft structure which operates from its own power source on 121.5 MHz and 243.0 MHz. It aids in locating downed aircraft by radiating a downward sweeping audio tone, two to four times per second. It is designed to function without human action after an accident.

**emergency safe altitude**: See *minimum safe altitude*.

**en route air traffic control services**: Air traffic control service provided aircraft on an IFR flight plan, generally by centers, when these aircraft are operating between departure and destination terminal areas. When equipment capabilities and controller workload permit, certain advisory/assistance services may be provided to VFR aircraft.

**en route charts**: See *aeronautical charts*.

**en route descent**: Descent from the en route cruising altitude which takes place along the route of flight.

**en route flight advisory service/flight watch**: A service specifically designed to provide, upon pilot request, timely weather information pertinent to the type of flight, intended route of flight and altitude. The FSSs providing this service are listed in Airport/Facility Directory. See *flight watch*.

**execute missed approach**: Instructions issued to a pilot making an instrument approach which means continue inbound to the missed approach point and execute the missed approach procedure as described on the Instrument Approach Procedure Chart, or as previously assigned by ATC. The pilot may climb immediately to the altitude specified by such procedure upon making a missed approach. No turns should be initiated prior to reaching the missed approach point. When conducting an ASR or PAR approach, execute the assigned missed approach procedure immediately upon receiving instructions to "execute missed approach."

**expect approach clearance (time)**: The time at which it is expected that an arriving aircraft will be cleared to begin an approach for landing. It is issued when the aircraft clearance limit is a designated initial, intermediate, or final approach fix for the approach in use and the aircraft is to be held. If delay is anticipated, the pilot should be advised of his EAC (Expected Approach Clearance) at least five minutes before the aircraft is estimated to reach the clearance limit.

**expect (altitude) at (time) or (fix)**: Used under certain conditions in a departure clearance to provide a pilot with an altitude to be used in the event of two-way communications failure.

**Expect Departure Clearance (Time) (EDCT)**: Used in *Fuel Advisory Departure* (FAD) program. The time the operator can expect a gate release. Excluding long distance flight, an EDCT will always be assigned even though it may be the same as the *Estimated Time of Departure* (ETD). The EDCT is calculated by adding the "ground delay" factor.

**Expect Further Clearance (time) (EFC)**: The time at which it is expected that additional clearance will be issued to an aircraft. It is issued when the aircraft clearance limit is a fix not designated as part of the approach procedure to be executed, and the aircraft will be held. If delay is anticipated, the pilot should be advised of his EFC at least five minutes before the aircraft is estimated to reach the clearance limit.

**expect further clearance via (airways, routes or fixes)**: Used to inform pilot of the routing he can expect if any part of the route beyond a short range clearance limit differs from that filed.

**fast file**: A system whereby a pilot files a flight plan via telephone that is tape recorded and then transcribed for transmission to the appropriate air traffic facility. Locations having a fast file capability are contained in the *Airport/Facility Directory* (refer to AIM).

**feathered propeller**: A propeller whose blades have been rotated so that the leading and trailing edges are nearly parallel with the aircraft flight path to stop or minimize drag and engine rotation. Normally used to indicate shutdown of a reciprocating or turboprop engine due to a malfunction.

**feeder route**: A route depicted on insturment approach procedure charts to designate routes for aircraft to proceed from the en route structure to the initial approach fix (IAF).

**ferry flight**: A flight for the purpose of returning an aircraft to base, delivering an aircraft from one location to another or moving an aircraft to and from a maintenance base. Ferry flights, under certain conditions, may be conducted under terms of a special flight permit.

**filed**: Normally used in conjunction with flight plans, meaning a flight plan has been submitted to ATC.

**final**: Commonly used to mean that an aircraft is on the final approach course or is aligned with a landing area.

**final approach course**: A straight line extension of a localizer, a final approach radial/bearing or a runway centerline, all without regard to distance.

**Final Approach Fix (FAF)**: The designated fix from or over which the final approach (IFR) to an airport is executed. The FAF identifies the beginning of the final approach segment of the instrument approach (Fig. G-14).

**final approach, IFR**: The flight path of an aircraft which is inbound to an airport on a final instrument approach course, beginning at the final

Fig. G-14. The 1980 Cessna Skylane. The Skylane first appeared in 1956 and was then simply a Cessna 180 with tricycle gear. More Skylanes have been built than any Cessna except the 172/Skyhawk (courtesy of Cessna Aircraft Company).

approach fix or point and extending to the airport or the point where a circle-to-land maneuver or a missed approach is executed.

**final approach point:** The point, within prescribed limits of an instrument approach procedure, where the aircraft is established on the final approach course and final approach descent may be commenced. A final approach point is applicable only in non-precision approaches where a final approach fix has not been established. In such instances, the pilot identifies the beginning of the final approach segment of the instrument approach.

**final approach segment:** See *segments of an instrument approach procedure*.

**final approach, VFR:** See *traffic pattern*.

**final controller:** The controller providing information and final approach guidance during PAR and ASR approaches utilizing radar equipment.

**fix:** A geographical position determined by visual reference to the surface, by reference to one or more radio navigation aids celestial plotting or by other navigational devices.

**fixed-wing special IFR:** Aircraft operating in accordance with a waiver and a letter of agreement within control zones specified in FAR Part 93.113. These operations are conducted by IFR-qualified pilots in IFR-equipped aircraft and by pilots of agricultural and industrial aircraft.

**flag or flag alarm:** A warning device incorporated in certain airborne navigation and flight instruments indicating that instruments are inoperative or otherwise not operating satisfactorily, or signal strength or quality of the received signal falls below acceptable values.

**flameout:** Unintended loss of combustion in turbine engine resulting in the loss of engine power.

**Flight Information Region (FIR):** An airspace of defined dimensions within which flight information service and alerting service are provided. Flight information service is provided for the purpose of giving advice and information useful for the safe and efficient conduct of flights. Alerting service is provided to notify appropriate organizations regarding aircraft in need of search and rescue aid, and to assist such organizations as needed.

**flight inspection-flight check:** Inflight investigation and evaluation of a navigational aid to determine whether it meets established tolerances.

**flight level:** A level of constant atmospheric pressure related to a reference datum of 29.92 inches of mercury. Each is stated in three digits that represent hundreds of feet. For example, flight level 250 represents a barometric altimeter indication of 25,000 feet; flight level 255 is an indication of 25,500 feet.

**flight path:** A line, course or track along which an aircraft is flying or intended to be flown.

**flight plan:** Specified information relating to the intended flight of an aircraft that is filed orally or in writing with an FSS or an ATC facility.

**flight recorder:** A general term applied to any instrument or device that records information about the performance of an aircraft in flight, or about conditions encountered in flight. Flight recorders may make records of airspeed, outside air temperature, vertical acceleration, engine RPM, manifold pressure and other pertinent variables for a given flight.

**Flight Service Station (FSS):** Air Traffic Service facilities within the *National Airspace System* (NAS) which provide pilot briefing and en route communications with VFR flights; assist lost IFR/VFR aircraft; assist aircraft having emergencies; relay ATC clearances; originate, classify and disseminate Notices to Airmen (NOTAMs); broadcast aviation weather and NAS information; receive and close flight plans; monitor radio NAVAIDS; notify search and rescue units of missing VFR aircraft; and operate the national weather teletypewriter systems. In addition, at selected locations, FSSs take weather observations, issue airport advisories, administer airmen written examinations and advise Customs and Immigration of trans-border flights.

**Flight Standards District Office (FSDO):** An FAA field office serving an assigned geographical area, staffed with Flight Standards personnel, who serve the aviation industry and the general public on matters relating to the certification and operation of air carrier and general aviation aircraft. Activities include surveillance of operational safety, certification of airmen and aircraft, accident prevention, investigation, enforcement, etc.

**flight test**: A fight for the purpose of investigating the operation/flight characteristic of an aircraft component or evaluating an applicant for a pilot certificate or rating.

**flight visibility**: See *visibility*.

**flight watch**: A shortened term for use in air-ground contacts on frequency 122.0 MHz to identify the Flight Service Station providing En Route Flight Advisory Service; e.g., "Oakland Flight Watch."

**FLIP**: See DOD FLIP.

**flow control**: Measures designed to adjust the flow of traffic into a given airspace, along a given route, or bound for a given airport so as to ensure the most effective utilization of the airspace.

**fly heading (degrees)**: Informs the pilot of the heading he should fly. The pilot may have to turn to, or continue on, a specific compass direction in order to comply with the directions. The pilot is expected to turn in the shorter direction to the heading, unless otherwise instructed by ATC.

**formation flight**: More than one aircraft which, by prior arrangement between the pilots, operate as a single aircraft with regard to navigation and position reporting. Separation between the aircraft within the formation is the responsibility of the flight leader and the pilots of the other aircraft in the flight. This includes transition periods when aircraft within the formation are maneuvering to attain separation from each other to effect individual control, and during join-up and breakaway (Fig. G-15).

A standard formation is one in which a proximity of no more than one mile laterally or longitudinally and within 100 feet vertically from the flight leader is maintained by each wingman.

Non-standard formations are those operating under any of the following conditions: when the flight leader had requested and ATC has

Fig. G-15. The Learjet is strictly a business machine. This Century III Series, 35A model is Eaton Corporation's sixth Learjet and was the 1,000th Learjet built. Delivery in March, 1980 (courtesy of Gates Learjet Corporation).

approved other than standard formation dimensions, when operating within an authorized altitude reservation (ALTRV) or under the provisions of a letter of agreement, or when the operations are conducted in airspace specifically designed for special activity.

**FSS**: See *Flight Service Station*.

**Fuel Advisory Departure (FAD)**: Procedures to minimize engine running time for aircraft destined for an airport experience prolonged arrival delays.

**fuel dumping**: Airborne release of usable fuel. This does not include the dropping of fuel tanks (see *jettisoning* of external stores).

**fuel siphoning or fuel venting**: Unintentional release of fuel caused by overflow, puncture, loose cap, etc.

**gate hold procedures**: Procedures at selected airports to hold aircraft at the gate or other ground location whenever departure delays exceed or are anticipated to exceed five minutes. The sequence for departure will be maintained in accordance with initial call-up unless modified by flow control restrictions. Pilots should monitor the ground/clearance delivery frequency for engine start-up advisories or new proposal start-time if the delay changes.

**general aviation**: That portion of civil aviation which encompasses all facets of aviation except air carriers holding a certificate of convenience and necessity, and large aircraft commercial operators.

**General Aviation District Office (GAD?)**: An FAA field office serving a designated geographical area, staffed with Flight Standards personnel, who have responsibility for serving the aviation industry and the general public on all matters relating to the certification and operation of general aviation aircraft.

**glide path (on/above/below)**: Used by ATC to inform an aircraft making a PAR approach of its vertical position (elevation) relative to the descent profile. The terms "slightly" and "well" are used to describe the degree of deviation: e.g., "slightly above glide path." Trend information is also issued with respect to the elevation of the aircraft and may be modified by the terms "rapidly" and "slowly," e.g., "well above glide path, coming down rapidly." See *PAR approach*.

**Glide Slope (GS)**: Provides vertical guidance for aircraft during approach and landing. The glide slope consists of electronic components emitting signals which provide vertical guidance by reference to airborne instruments during instrument approaches such as ILS, or visual ground aids such as VASI which provides vertical guidance for VFR approach or for the visual portion of an instrument approach and landing.

**glide slope intercept altitude**: The minimum altitude of the intermediate approach segment prescribed for a precision approach which assures required obstacle clearance. It is depicted on instrument approach procedure charts.

**go ahead**: Proceed with your message. Not to be used for any other purpose.

**go around**: Instructions for a pilot to abandon his approach to landing. Additional instructions may follow. Unless otherwise advised by ATC, a VFR aircraft or an aircraft conducting a visual approach should overfly the runway while climbing to traffic pattern altitude and enter the traffic pattern via the crosswind leg. A pilot on an IFR flight plan making an instrument approach should execute the published missed approach procedure or proceed as instructed by ATC: e.g., "go around," plus additional instructions as required (Fig. G-16).

**graphic notices and supplemental data**: A publication designed primarily as a pilot's operational manual containing a tabulation of parachute jump areas, special notice-area graphics, terminal radar service area graphics, olive branch routes and other data not requiring frequent change.

**ground clutter**: A pattern produced on the radar scope by ground returns which may degrade other radar returns in the affected area. The effect of ground clutter is minimized by the use of moving target indicator (MTI) circuits in the radar equipment resulting in a radar presentation which displays only targets which are in motion.

**Ground Controlled Approach (GCA)**: A radar approach system operated from the ground by air traffic control personnel transmitting instructions to the pilot by radio. The approach may be conducted with surveillance radar (ASR) only or with both surveillance and precision

Fig. G-16. The E33A Bonanza, built 1968-69, is essentially the same as the C33A Debonair (1966-67), which is to say that it is essentially the same as the latest F33 Bonanza. After the first 20 years of production, there was not much left to refine on the Bonanzas (courtesy of Beech Aircraft Corporation).

approach radar (PAR). Usage of the term "GCA" by pilots is discouraged except when referring to a GCA facility. Pilots should specifically request a "PAR" approach when a precision radar approach is desired, or request an "ASR" or "surveillance" approach when a non-precision radar approach is desired. See *radar approach*.

**ground speed**: The speed of an aircraft relative to the surface of the earth.

**ground visibility**: See *visibility*.

**handoff**: Transfer of radar identification of an aircraft from one controller to another, either within the same facility or interfacility. Actual transfer of control responsibility may occur at the time of the handoff, or at a specified time, point or altitude.

**have numbers**: Used by pilots to inform ATC that they have received runway and wind information only.

**heavy aircraft**: See *aircraft classes*.

**Height Above Airport (HAA)**: The height of the minimum descent altitude above the published airport elevation. This is published in conjunction with circling minimums. See *minimum descent altitude*.

**Height Above Landing (HAL)**: The height above a designated helicopter landing area used for helicopter instrument approaches. Refer to FAR Part 97.

**Height Above Touchdown (HAT)**: The height of the decision height or minimum descent altitude above the highest runway elevation in the touchdown zone (first 3,000 feet of the runway). HAT is published on instrument approach charts in conjunction with all straight-in minimums. See *decision height* and minimum descent altitude.

**helicopter**: Rotorcraft that, for its horizontal motion, depends principally upon its engine-driven rotors.

**helipad**: That part of the landing and takeoff area designed for helicopters.

**heliport**: Land, water, or structure used or intended to be used for the landing and takeoff of helicopters.

**hertz (Hz)**: The standard radio equivalent of frequency in cycles per second of an electromagnetic wave. Kolohertz (kHz) is a frequency of one thousand cycles per second. Megahertz (MHz) is a frequency of one million cycles per second.

**high frequency communications**: High radio frequencies (HF) between 3 and 30 MHz used for air-ground voice communication in overseas operations.

**High Frequency (HF)**: The frequency band between 3 and 30 MHz.

**high speed taxiway/exit/turnoff**: A long radius taxiway designed and provided with lighting or marking to define the path of aircraft, traveling at high speed (up to 60 kts), from the runway center to a point on the center of a taxiway. Also referred to as long radius exit or turn-off taxiway. The high speed taxiway is designed to expedite aircraft turning off the runway after landing, thus reducing runway occupancy time.

**hold holding/procedure:** A predetermined maneuver which keeps aircraft within a specified airspace while awaiting further clearance from ATC. Also used during ground operations to keep aircraft within a specified area or at a specified point while awaiting further clearance. See *holding fix*.

**holding fix:** A specified fix identifiable to a pilot by NAVAIDS or visual reference to the ground used as a reference point in establishing and maintaining the position of the aircraft while holding.

**homing:** Flight toward a NAVAID, without correcting for wind, by adjusting the aircraft heading to maintain a relative bearing or zero degrees. See *bearing*.

**how do you hear me:** A question relating to the quality of the transmission or to determine how well the transmission is being received.

**ident:** A request for a pilot to activate the aircraft transponder identification feature. This will help the controller to confrim an aircraft identity or to identify an aircraft.

**ident feature:** The special feature in the ATC Radar Beacon System (ATCRBS) equipment and the "I/P" feature in certain Selective Identification Feature (SIF) equipment. It is used to immediately distinguish one displayed beacon target from other beacon targets.

**IFR aircraft/IFR flight:** An aircraft conducting flight in accordance with instrument flight rules.

**IFR conditions:** Weather conditions below the minimum for flight under VFR (Visual Flight Rules). See *instrument meteorological conditions*.

**IFR departure procedure:** See *IFR takeoff minimums and departure* procedures.

**IFR military training routes:** Routes used by the Department of Defense and associated Air Reserve and Air Guard units, for the purpose of conducting low-altitude navigation and tactical training in both IFR and VFR weather conditions below 10,000 feet MSL at airspeeds in excess of 250 kts IAS.

**IFR over the top:** The operation of an aircraft over the top on an IFR flight plan when cleared by air traffic control to maintain VFR conditions or VFR conditions on top.

**IFR takeoff minimums and departure procedures:** FAR, Part 91, prescribes standard takeoff rules for certain civil users. At some airports, obstructions or other factors require the establishment of nonstandard takeoff minimums, departure procedures, or both, to assist pilot in avoiding obstacles during climb to the minimum en route altitude. Those airports are listed in *NOS/DOD Instrument Approach Charts* (IAPs) under a section entitled "IFR Takeoff Minimums and Departure Procedures." The NOS/DOD IAP chart legend illustrates the symbol used to alert the pilot to nonstandard takeoff minimums and departure procedures. When departing IFR from such airports, or from any airports where there are no departure procedures, SIDs, or ATC facilities available, pilots should advise ATC of any departure limitations. Controllers may query a pilot to determine acceptable departure directions, turns or headings after takeoff. Pilots should be familiar with the departure procedures and must assure that their aircraft can meet or exceed any specified climb gradients.

**ILS categories**: *ILS Category I* is an ILS approach procedure which provides for approach to a height above touchdown of not less than 200 feet and with runway visual range of not less than 1800 feet.

*ILS Category II* is an ILS approach procedure which provides for

Fig. G-17. Piper's Turbo Arrow IV. The promise of greater efficiency has resurrected the turbocharger on light aircraft. First offered in the mid-sixties, turbocharging was not widely accepted, and is probably not worth the extra cost to many private pilots today (courtesy of Piper Aircraft Corporation).

approach to a height above touchdown of not less than 100 feet and with runway visual range of not less than 1200 feet.

Three procedures comprise *ILS Category III*: IIIA, An ILS approach procedure which provides for approach without a decision height minimum and a runway visual range of not less than 700 feet, IIIB, an ILS approach procedure which provides for an approach without a decision height minimum and with a runway visual range of not less than 150 feet; and an ILS approach procedure which provides for approach without a decision height minimum and without runway visual range minimum (Fig. G-17).

**immediately**: Used by ATC when such action compliance is required to avoid an imminent situation.

**Information Request (INREQ)**: A request originated by an FSS for information concerning an overdue VFR aircraft.

**Initial Approach Fix (IAF)**: The fixes depicted on instrument approach procedure charts that identifies the beginning of the initial approach segment(s).

**initial approach segment**: See *segments of an instrument approach procedure*.

**Inner Marker (IM)**: A marker beacon used with an ILS (CAT II) precision approach located between the middle marker and the end of the ILS runway. It transmits a radiation pattern keyed at six dots per second and indicates to the pilot, both aurally and visually, that he is at the designated decision height (DH), normally 100 feet above the touchdown zone elevation, on the ILS CAT II approach. It also marks progress during a CAT III approach.

**Instrument Approach Procedure (IAP)**: A series of predetermined maneuvers for the orderly transfer of an aircraft under instrument flight conditions from the beginning of the initial approach to a landing, or to a point from which a landing may be made visually. It is prescribed and approved for a specific airport by competent authority . (Refer to FAR Part 91.) United States civil standard instrument approach procedures are approved by the FAA as prescribed under FAR, Part 97. American military standard instrument approach procedures are approved and published by the Department of Defense. Special instrument approach procedures are approved by the FAA for individual operators, but are not published in FAR, Part 97.

**Instrument Flight Rules (IFR)**: Rules governing the procedures for conducting instrument flight. Also, a term used by pilots and controllers to indicate type of flight plan.

**Instrument Landing System (ILS)**: A precision instrument approach system which normally consists of the following electronic components and visual aids: localizer, glide slope, outer marker, middle marker and approach lights.

**Instrument Meteorological Conditions (IMC):** Meteorological conditions expressed in terms of visibility, distance from cloud, and ceiling less than the minimums specified for visual meteorological conditions.

**instrument runway:** A runway equipped with electronic and visual navigation aids for which a precision or non-precision approach procedure having straight-in landing minimums has been approved.

**Intermediate Fix (IF):** The fix that identifies the beginning of the intermediate approach segment of an instrument approach procedure. The fix is not normally identified on the instrument approach chart as an IF.

**international airport:** Relating to international flight it means: an airport of entry which has been designated by the Secretary of Treasury or Commissioner of Customs as an international airport for customs service, a landing rights airport at which specific permission to land must be obtained from customs authorities in advance, or an airport designated under the Convention on International Civil Aviation as an airport for use by international commercial air transport and/or international general aviation.

**International Civil Aviation Organization (ICAO):** A specialized agency of the United Nations whose objective is to develop the principles and techniques of international air navigation and to foster planning and development of international civil air transport.

**International Flight Information Manual (IFIM):** A publication designed primarily as a pilot's preflight planning guide for flights into foreign airspace and for flights returning to the United States from foreign locations.

**interrogator:** The ground-based surveillance radar beacon transmitter-receiver which normally scans in synchronism with a primary radar, transmitting discrete radio signals which repetitiously request all transponders, on the mode being used, to reply. The replies received are mixed with the primary radar returns and displayed on the same plan position indicator (radar scope). This term is also applied to the airborne element of the TACAN/DME system. See *transponder*.

**intersection** A point defined by any combination of courses, radials or bearings of two or more navigational aids. Used to describe the point where two runways cross, a taxiway and a runway cross, or two taxiways cross.

**intersection departure/intersection takeoff:** A takeoff or proposed takeoff on a runway from an intersection.

**I say again:** Means the message will be repeated.

**Jamming:** Electronic or mechanical interference which may disrupt the display of aircraft on radar or the transmission or reception of radio communications/navigation.

**jet blast**: Jet engine exhaust; thrust stream turbulence. Also, see *wake turbulence*.

**jet route**: A route designed to serve aircraft operations from 18,000 feet MSL up to and including flight level 450. The routes are referred to as "J" routes with numbering to identify each: e.g., J 105. Refer to FAR, Part 71.

**jet stream**: A migrating stream of high-speed winds present at high altitudes.

**jettisoning of external stores**: Airborne release of external stores: e.g., tiptanks, ordinances. Refer to FAR, Part 91.

**joint use restricted area**: See *restricted area*.

**known traffic**: With respect to ATC clearances, it means aircraft whose altitude, position and intentions are known to ATC.

**landing area**: Any locality, either of land or water, including airports and intermediate landing fields, which is used, or intended to be used, for the landing and takeoff of aircraft whether or not facilities are provided for the shelter, servicing, receiving or discharging passengers or cargo.

**landing direction indicator**: A device which visually indicates the direction in which landings and takeoffs should be made. See *tetrhedron*.

**landing minimums/IFR landing minimums**: The minimum visibility prescribed for landing a civil aircraft while using an instrument approach procedure. The minimum applies with other limitations set

Fig. G-18. The Rockwell Jetprop Commander 980 is aimed at the corporate aircraft market—that large segment of business/industrial users whose requirements take them out of the piston-engine class but who cannot justify operation of a pure jet.

torth in FAR, Part 91, with respect to the *minimum Descent Altitude (MDA)* or *Decision Height (DH)* prescribed in the instrument approach procedures as follows: *straight-in landing minimums*, a statement of MDA and visibility, or DH and visibility, required for straight-in landing on a specified runway; or circling minimums, a statement of MDA and visibility required for the circle-to-land maneuver.

Descent below the established MDA or DH is not authorized during an approach unless the aircraft is in a position from which a normal approach to the runway of intended landing can be made, and adequate visual reference to required visual cues is maintained.

**landing roll**: The distance from the point of touchdown to the point where the aircraft can be brought to a stop or exit the runway.

**landing sequence**: The order in which aircraft are positioned for landing. (Fig. G-18).

**last assigned altitude**: The last altitude/flight level assigned by ATC and acknowledged by the pilot.

**lateral separation**: The lateral spacing of aircraft at the same altitude by requiring operation on different routes or in different geographical locations.

**lighted airport**: An airport where runway and obstruction lighting is available.

**light gun**: A handheld directional light signaling device which emits a brilliant narrow beam of white, green or red light as selected by the tower controller. The color and type of light transmitted can be used to approve or disapprove anticipated pilot actions where radio communication is not available. The light gun is used for controlling traffic operating in the vicinity of the airport and on the airport movement area.

**limited remote communications outlet (LRCO)**: An unmanned satellite air/ground communications facility which may be associated with a VOR. These outlets effectively extend the service range of the FSS and provide greater communications reliability. LRCOs are depicted on *en route charts*.

**localizer**: The component of an ILS which provides course guidance to the runway.

**localizer-type directional aid (LDA)**: A NAVAID, used for non-precision instrument approaches, with utility and accuracy comparable to a localizer but which is not part of a complete ILS. It is not aligned with the runway (Fig. G-19).

**localizer usable distance**: The maximum distance from the localizer transmitter at a specified altitude, as verified by flight inspection, at which reliable course information is continuously received.

**local traffic**: Aircraft operating in the traffic pattern or within sight of the tower, aircraft known to be departing or arriving from flight in local

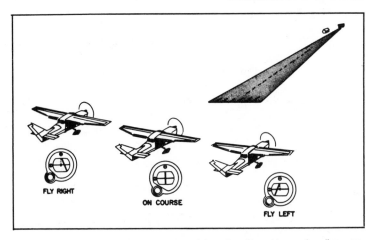

FLY RIGHT

ON COURSE

FLY LEFT

Fig. G-19. Cockpit indications obtained by aircraft making a localizer approach (courtesy of FAA).

practice areas, or aircraft executing practice instrument approaches at the airport.

**longitudinal separation**: The longitudianal spacing of aircraft at the same altitude by a minimum distance expressed in units of time or miles.

**loran/long range navigation**: An electronic navigational system by which hyperbolic lines of position are determined by measuring the difference in the time of reception of synchronized pulse signals from two fixed transmitters. Loran A operates in the 1750-1950 kHz frequency band. Loran C and D operate in the 100-110 kHz frequency band.

**lost communications/two-way radio communications failure**: Loss of the ability to communicate by radio. Aircraft are sometimes refered to as "NORDO" (no radio). Standard pilot procedures are specified in FAR, Part 91. Radar controllers issue procedures for pilots to follow in the event of lost communications during a radar approach, when weather reports indicate that an aircraft will likely encounter IFR conditions during the approach.

**low altitude airway structure/federal airways**: The network of airways serving aircraft operations up to but not including 18,000 feet MSL.

**low altitude alert, check your altitude immediately**: See *Safety Advisory*.

**low approach**: An approach over an airport or runway following an instrument approach of a VFR approach, including the go-around maneuver where the pilot intentionally does not make contact with the runway.

**Low Frequency (LF)**: The frequency band between 30 and 300 kHz.

**mach number**: The ratio of true airspeed to the speed of sound: e.g., Mach .82, Mach 1.6.

**maintain**: Concerning altitude/flight level, the term means to remain at the altitude/flight level specified. The phrases "climb and" and "descend and" normally precede "maintain" and the altitude assignment: e.g., "descend and maintain 5000." If a SID procedure is assigned in the initial or subsequent clearance, the altitude restrictions in the SID procedure, if any, will apply unless otherwise advised by ATC. Concerning other ATC instructions, the term is used in its literal sense: e.g., "maintain VFR."

**make short approach**: Used by ATC to inform a pilot to alter his traffic pattern so as to make a short final approach.

**marker beacon**: An electronic navigation facility transmitting a 75 MHz vertical fan or bone-shaped radiation pattern. Marker beacons are identified by their modulation frequency and keying code. When received by compatible airborne equipment, they indicate to the pilot, both aurally and visually, that he is passing over the facility.

**Maximum Authorized Altitude (MAA)**: A published altitude representing the maximum usable altitude or flight level for an airspace structure or route segment. It is the highest altitude on a Federal Airway, Jet Route, area navigation low or high route, or other direct route for which an MEA is designated in FAR, Part 95, at which adequate reception of navigation and signals is assured.

**mayday**: The international radio-telephony distress signal. When repeated three times, it indicates imminent and grave danger and that immediate assistance is required. See **PAN**.

**metering**: A method of time-regulating arrival traffic into a terminal area.

**metering fix**: A fix along an established route from over which aircraft will be "metered" prior to entering terminal airspace. Normally, this fix should be established at a distance from the airport which will facilitate a profile descent 10,000 feet above airport elevation (AAE) or above.

**Microwave Landing System (MLS)**: An instrument landing system operating in the microwave spectrum which provides lateral and vertical guidance to aircraft having compatible avionics equipment.

**middle compass locator**: See *compass locator*.

**Middle Marker (MM)**: A marker beacon that defines a point along the glide slope of an ILS normally located at or near the point of decision height (DH) for ILS CAT I. It is keyed to transmit alternate dots and dashes, two per second, on a 1300 HZ tone which is received aurally and visually by compatible airborner equipment. See *marker beacon* and *Instrument Landing System*.

**mid RVR**: See *visibility*.

**Military authority asumes responsibility for separation of aircraft (marsa)**: A condition whereby the military servics involved assume responsibility for a separation between participating military aircraft in the ATC system. it is used only for required IFR operations which are specified in letters of agreement or other appropriate FAA or military documents.

**Military Operations Area (MOA)**: See *special use airspace*.

**Minimum Crossing Altitude (MCA)**: The lowest altitude at certain fixes which an aircraft must cross when proceeding in the direction of a higher minimum en route IFR altitude (MEA).

**Minimum Descent Altitude (MDA)**: The lowest altitude, expressed in feet above MSL, to which descent is authorized on final approach or during circle-to-land maneuvering in execution of a standard instrument approach procedure where no electronic glide slope is provided. See *non-precision approach*.

**Minimum En Route IFR Altitude (MEA)**: The lowest published altitude between radio fixes which assures acceptable navigational signal coverage and meets obstacle clearance requirements between those fixes. The MEA prescribed for a federal airway or segment thereof, area navigational low or high route, or other direct route, applies to the entire width of the airway, segment or route between the radio fixes defining the airway, segment or route.

**minimum fuel**: Indicates that an aircraft's fuel supply has reached a state where, upon reaching the destination, it can accept little or no delay. This is not an emergency situation, but merely indicates that an emergency is possible if any undue delay should occur.

**Minimum Holding Altitude (MHA)**: The lowest altitude prescribed for a holding pattern which assures navigational signal coverage, communications and meets obstacle clearance requirements.

**minimum IFR altitudes**: Minimum altitudes for IFR operations as prescribed in FAR, Part 91. These altitudes are published on aeronautical charts and prescribed in FAR, part 95, for airways and routes, and in Part 97 for standard instrument approach procedures. If no applicable minimum altitude is prescribed in Parts 95 or 97, the following minimum IFR altitude applies: in designated mountainous areas, 2000 feet above the highest obstacle within a horizontal distance of five statute miles from the course to be flown; or other than mountainous areas, 1000 feet above the highest obstacle within a horizontal distance of five statute miles from the course to be flown; or as otherwise authorized by the administrator or assigned by ATC.

**Minimum Obstruction Clearance Altitude (MOCA)**: The lowest published altitude in effect between radio fixes on VOR airways, off-airway routes, or route segments which meets obstacle clearance requirements for the entire route segment and which assures acceptable navigation signal coverage only within 22 nautical miles of a VOR.

**Minimum Reception Altitude (MRA)**: The lowest altitude at which an intersection can be determined.

**Minimum Safe Altitude (MSA)**: The minimum altitude specified in FAR, Part 91, for various aircraft operations. Altitudes depicted on approach charts which provide at least 1000 feet of obstacle clearance for emergency use within a specified distance from the navigation facility upon which a procedure is predicated. These altitudes will be identified as minimum sector altitudes or emergency safe altitudes and are established as follows.

**minimum sector altitudes**: Altitudes depicted on approach charts which provide at least 1000 feet of obstacle clearance within a 25-mile radius of the navigation facility upon which the procedure is predicated. Sectors depicted on approach charts must be at least 90 degrees in scope. These altitudes are for emergency use only and do not necessarily assure acceptable navigational signal coverage.

Altitudes may be depicted on approach charts which provide at least 1000 feet of obstacle clearance within a 100-mile radius of the navigation facility upon which the procedure is predicated, and are normally used only in military procedures. These altitudes are identified on published procedures as "emergency safe altitudes."

**Minimum Safe Altitude Warning (MSAW)**: A function of the ARTS III computer that aids the controller by alerting him when a tracked Mode C equipped aircraft is below or is predicted by the computer to go below a predetermined minimum safe altitude.

**minimums/minima**: Weather conditions requirements established for a particular operation or type of operation: e.g., IFR takeoff or landing, alternate airport for IFR flight plans, VFR flight.

**Minimum Vectoring Altitude (MVA)**: The lowest MSL altitude at which an IFR aircraft will be vectored by a radar controller, except as otherwise authorized for radar approaches, departures and missed approaches. The altitude meets IFR obstacle clearance criteria. It may be lower than the published MEA along an airway or J-route segment and may be utilized for radar vectoring only upon the controller's determination that an adequate radar return is being received from the aircraft. Charts depicting minimum vectoring altitudes are normally available only to the controllers and not to pilots.

**missed approach**: A maneuver conducted by a pilot when an instrument approach cannot be completed to a landing. The route of flight and altitude are shown on instrument approach procedure charts. A pilot executing a missed approach prior to the Missed Approach Point (MAP) must continue along the final approach to the MAP. The pilot may climb immediately to the altitude specified in the missed approach procedure. Also, a term used by the pilot to inform ATC that he is executing the missed approach. At locations where ATC radar service is provided, the pilot should conform to radar vectors, when provided by ATC, in lieu of the published missed approach procedure.

**Missed Approach Point (MAP):** A point prescribed in each instrument approach procedure at which the procedure shall be executed if the required visual reference does not exist.

**mode:** The letter or number assigned to a specific pulse spacing of radio signals transmitted or received by ground interrogator or airborne transponder components of the ATC Radar Beacon System (ATCRBS). Mode A (military Mode 3) and Mode C (altitude reporting) are used in air traffic control.

**movement area:** The runways, taxiways, and other areas of an airport which are utilized for taxiing, takeoff and landing of aircraft, exclusive of loading ramp and parking areas. At those airports with a tower, specific approval for entry onto the movement area must be obtained from ATC.

**Moving Target Indicator (MTI):** An electronic device which will permit radar scope presentation only from targets which are in motion. A partial remedy for ground clutter.

**MSAW:** See *Minimum Safe Altitude Warning.*

**NAS stage A:** The en route ATC system's radar, computers and computer programs, controller plan view displays PVDs/radar scopes, input/output devices, and the related communications equipment which are integrated to form the heart of the automated IFR air traffic control

Fig. G-20. Over 15 years of product improvement. A 1980 Learjet Longhorn 50 series is in the foreground accompanied by an early model Learjet 23. The Longhorn 50 can transport 10 passengers well over 3,000 miles at altitudes to 51,000 feet. The original 23 carries six up to 1,400 miles and is certified to 41,000 feet (courtesy of Gates Learjet Corporation).

system. This equipment performs Flight Data Processing (FDP) and Radar Data Processing (RDP). It interfaces with automated terminal systems and is used in the control of en route IFR aircraft.

**NAS stage A conflict alert function**: An aid to the radar controller in detecting impending situations where loss of radar separation minimums for IFR aircraft may occur. Using inputs from automatic tracking, the Conflict Alert Function provides the ARTCC controller with an alert on the radar display when aircraft flying above 18,000 feet MSL are positioned so that violations of separation standards could occur in a short time (approximately two minutes) (Fig. G-20).

**National Airspace System (NAS)**: The common network of American airspace, air navigation facilities, equipment and services, airports or landing areas, aeronautical charts, information and services, rules, regulations and procedures, technical information, and manpower and material. Included are system components shared jointly with the military.

**national beacon code allocation plan airspace**: Airspace over U.S. territory located within the North American continent between Canada and Mexico, including adjacent territorial waters outward to abut boundaries of oceanic control areas (CTA)/Flight Information Regions (FIR).

**National Flight Data Center (NFDC)**: A facility in Washington, D.C., established by the FAA to operate a central aeronautical information service for the collection, validation and dissemination of aeronautical data in support of the activities of government, industry and the aviation community. The information is published in the National Flight Data Digest.

**National Flight Data Digest (NFDD)**: A daily (except weekends and federal holidays) publication of flight information appropriate to aeronautical charts, aeronautical publications, Notices to Airmen (NOTAMs) or other media serving the purpose of providing operational flight data essential to safe and efficient aircraft operations.

**national search and rescue plan**: An inter-agency agreement which provides for the effective utilization of all available facilities in all types of search and rescue missions.

**NAVAID classes**: VOR, VORTAC, and TACAN aids are classed according to their operational use. The three classes of NAVIDS are: T, Terminal; L, Low altitude; and H, High altitude.

The normal service range for T, L, and H class aids is found in AIM. Certain operational requirements make it necessary to use some of these aids at greater ranges than specified. Extended range is made possible through flight inspection determinations. Some aids also have lesser service range due to location, terrain, frequency protection, etc. Restrictions to service range are listed in the Airport/Facility Directory.

**navigable airspace:** Airspace at and above the minimum flight altitudes prescribed in the FARs including airspace needed for safe takeoffs and landings.

**Navigational aid (NAVAID):** Any visual or electronic device airborne or on the surface which provides point to point guidance information or position data to aircraft in flight.

**NDB:** See Non-directional Beacon.

**negative:** "No," "Permission not granted," or "That is not correct."

**negative contact:** Used by pilots to inform ATC that previously issued traffic is not in sight. It may be followed by a pilot's request for the controller to provide assistance in avoiding the traffic. Negative contact is also used when pilots are unable to contact ATC on a particular frequency.

**night:** The time between the end of the evening civil twilight and the beginning of morning civil twilight, as published in the American Air Almanac, converted to local time.

**no gyro approach/vector:** A radar approach/vector provided in case of a malfunctioning gyrocompass or directional gyro. Instead of providing the pilot with headings to be flown, the controller observes the radar track and issues control instructions "turn right/left" or "stop turn" as appropriate.

**non-composite separation:** Separation in accordance with minima other than the composite separation minimum specified for the area concerned.

**Non-Directional Beacon/Radio Beacon (NDB):** An L/MF or UHF radio beacon transmitting non-directional signals whereby the pilot of an aircraft equipped with direction finding equipment can determine his bearing to or from the radio beacon and "home" on, or track to or from the station. When the radio beacon is installed in conjunction with the Instrument Landing System marker, it is normally called a *Compass Locator*.

**nonprecision approach procedure:** A standard instrument approach procedure in which no electronic glide slope is provided: e.g., VOR, TACAN, NDB, LOC, ASR, LDA or SDF approaches.

**nonradar:** Precedes other terms and generally means without the use of radar.

*Nonradar route* is a flight path or route over which the pilot is performing his own navigation. The pilot may be receiving radar separation, radar monitoring or other ATC services while on a nonradar route (Fig. G-21). See *radar route*.

*Nonradar approach* is used to describe instrument approaches for which course guidance on final approach is not provided by ground based precision or surveillance radar. Radar vectors to the final approach course may or may not be provided by ATC. Examples of

175

Fig. G-21. Totally trust the line boy if you like adventure. The wrong kind of fuel or an oil filler cap left off will become your problem, not his.

nonradar approaches are VOR, ADF, TACAN, and ILS approaches.

*Nonradar separation* is the spacing of aircraft in accordance with established minima without the use of radar: e.g., vertical, lateral or longitudinal separation.

*Nonradar arrival* is an arriving aircraft that is not being vectored to the final approach course for an instrument approach or towards the airport for a visual approach. The aircraft may or may not be in a radar environment and may or may not be receiving radar separation, radar monitoring or other services provided by ATC.

**nonradar approach control**: An ATC facility providing approach control service without the use of radar.

**NORDO**: See *lost communications*.

**North American Route**: A numerically coded route preplanned over existing airway and route systems to and from specific coastal fixes serving the North Atlantic. North American routes consist of the following.

*Common route/portion* is that segment of a North American Route between the inland navigation facility and the coastal fix.

*Non-common route/portion* is that segment of a North American route between the inland navigation facility and a designated North American terminal.

*Inland navigation facility* is a navigation aid on a North American Route at which the common route and/or the non-common route begins or ends.

*Coastal fix* is a navigation aid or intersection where an aircraft transitions between the domestic route structure and the oceanic route structure.

**Notices To Airmen**: A publication designed primarily as a pilot's operational manual containing current NOTAM information. A notice containing information, not known sufficiently in advance to publicize by other means, concerning the establishment, condition or change in any facility, service or procedure of or hazard in the *National Airspace System*.

NOTAM (D) is a NOTAM given distant dissemination (in addition to local dissemination) via teletypewriter beyond the area of responsibility of the FSS. These NOTAMS will be stored and repeated hourly until canceled.

NOTAM (L) is a NOTAM given local dissemination by voice (teletype where applicable) and a wide variety of means such as *Tel-autograph*, teleprinter, facsimile reproduction, hot line, telecopier, telegraph and telephone to satisfy local user requirements.

*FDC NOTAM* is a NOTAM, regulatory in nature, transmitted by NFDC and given all-circuit dissemination.

**numerous targets vicinity (location)**: A traffic advisory issued by ATC to advise pilots that targets on the radar scope are too numerous to issue individually.

**obstacle**: An existing object, object of natural growth, or terrain at a fixed geographical location or which may be expected at a fixed location within a prescribed area, with reference to which vertical clearance is or must be provided during flight operation.

**obstruction**: An object which penetrates an imaginary surface described in FAR, Part 77.

**obstruction light**: A light, or one of a group of lights, usually red or white, frequently mounted on a surface structure or natural terrain to warn pilots of the presence of an obstruction.

**off-route vector**: A vector by ATC which takes an aircraft off a previously assigned route. Altitudes assigned by ATC during such vectors provide required obstacle clearance.

**offset parallel runways**: Staggered runways having centerlines which are parallel.

**Olive Branch routes (OB routes) All Weather Low Altitude Routes (AWLARS)**: Training routes used by the USAF and USN jet aircraft in both VFR and IFR weather conditions from the surface to the published altitude. Routes, their altitudes and times of operation are shown in *Graphic Notices and Supplemental Data* and the DOD FLIP. Graphic information and weather requirements necessary for IFR and VFR training are also shown in Graphic Notices and Supplemental Data. The current operational status of a particular route may be obtained by calling an FSS near the route.

**on course**: Used to indicate that an aircraft is established on the route centerline. It is also used by ATC to advise a pilot making a radar approach that his aircraft is lined up on the final approach course.

**on-course indication**: An indication of an instrument which provides the pilot a visual means of determining that the aircraft is located on the centerline of a given navigational track; or an indication on a radar scope that an aircraft is on a given track.

**option approach**: An approach requested and conducted by a pilot which will result in either a touch-and-go, missed approach, low approach, stop-and-go or full stop landing.

**organized track system**: A movable system of oceanic tracks that traverses the North Atlantic between Europe and North America the physical position of which is determined twice daily by taking the best advantage of the winds aloft.

**out**: The conversation is ended and no response is expected.

**outer compass locator**: See *compass locator*.

**outer fix**: A general term used within ATC to describe fixes in the terminal area, other than the final approach fix. Aircraft are normally cleared to these fixes by an Air Route Traffic Control Center (ARTCC) or an approach control facility. Aircraft are normally cleared from these fixes to the final approach fix or final approach course.

**Outer Marker (OM)**: A marker beacon at or near the glide slope intercept altitude of an ILS approach. It is keyed to transmit two dashes per second on a 400 HZ tone which is received aurally and visually by compatible airborne equipment. The OM is normally located four to seven miles from the runway threshold on the extended centerline of the runway.

**over**: My transmission is ended; I expect a response.

**overhead approach/360 overhead**: A series or predetermined maneuvers prescribed for VFR arrival of military aircraft (often in formation) for entry into the VFR traffic pattern and to proceed to a landing. The pattern usually specifies the following: the radio contact required of the pilot, an initial approach three to five miles in length, the speed to be maintained, an elliptical pattern consisting of two 180-degree turns, a break point at which the first 180-degree turn is started, the direction of turns, altitude (at least 500 feet above the conventional pattern), and, a "roll-out" on final approach not less than ¼-mile from the landing threshold and not less than 300 feet above the surface.

**PAN**: The international radio-telephony urgency signal. When repeated three times it indicates uncertainty or alert, followed by the nature of the urgency. See *mayday*.

**parallel ILS approaches**: ILS approaches to parallel runways by IFR aircraft which, when established inbound toward the airport on the

Fig. G-22. The Cessna Centurion is in the Bonanza class performance-wise. Pictured is a 1977 model, like the Bonanza the Centurion hasn't changed much in recent years (courtesy of Cessna Aircraft Company).

adjacent localizer courses, are radar-separated by at least two miles. (Fig. G-22).

**parallel offset route**: A parallel track to the left or right of the designated or established airway/route. Normally associated with area navigation (RNAV) operations.

**parallel runways**: Two or more runways at the same airport whose centerlines are parallel. In addition to runway number, parallel runways are designated as L (left) and R (right) or, if three parallels exist, L, R and C (center).

**par approach**: A precision instrument approach wherein the air traffic controller issues guidance instructions, for pilot compliance, based on the aircraft's position in relation to the final approach course (azimuth), the glide slope (elevation), and the distance (range) from the touchdown point on the runway as displayed on the controller's radar scope.

**permanent echo**: Radar signals reflected from fixed objects on the earth's surface: e.g., buildings, towers and terrain. Permanent echos are distinguished from ground clutter by being definable locations rather than large areas. Under certain conditions they may be used to check radar alignment.

**Photo Reconnaissance (PR)**: Military activity that requires locating individual photo targets and navigating to the targets at a preplanned angle and altitude. The activity normally requires a lateral route width of 16 nm and altitude range of 1500 feet to 10,000 feet AGL.

**pilot briefing/pre-flight pilot briefing**: A service provided by the FSS to assist pilots in flight planning. Briefing items may include weather information, NOTAMS, military activities, flow control information and other items as requested.

**Pilot In Command (PIC)**: The pilot responsible for the operation and safety of an aircraft during flight time.

**Pilots' Automatic Telephone Weather Answering Service (PATWAS)**: A continuous telephone recording containing current and forecast weather information for pilots.

**pilot's discretion**: When used in conjunction with altitude assignments, it means that ATC has offered the pilot the option of starting climb or descent at any rate he wishes. He may temporarily level off at any intermediate altitude. However, once he has vacated an altitude he may not return to that altitude.

**Pilot Weather Report (PIREP)**: A report of meteorological phenomena encountered by aircraft in flight.

**position report/progress report**: A report over a known location as transmitted by an aircraft to ATC.

**position symbol**: A computer generated indication shown on a radar display to indicate the mode of tracking.

**positive control**: The separation of all air traffic, within designated airspace, by air traffic control.

**Positive Control Area (PCA)**: Airspace designated in FAR, Part 71, wherein aircraft are required to be operated under Instrument Flight Rules (IFR). Vertical extent of PCA is from 18,000 feet to and including flight level 600 throughout most of the conterminous United States. In Alaska, it includes the airspace over the State of Alaska from 18,000 feet up to and including flight level 600, but not including the airspace less than 1500 feet above the surface, and the Alaskan Peninsula west of longitude 160 degrees W. Rules for operating in positive control areas are found in FARS 91.97 and 91.24.

**precipitation**: Any or all forms of water particles (rain, sleet, hail or snow) that fall from the atmosphere and reach the surface.

**precision approach procedure/precision approach**: A standard instrument approach procedure in which an electronic glide slope is provided: e.g., ILS and PAR.

**Precision Approach Radar (PAR)**: Radar equipment in some ATC facilities serving military airports, which is used to detect and display the azimuth, range and elevation of an aircraft on the final approach course to a runway. It is used by air traffic controllers to provide the pilot with a precision approach, or to monitor certain nonradar approaches.

**preferential routes**: Preferential routes (PDRs, PARs and PDARs) are adapted in ARTCC computers to accomplish inter/intra-facility controller coordination and to assure that flight data is posted at the proper control positions. Locations having a need for these specific inbound and outbound routes normally publish such routes in local facility bulletins, and their use by pilots minimizes flight plan route amendments. When the workload or traffic situation permits, controllers normally provide radar vectors or assign requested routes to minimize circuitous routing. Preferential routes are usually confined to one ARTCC area and are referred to by the following names or acronyms:

*Preferential Departure Route (PDR)* is a specific departure route from an airport or terminal area to an en route point where there is no further need for flow control. It may be included in a Standard Instrument Departure (SID) or a preferred IFR Route.

*Preferential Arrival Route (PAR* is a specific arrival route from an appropriate en route point to an airport or terminal area. It may be included in a Standard Terminal Arrival Route (STAR) or a Preferred IFR Route. The abbreviation PAR is used primarily within the ARTCC and should not be confused with the abbreviation for Precision Approach Radar.

*Preferential Departure and Arrival Route (PDAR)* is a route between two terminals which are within or immediately adjacent to one ARTCC area. PDARs are not synonomous with Preferred IFR Routes but may be listed as they do accomplish essentially the same purpose.

**Preferred IFR Routes**: Routes established between busier airports to increase system efficiency and capacity. They normally extend through one or more ARTCC areas and are designed to achieve balanced traffic flows among high density terminals. IFR clearances are issued on the basis of these routes except when severe weather avoidance procedures or other factors dictate otherwise. Preferred IFR Routes are listed in the Airport/Facility Directory. If a flight is planned to or from an area having such routes, but the departure or arrival point is not listed in the Airport/Facility Directory, pilots may use that part of a Preferred IFR Route which is appropriate for the departure or arrival point that is listed. Preferred IFR Routes are correlated with SIDs and STARs may be defined by airways, jet routes, direct routes between NAVAIDS, Waypoints, NAVAID radials/DME or any other combinations thereof.

**prevailing visibility**: See *visibility*.

**procedure turn inbound**: That point of a procedure turn maneuver where course reversal has been completed and an aircraft is established inbound on the intermediate approach segment of final approach course. A report of "procedure turn inbound" is normally used by ATC as a position report for separation purposes.

**Procedure Turn (PT)**: The maneuver prescribed when it is necessary to reverse direction to establish an aircraft on the intermediate approach segment or final approach course. The outbound course, direction of turn, distance within which the turn must be completed and minimum altitude are specified in the procedure. However, the point at which the turn may be commenced, and the type and rate of turn, are left to the discretion of the pilot.

**profile descent**: An uninterrupted descent (except where level flight is required for speed adjustment: e.g., 250 kts at 10,000 feet MSL) from cruising altitude/level to interception of a glide slope, or to a minimum altitude specified for the initial or intermediate approach segment of a non-precision instrument approach. The profile descent normally terminates at the approach gate or where the glide slope or other appropriate minimum altitude is intercepted.

**prohibited area**: See *special use airspace*.

**Proposed Boundary Crossing Time (PBCT)**: Each center has a PBCT parameter for each internal airport. Proposed internal flight plans are transmitted to the adjacent center if the flight time along the proposed route from the departure airport to the center boundary is less than or equal to the value of PBCT, or if airport adaption specifies transmission regardless of PBCT.

**published**: Depicted on aeronautical charts or described in other aeronautical publications and approved for use in the National Airspace System.

**published route**: A route for which an IFR altitude has been established and published: e.g., *Federal Airways*, *Jet Routes*, *Area Navigation Routes* and *Specified Direct Routes*.

**quadrant**: A quarter of a circle, centered on a NAVAID, oriented clockwise from magnetic north as follows: NE quadrant 000-089, SE quadrant 090-179, SW quadrant 180-269 and NW quadrant 270-359 degrees.

**quick look**: A feature of NAS Stage A and ARTS which provides the controller the capability to display full data blocks of tracked aircraft from other control positions.

**quota flow control (QFLOW)**: A flow control procedure by which the *Central Flow Control Function (CFCF)* restricts traffic to the ARTC Center area having an impacted airport, thereby avoiding sector/area saturation.

**radar advisory**: The provision of advice and information based on radar observations. See *Advisory Service*.

**Radar Air Traffic Control Facility (RATCF)**: An air traffic control facility, located at a U.S. Navy or Marine Corps Air Station, utilizing surveillance and, normally, precision approach radar and air/ground communications equipment to provide approach control services to aircraft arriving, departing or transiting the airspace controlled by the facility. The facility may be operated by the FAA, the USN or USMC, and service may be provided to both civil and military airports. Similar to TRACON (FAA), RAPCON (USAF), RATCF (Navy) and ARAC (Army).

**radar approach**: An instrument approach procedure which utilizes *Precision Approach Radar (PAR)* or *Airport Surveillance Radar (ASR)*.

Fig. G-23. The Mooneys are designed with great attention to aerodynamic detail and probably return more speed per horsepower than any other light aircraft. Pictured is the 1970 Statesman, a stretched version of the Ranger and Mark 21, known today as the 201 (courtesy of Mooney Aircraft Corporation).

**Radar Approach Control (RAPCON)**: An air traffic control facility, located at a USAF base, utilizing surveillance and, normally, precision approach radar and air/ground communications equipment to provide approach control services to aircraft arriving, departing or transiting the airspace controlled by the facility. See *Radar Air Traffic Control Facility*.

**radar arrival**: An arriving aircraft which is being vectored to the final approach course for an instrument approach or toward the airport for a visual approach (Fig. G-23). See *radar approach*.

**radar contact**: Used by ATC to inform an aircraft that it is identified on the radar display and radar service may be provided until radar identification is lost or radar service is terminated. When a pilot is informed of "radar contact," he must automatically discontinue reporting over compulsory reporting points. It also means the term the air traffic controller uses to inform the transferring controller that the target being transferred is identified on his radar display.

**radar contact lost**: Used by ATC to inform a pilot that radar identification of his aircraft has been lost. The loss may be attributed to several things including the aircraft merging with weather or ground clutter, the aircraft flying below the radar line-of-sight, the aircraft entering an area of poor radar return, or a failure of the aircraft transponder or ground radar equipment.

**radar environment**: An area in which radar service may be provided.

**radar flight following**: The observation of the progress of radar-identified aircraft, whose primary navigation is done by the pilot, wherein the controller retains and correlates the aircraft identity with the appropriate target symbol displayed on the radar scope.

**radar identification**: The process of ascertaining that an observed radar target is the radar return from a particular aircraft.

**radar identified aircraft**: An aircraft whose position has been correlated with an observed target or symbol on the radar display.

**radar monitoring**: See *radar service*.

**radar point out/point out**: Used between controllers to indicate radar handoff action where the initiating controller plans to retain communications with an aircraft penetrating the other controller's airspace and additional coordination is required.

**radar/radio detection and ranging**: A device which measures the time interval between transmission and reception of radio pulses and correlates the angular orientation of the radiated antenna beam or beams in azimuth and/or elevation of objects in the path of the transmitted pulses.

*Primary Radar* is a radar system in which a minute portion of a radio pulse transmitted from a site is reflected by an object and then received back at that site, for processing and display at an air traffic control facility.

*Secondary radar/radar beacon/ATCRBS* is a radar system in which the object to be detected is fitted with cooperative equipment in the form of a radio receiver/transmitter (transponder). Radar pulses transmitted from the searching transmitter/receiver (interrogator) site are received in the cooperative equipment and used to trigger a distinctive transmission from the transponder. This reply transmission, rather than a reflected signal, is then received back at the interrogator site for processing and display at an air traffic control facility.

**Radar Route**: A flight path or route over which an aircraft is vectored. Navigational guidance and altitude assignments are provided by ATC.

**radar separation**: See *radar service*.

**radar service**: A term which encompasses one or more of the following services based on the use of radar which can be provided by a controller to a pilot of a radar-identified aircraft. *Radar separation* is the radar spacing of aircraft in accordance with established minima. *Radar navigational guidance* involves vectoring aircraft to provide course guidance. *Radar monitoring* is the radar flight following of aircraft, whose primary navigation is being performed by the pilot, to observe and note deviations from its authorized flight path, airway or route. When being applied specifically to radar monitoring of instrument approaches with precision approach radar (PAR) or radar monitoring of simultaneous ILS approaches, it includes advice and instructions whenever an aircraft nears or exceeds the prescribed PAR safety limit or simultaneous ILS no transgression zone (Fig. G-24).

**radar service terminated**: Used by ATC to inform a pilot that he will no longer be provided any of the services that could be received while

Fig. G-24. One of the best buys in today's used plane market for low cost pleasure flying is the Luscombe Silvaire, produced from 1937 to 1960 (by several different companies), with engines ranging from 50 to 90 hp. In background is a Bellanca Cruisair (courtesy of Jeffery Ethell).

under radar contact. Radar service is automatically terminated and the pilot is not advised in the following cases: an aircraft cancels its IFR flight plan, except within a TCA, TRSA, or where Stage II service is provided at the completion of a radar approach; when an arriving aircraft receiving Stage I, II, or III service is advised to contact the tower; when an aircraft conducting a visual approach or contact approach is advised to contact the tower; and when an aircraft making an instrument approach has landed or the tower has the aircraft in sight, whichever occurs first.

**radar surveillance**: The radar observation of a given geographical area for the purpose of performing some radar function.

**radar traffic advisories**: See *traffic advisories*.

**radial**: A magnetic bearing extending from a VOR/VORTAC or TACAN navigation facility.

**radio**: A device used for communication. The term is also used to refer to a Flight Service Station (FSS): e.g., "Seattle Radio" is used to call Seattle FSS.

**radio altimeter/radar altimeter**: Aircraft equipment which makes use of the reflection of radio waves from the ground to determine the height of the aircraft above the surface.

**radio beacon**: See *non-directional beacon*.

**Radio Magnetic Indicator (RMI)**: An aircraft navigational instrument coupled with a gyro compass or similar compass that indicates the direction of a selected NAVAID and indicates bearing with respect to the heading of the aircraft.

**ramp**: See *apron*.

**read back**: Repeat my message back to me.

**receiving controller/facility**: A controller/facility receiving control of an aircraft from another controller or facility.

**reduce speed to**: See *speed adjustment*.

**release time**: A departure time restriction issued to a pilot by ATC when necessary to separate a departing aircraft from other traffic.

**Remote Comunications Air/Ground facility (RCAG)**: An unmanned VHF/UHF transmitter/receiver facility which is used to expand ARTCC air/ground communications coverage and to facilitate direct contact between pilots and controllers. RCAG facilities are sometimes not equipped with emergency frequencies 121.5 MHz and 243.0 MHz.

**Remote Communications Outlet (RCO)**: An unmanned air/ground communications station remotely controlled, providing UHF and VHF transmit and receive capability to extend the service range of the FSS.

**report**: Used to instruct pilots to advise ATC of specified information: e.g., "Report passing Hamilton VOR."

**reporting point**: A geographical location in relation to which the position of an aircraft is reported. See *compulsory reporting point*.

**request Full Route Clearance (FRC)**: Used by pilots to request that the entire route of flight be read verbatim in an ATC clearance. Such request should be made to preclude receiving an ATC clearance based on the original filed flight plan when a filed IFR flight plan has been received by the pilot, company or operations prior to departure.

**Rescue Coordination Center (RCC)**: A search and rescue (SAR) facility equipped and manned to coordinate and control SAR operations in an area designated by the SAR plan. The U.S. Coast Guard and the USAF have responsibility for the operation of RCCs.

**restricted area**: See *special use airspace*.

**resume own navigation**: Used by ATC to advise a pilot to resume his own navigational responsibility. It is issued after completion of a radar vector or when radar contact is lost while the aircraft is being radar vectored.

**RNAV**: See *area navigation*.

**RNAV approach**: An instrument approach procedure which relies on aircraft area navigation equipment for guidance.

**road reconnaissance (RC)**: Military activity requiring navigation along roads, railroads and rivers. Reconnaissance route/route segments are seldon along a straight line and normally require a lateral route width of 10 nm to 30 nm and altitude range of 500 feet to 10,000 feet AGL (Fig. G-25).

**roger**: I have received all of your last transmission. It should not be used to answer a question requiring a yes or no answer. See *affirmative and negative*.

**rollout RVR**: See *visibility*.

**route**: A defined path, consisting of one or more courses in a horizontal

Fig. G-25. Piper Tomahawk turns from base to final at an uncontrolled field with a right-hand traffic pattern.

plane, which aircraft traverse over the surface of the earth.

**route segment**: As used in air traffic control, a part of a route that can be defined by two navigational fixes, two NAVAIDS, or a fix and a NAVAID.

**runway**: A defined rectangular area, on a land aerodrome prepared for the landing and takeoff of aircraft. Runways are normally numbered in relation to their magnetic direction rounded off to the nearest 10 degrees, such as Runway 25.

**Runway Condition Reading (RCR)**: Numerical decelerometer readings relayed by air traffic controllers at USAF and certain civil bases/airports for use by the pilot in determining runway braking action. These readings are routinely relayed only to USAF and Air National Guard aircraft.

**runway end identifier lights**: See *airport lighting*.

**runway gradient**: The average slope, measured in percent, between two ends or two points on a runway. Runway gradient is depicted on government aerodrome sketches when total runway gradient exceeds 0.3 per cent.

**runway in use/active runway/duty runway**: Any runway or runways currently in use for takeoff or landing. When multiple runways are used, they are all considered active runways.

**runway lights**: See *airport lighting*.

**runway markings**: *Basic markings* on runways are used for operations under visual flight rules consisting of centerline marking and runway direction numbers and, if required, letters.

Instrument markings are on runways served by nonvisual navigation aids and intended for landings under instrument weather conditions, consisting of basic marking plus threshold marking.

All-weather (precision instrument) markings are on runways served by nonvisual precision approach aids and on runways having special operational requirements, consisting of instrument markings plus landing zone markings and side strips.

**runway profile descent**: An instrument flight rules (IFR) air traffic control arrival procedure to a runway published for pilot use in graphic of textual form and which may be associated with a STAR. Runway profile descents provide routing and may depict crossing altitudes, speed restrictions and headings to be flown from the en route structure to the point where the pilot will receive clearance for and execute an instrument approach procedure. A runway profile descent may apply to more than one runway if so stated on the chart.

**runway visual range**: See *visibility*.

**safety advisory**: A safety advisory issued by ATC to aircraft under their control if ATC is aware the aircraft is at an altitude which, in the controller's judgment, places the aircraft in unsafe proximity to terrain, obstructions or other aircraft. The controller may discontinue the issuance of further advisories if the pilot advises he is taking action to correct the situation or has the other aircraft in sight.

*Terrain/obstruction advisory* is issued by ATC to aircraft under their control if ATC is aware the aircraft is at an altitude which, in the controller's judgment, places the aircraft in unsafe proximity to terrain or obstructions. An example would be, "Low altitude alert; check your altitude immediately."

An *aircraft conflict advisory* is issued by ATC to aircraft under their control if ATC is aware of an aircraft that is not under their control at an altitude which, in the controller's judgment, places both aircraft in unsafe proximity to each other. With the alert, the ATC will offer the pilot an alternate course of action when feasible, "Traffic alert; advise you turn right, heading zero niner zero, or climb to eight thousand immediately."

The issuance of a safety advisory is contingent upon the capability of the controller to have an awareness of an unsafe condition. The course of action provided will be predicated on other traffic under ATC control. Once the advisory is issued, it is solely the pilot's prerogative to determine what course of action, if any, he will take (Fig. G-26).

**say again**: Used to request a repeat of the last transmission. Usually specifies transmission or portion thereof not understood or received, "Say again all after Hobart VOR."

Fig. G-26. The Boeing-Stearman PT-13 through PT-17 (depending upon engine installation) was a WW-II military trainer, a favorite with agricultural applicator pilots for nearly three decades after that, and a coveted find for old airplane buffs today.

**say altitude**: Used by ATC to ascertain an aircraft's specific altitude/flight level. When the aircraft is climbing or descending, the pilot should state the indicated altitude rounded to the nearest 100 feet.

**say heading**: Used by ATC to request an aircraft heading. The pilot should state the actual heading of his aircraft.

**search and rescue facility**: A facility responsible for maintaining and operating a search and rescue (SAR) service to render aid to persons and property in distres. It is any SAR unit, station, NET or other operational activity which can be usefully employed during an SAR mission; e.g., a Civil Air Patrol Wing or a Coast Guard Station.

**search and rescue (SAR)**: A service which seeks missing aircraft and assists those found to be in need of assistance. It is a cooperative effort using the facilities and services of available federal, state and local agencies. The U.S. Coast Guard is responsible for coordination of search and rescue for the Maritime Region, and the USAF is responsible for search and rescue for the Inland Region. Information pertinent to search and rescue should be passed through any air traffic facility or be transmitted directly to the Rescue Coordination Center by telephone. See *Flight Service Station.*

**see and avoid**: A visual procedure wherein pilots of aircraft flying in visual meteorological conditions (VMC), regardless of type of flight plan, are charged with the responsibility to observe the presence of other aircraft and to maneuver their aircraft as required to avoid the other aircraft. Right-of-way rules are contained in FAR, Part 91.

**segmented circle**: A system of visual indicators designed to provide traffic pattern information at airports without operating control towers.

**segments of an instrument approach procedure:** An instrument approach procedure may have as many as four separate segments depending on how the approach procedure is structured. *Initial approach* is the segment between the initial approach fix and the intermediate fix, or the point where the aircraft is established on the intermediate course or final approach course. *Intermediate approach* is the segment between the intermediate fix or point and the final approach fix. *Final approach* is the segment between the final approach fix or point and runway, airport or missed approach point. *Missed approach* is the segment between the missed approach point, or point of arrival at decision height, and the missed approach fix at the prescribed altitude (refer to FAR, Part 97).

**separation:** In air traffic control, the spacing of aircraft to achieve their safe and orderly movement in flight and while landing and taking off.

**severe weather avoidance plan (SWAP:** A plan to reroute traffic to avoid severe weather in the New York ARTCC area to provide the least disruption to the ATC system when large portions of airspace are unusable due to severe weather.

**short range clearance:** A clearance issued to a departing IFR flight which authorizes IFR flight to a specific fix short of the destination while air traffic control facilities are coordinating and obtaining the complete clearance.

**short takeoff and landing aircraft (STOL aircraft):** An aircraft which, at some weight within its approved operating weight range, is capable of operating from a STOL runway in compliance with the applicable STOL characteristics, airworthiness, operations, noise and pollution standards.

**sidestep maneuver:** A visual maneuver accomplished by a pilot at the completion on an instrument approach to permit a straight-in landing on a parallel runway not more than 1200 feet to either side of the runway to which the instrument approach was conducted.

**SIGMET (Significant Meteorological Information):** A weather advisory issued concerning weather significant to the safety of all aircraft. SIGMET advisories cover tornadoes, lines of thunderstorms, embedded thunderstorms, large hail, severe and extreme turbulence, severe icing, and widespread dust or sandstorms that reduce visibility to less than three miles.

**Simplified Directional Facility (SDF):** A NAVAID used for nonprecision instrument approaches. The final approach course is similar to that of an ILS localizer except that the SDF course may be wider than the localizer, resulting in a lower degree of accuracy.

**Simulated Flameout (SFO):** A practice approach by a jet aircraft (normally military) at idle thrust to a runway. The approach may start at a relatively high altitude over a runway (high key) and may continue on a relatively high and wide downwind leg with a high rate of descent and a continuous turn to final. It teminates in a landing or low approach. The purpose of this approach is to simulate a flameout.

**simultaneous ILS approaches**: An approach system permitting simultaneous ILS approaches to airports having parallel runways separated by at least 4,300 feet between centerlines. Integral parts of a total system are ILS, radar, communications, ATC procedures and appropriate airborne equipment.

**single direction routes**: Preferred IFR Routes which are sometimes depicted on high altitude en route charts and which are normally flown in one direction only. See preferred IFR route.

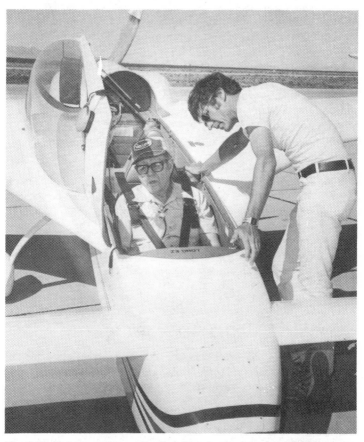

Fig. G-27. Veteran aviation writer Don Downie checks out in the Rutan Long EZ. Enthusiastic reports on the Rutan airplanes from pilots like Downie—who soloed in 1937, flew C-46s over the Hump in WW-II, and can count more than 150 different types of aircraft in his stack of logbooks—are adding fuel to the "Rutan Revolution."

**Single Frequency Approach (SFA)**: A service provided under a letter of agreement to military single-piloted jet aircraft which permits use of a single UHF frequency during approach for landing (Fig. G-27). Pilots will not normally be required to change frequency from the beginning of the approach to touchdown except that pilots conducting an en route descent are required to change frequency when control is transferred from the ARTCC to the terminal facility. The abbreviation "SFA" in the DOD FLIP IFR Supplement under "Communication" indicates this service is available at an aerodrome.

**Single Frequency Outlets (SFO) and Simultaneous Single Frequency Outlets (SSFO)**: Frequency outlets commissioned at locations in Alaska not served by air traffic control facilities and remotely controlled by adjacent FSSs. They are subject to undetected and prolonged outages.

**single-piloted aircraft**: A military turbojet aircraft possessing one set of flight controls, a consideration by ATC when determining the appropriate air traffic service to be applied.

**slash**: A radar beacon reply displayed as an elongated target.

**special emergency**: A condition of air piracy or other hostile act by a person(s) aboard an aircraft which threatens the safety of the aircraft or its passengers.

**special IFR**: See *fixed-wing special IFR*.

**special use airspace**: Airspace of defined dimensions identified by an area on the surface of the earth wherein activities must be confined because of their nature. Limitations may be imposed upon aircraft operations that are not a part of those activities. The following are types of special use airspace.

*Alert area* is airspace which may contain a high volume of pilot training activities or an unusual type of aerial activity—neither of which is hazardous to aircraft. Alert areas are depicted on aeronautical charts for the information of non-participating pilots. All activities within an alert area are conducted in accordance with FARs and pilots of participating aircraft. Pilots transiting the area are equally responsible for collision avoidance.

A *controlled firing area* is airspace wherein activities are conducted under conditions so controlled as to eliminate hazards to non-participating aircraft and to ensure the safety of persons and property on the ground.

*Military Operations Area (MOA)* is an airspace assignment of defined vertical and lateral dimensions established outside positive control areas to separate/segregate certain military activities from IFR traffic, and to identify for VFR traffic where these activities are conducted.

A *prohibited area* is designated airspace within which the flight of aircraft is prohibited.

A *restricted area* is airspace designated under FAR, Part 73, within which the flight of aircraft, while not wholly prohibited, is subject to restriction. Most restricted areas are designated joint use and IFR/VFR operations in the area may be authorized by the controlling ATC facility when it is not being utilized by the using agency. Restricted areas are depicted on en route charts. Where joint use is authorized, the name of the ATC controlling facility is also shown.

A *warning area* is airspace which may contain hazards to non-participating aircraft in international airspace.

**special VFR conditions**: Weather conditions in a control zone which are less than basic VFR and in which some aircraft are permitted flight under Visual Flight Rules (refer to FAR, Part 91).

**special VFR operations**: Aircraft operating in accordance with clearances within control zones in weather conditions less than the basic VFR minima. Such operations must be requested by the pilot and approved by ATC.

**speed adjustment**: An ATC procedure used to request pilots to adjust aircraft speed to a specific value for the purpose of providing desired spacing. Speed adjustments are always expressed as indicated airspeed. Pilots are expected to maintain a speed of plus or minus 10 kts of the specified speed. Examples of speed adjustments are, "Increase speed to (speed)" or "Increase speed (number of) knots." "Reduce speed to (speed)" or "Reduce speed (number of) knots."

**squawk (mode, code and function)**: Activate specific modes/codes/functions on the aircraft transponder, "Squawk three alpha, two one zero five, low." See *transponder*.

**Stage I/II/III**: See *terminal radar program*.

**standard instrument approach procedure**: See *instrument approach procedure*.

**Standard Instrument Departure (SID)**: A preplanned instrument flight rule (IFR) air traffic control departure procedure printed for pilot use in graphic and/or textual form. SIDs provide transition from the terminal to the appropriate en route structure.

**standard rate turn**: A turn of three degrees per second.

**Standard Terminal Arrival Route (STAR)**: A preplanned instrument flight rule (IFR) air traffic control arrival route published for pilot use in graphic and/or textual form. STARs provide transition from the en route structure to a fix or point from which an approach can be made.

**stand by**: Means the controller or pilot must pause for a few seconds, usually to attend to other duties of a higher priority. Also means to "wait" as in "stand by for clearance." If a delay is lengthy, the caller should re-establish contact.

**stationary reservations**: Altitude reservations which encompass activities in a fixed area. These may include activities such as weapons

Fig. G-28. The 1980 Cessna Stationair Six evolved from stretched versions of the popular Skylane, and is sort of an aerial station wagon (courtesy of Cessna Aircraft Company).

systems test, U.S. Navy carrier and anti-submarine operations, rocket, missile and drone operations, along with aerial refueling, etc.

**stepdown fix:** A fix permitting additional descent within a segment of an instrument approach procedure by identifying a point at which a controlling obstacle has been safely overflown (Fig. G-28).

**stop altitude squawk:** Used by ATC to inform an aircraft to turn off the automatic altitude reporting feature of its transponder. It is issued when the verbally reported altitude varies 300 feet or more from the automatic altitude report.

**stop and go:** A procedure wherein an aircraft will land, make a complete stop on the runway, and then commence a takeoff from that point.

**stop-over flight plan:** A flight plan which includes two or more separate en route flight segments with a stopover at one or more intermediate airports.

**stop squawk (mode or code:** Used by ATC to tell the pilot to turn off specified functions of the aircraft transponder.

**stop stream (or burst or buzzer):** Used by ATC to request a military pilot to suspend electronic counter-measure activity. See *jamming*.

**straight-in approach, IFR:** An instrument approach wherein final approach is begun without first having executed a procedure turn. Not necessarily completed with a straight-in landing or made to straight-in landing minimums.

**straight-in approach, VFR:** Entry into the traffic pattern by interception of the extended centerline (final approach course) without executing any other portion of the traffic pattern.

**straight-in landing:** A landing made on a runway aligned within 30 degrees of the final approach course following completion of an instrument approach.

**straight-in landing minimums**: See *landing minimums*.

**substitute route**: A route assigned to pilots when any part of an airway or route is unusable because of NAVAID failure. These routes consist of substitute routes which are shown on U.S. government charts; routes defined by ATC as specified NAVAID radials or courses; and routes defined by ATC as direct to or between NAVAIDs.

**sunset and sunrise**: The mean solar times of sunset and sunrise as published in the *Nautical Almanac*, converted to local standard time for the locality concerned. Within Alaska, the end of evening civil twilight and the beginning of morning civil twilight, as defined for each locality.

**surveillance approach**: An instrument approach wherein the air traffic controller issues instructions, for pilot compliance, based on aircraft position in relation to the final approach course (azimuth), and the distance (range) from the end of the runway as displayed on the controller's radar scope. The controller will provide recommended altitudes on final approach if requested by the pilot. See PAR approach.

**TACAM (Tactical Air Navigation)**: An ultra-high frequency electronic rho-theta air navigation aid which provides suitably equipped aircraft a continuous indication of bearing and distance to the TACAN station. See VORTAC.

**target**: The indication shown on a radar display resulting from a primary radar return or a radar beacon reply.

**target symbol**: A computer-generated indication shown on a radar display resulting from a primary radar return or a radar beacon reply.

**taxi into position and hold**: Used by ATC to inform a pilot to taxi onto the departure runway in takeoff position and hold. It is not authorization for takeoff. It is used when takeoff clearance cannot immediately be issued because of traffic or other reasons.

**taxi patterns**: Patterns established to illustrate the desired flow of ground traffic for the different runways or airport areas available for use (Fig. G-29).

**terminal area**: A general term used to describe airspace in which approach control service or airport traffic control service is provided.

**Terminal Control Area (TCA)**: See *controlled airspace*.

**Terminal Radar Approach Control (TRACON)**: An FAA air traffic control facility using radar and air/ground communications to provide approach control services to aircraft arriving, departing or transiting the airspace controlled by the facility. Service may be provided to both civil and military airports. A TRACON is similar to a RAPCON (USAF), RATCF (Navy) and ARAC (Army).

**terminal radar program**: A national program instituted to extend the terminal radar services provided IFR aircraft to VFR aircraft. Pilot participation in the program is urged but not mandatory. The progressive stages of the program are referred to as Stages I, II and III. The

195

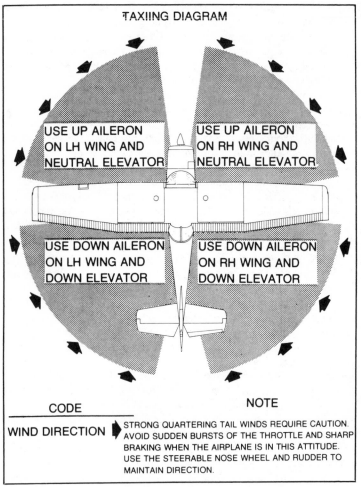

Fig. G-29. Flight control positions for taxiing in surface winds (courtesy of Cessna Aircraft Company).

stage of service provided at a particular location is contained in the Airport/Facility Directory.

Stage I/radar advisory service for VFR aircraft provides traffic information and limited vectoring to VFR aircraft on a workload permitting basis.

Stage II/radar advisory and sequencing for VFR aircraft provides, in addition to Stage I service, vectoring and sequencing on a full-time basis to arriving VFR aircraft. The purpose is to adjust the flow of arriving VFR aircraft into the traffic pattern in a safe and orderly manner and to provide traffic advisory to departing VFR aircraft.

Stage III/radar sequencing and separation service for VFR aircraft provides, in addition to Stage II services, separation between all participating aircraft within the airspace defined as a Terminal Radar Service Area (TRSA) or Terminal Control Area (TCA).

**Terminal Radar Service Area (TRSA)**: Airspace surrounding designated airports wherein ATC provides radar vectoring, sequencing and separation on a full-time basis for all IFR and participating VFR aircraft. Service provided in a TRSA is called Stage III service. Graphics depicting TRSA layout and communications frequencies are shown in Graphic Notices and Supplemental Data.

**Terrain Following (TF)**: The flight of a military aircraft maintaining a constant AGL altitude above the terrain of the highest obstruction. The altitude of the aircraft will constantly change with the varying terrain.

**tetrahedron**: A device normally located on uncontrolled airports and used as a landing direction indicator. The small end of a tetrahedron points in the direction of landing. At controlled airports, the tetrahedron should be disregarded because tower instructions supersede the indicator.

**threshold**: The beginning of that portion of the runway usable for landing (Fig. G-30).

**Threshold Crossing Height (TCH)**: The height of the glide slope above the runway threshold.

**threshold lights**: See *airport lighting*.

Fig. G-30. Airliner requirements provide the private pilot with some benefits. When flying a lightplane off a runway that stretches halfway to Dallas, even that one-in-a-million chance of engine failure on takeoff is no problem.

197

**thunderstorm intensity levels**: Existing radar systems cannot detect turbulence per se. However, because there is a direct correlation between thunderstorm precipitation density and storm intensity, the NWS is able to measure the strength of radar weather echoes for the purpose of categorizing the strength of the storm: level 1 (weak) and level 2 (moderate), moderate to severe turbulence possible; level 3 (strong), severe turbulence possible, lightning; level 4 (very strong), severe turbulence likely, lightning; level 5 (intense), severe turbulence, lightning, organized wind gusts along with hail likely; level 6 (extreme, severe turbulence, large hail, lightning and extensive wind gusts.

**time group**: Four digits representing the hour and minutes from the 24-hour clock. Time group without time zone indicators are understood to be GMT (Greenwich Mean Time); for example "0205." A time zone indicator is used to indicate local time, "0205m." The end and beginning of the day are shown by "2400" and "0000" respectively.

**torching**: The burning of fuel at the end of an exhaust pipe or stack of a reciprocating aircraft engine, the result of an excessive richness in the fuel air mixture.

**touch and go/touch and go landing**: An operation by an aircraft that lands and departs on a runway without stopping or exiting the runway.

**touchdown**: The point at which an aircraft makes contact with the landing surface. Concerning a precision radar approach (PAR), it is the point where the glide path intercepts the landing surface.

**touchdown RVR**: See *visibility*.

**touchdown zone**: The first 3,000 feet of the runway beginning at the threshold. The area is used for determination of *Touchdown Zone Elevation* in the development of straight-in landing minimums for instrument approaches.

**Touchdown Zone Elevation (TDZE)**: The highest elevation in the first 3000 feet of the landing surface. TDZE is indicated on the instrument approach procedure chart when straight-in minimums are authorized.

**touchdown zone lighting**: See *airport lighting*.

**tower/airport traffic control tower**: A terminal facility which through the use of air/ground communications, visual signaling and other devices provides ATC services to airborne aircraft operating in the vicinity of an airport and to aircraft operating on the movement area.

**tower en route control service/tower to tower**: The control of IFR en route traffic within delegated airspace between two or more adjacent approach control facilities. This service is designed to expedite traffic and reduce control and pilot communication requirements.

**TPX 42**: A numeric beacon decoder equipment/system. It is designed to be added to terminal radar systems for beacon decoding. It provides rapid target identification, reinforcement of the primary radar target and altitude information from Mode C.

**track**: The actual flight path of an aircraft over the surface of the earth.

**traffic alert**: See *safety advisory*.

**traffic advisories**: Advisories issued to alert a pilot to other known or observed IFR/VFR air traffic which may be in such proximity to his aircraft's position or intended route of flight to warrant his attention. Such advisories may be based on visual observation from a control tower, observation of radar identified and non-identified aircraft targets on an ARTCC/Approach Control radar scope, or verbal reports from pilots or other facilities.

Controllers use the word "traffic" followed by additional information, if known, to provide such advisories, "Traffic, two o'clock, one zero miles, southbound, fast moving, altitude readout seven thousand five hundred." Traffic advisory service will be provided to the extent possible depending on higher priority duties of the controller or other limitations imposed by equipment, volume of traffic frequency congestion or controller workload. Radar/nonradar traffic advisories do not relieve the pilot of his responsibility for continual vigilance to see and avoid other aircraft. IFR and VFR aircraft are cautioned that there are many times when the controller is not able to give traffic advisories concerning all traffic in the aircraft's proximity; in other words, when a pilot requests or is receiving traffic advisories, he should not assume that all traffic will be issued.

**traffic in sight**: Used by pilots to inform a controller that previously issued traffic is in sight.

**traffic pattern**: The traffic flow that is prescribed for aircraft landing at, taxiing on or taking off from an airport. The components of a typical traffic pattern are upwind leg, crosswind leg, downwind leg, base leg and final approach.

*Upwind leg* is a flight path parallel to the landing runway in the direction of the landing. *Crosswind leg* is a flight path at right angles to the landing runway off its upwind leg. *Downwind leg* is a flight path parallel to the landing runway in the direction opposite to the landing. The downwind leg normally extends between the crosswind leg and the base leg (Fig. G-31). *Base leg* involves a flight path at right angles to the landing runway off its approach end. The base leg normally extends from the downwind leg to the intersection of the extended runway centerline. *Final approach* is a flight path in the direction of landing along the extended runway centerline. The final approach normally extends from the base leg to the runway. An aircraft making a straight-in approach VFR is also considered to be on final approach.

**Transcribed Weather Broadcast (TWEB)**: A continuous recording of meteorological and aeronautical information that is broadcast on L/MF and VOR facilities for pilots.

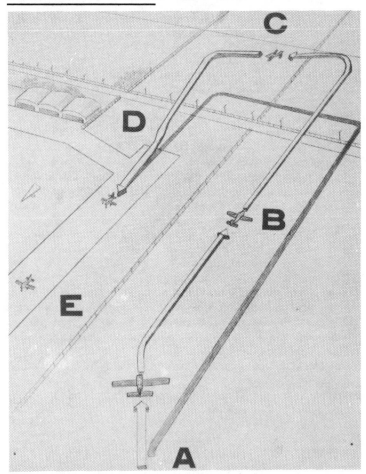

Fig. G-31. Standard traffic pattern. (A) Enter downwind leg at a 45-degree angle so that you may best observe other traffic. (B) Select your touchdown point. (C) Length of downwind and base legs will be determined by wind conditions. Flare out at (D), holding the nosewheel off. (E) Ease down nosewheel as speed dissipates.

**transfer of control**: That action whereby the responsibility for the separation of an aircraft is transferred from one controller to another.

**transferring controller/facility**: A controller/facility transferring control of an aircraft to another controller or facility.

**transition**: The general term that describes the change from one phase of flight or flight condition to another: e.g., transition from en route flight to the approach, or transition from instrument flight to visual flight.

Also, a published route (SID Transition) used to connect the basic SID to one of several en route airways/jet routes; or, a published route STAR Transition) used to connect one of several en route airways/jet routes to the basic STAR. Refer to SID/STAR charts.

**transition area:** See *controlled airspace*.

**transmissometer:** An apparatus used to determine visibility by measuring the transmission of light through the atmosphere. It is the measurement source for determining runway visual range (RVR) and runway visibility value (RVV).

**transmitting in the blind/blind transmission:** A radio transmission from one station to other stations in circumstances where two-way communications cannot be established, but where it is believed that the called stations may be able to receive the transmission.

**transponder:** The airborne radar beacon receiver/transmitter portion of the *Air Traffic Control Radar Beacon System (ATCRBS)* which automatically receives radio signals from interrogators on the ground, and selectively replies with a specific reply pulse or pulse group only to those interrogations being received on the mode to which it is set to respond.

**T-VOR (terminal-very high frequency omnidirectional range station):** A VOR station located on or near an airport and used as an approach aid.


**ultrahigh frequency (UHF):** The frequency band between 300 and 3000 MHz. The bank of radio frequencies used for military air/ground voice communications. In some instances these frequencies may go as low as 225 MHz and still be referred to as UHF.

**unable:** Indicates inability to comply with a specific instruction, request or clearance.

**uncontrolled airspace:** That portion of the airspace that has not been designated as continental control area, control area, control zone, terminal control area or transition area.

**under the hood:** Indicates that the pilot is using a hood to restrict visibility outside the cockpit while simulating instrument flight. An appropriately rated pilot is required in the other control seat while this operation is being conducted. Refer to FAR, Part 91.

**UNICOM:** A non-government air/ground radio communication facility which may provide airport advisory service at certain airports. Locations and frequencies of UNICOMs are shown on aeronautical charts and publications.

**unpublished route:** A route for which no minimum altitude is published or charted for pilot use. It may include a direct route between NAVAIDS, a radial, a radar vector or a final approach course beyond the segments of an instrument approach procedure.

**vector**: A heading issued to an aircraft to provide navigational guidance by radar.

**verify**: Request confirmation of information, "Verify assigned altitude."

**verify specific direction of takeoff (or turns after takeoff):** Used by ATC to ascertain an aircraft's direction of takeoff and/or direction of turn after takeoff. It is normally used for IFR departures from an airport not having a control tower. When direct communication with the pilot is not possible, the request and information may be relayed through an FSS, dispatcher or by other means. See IFR Takeoff Minimums and Departure Procedures.

**vertical separation**: Separation established by assignment of different altitudes or flight levels.

**vertical takeoff and landing aircraft (VTOL aircraft):** Aircraft capable of vertical climbs and/or descents and of using very short runways or small areas for takeoff and landings. These aircraft include but are not limited to helicopters.

**very high frequency (VHF)**: The frequency band between 30 and 300 MHz. Portions of this band, 108 to 118 MHz, are used for certain NAVAIDS; 118 to 136 MHz are used for civil air/ground voice communications. Other frequencies in this band are used for purposes not related to air traffic control.

**very low frequency (VLF)**: The frequency band between 3 and 30 KHz.

**VFR aircraft/VFR flight**: An aircraft conducting flight in accordance with Visual Flight Rules.

**VFR low altitude training routes (TR)**: Routes used by the Department of Defense and associated Reserve and Air Guard units for the purpose of conducting low altitude navigation and tactical training under VFR rules at or below 1500 feet AGL at airspeeds in excess of 250 kts IAS.

**VFR military training routes (VR)**: Routes used by the Department of Defense and associated Reserve and Air Guard units for the purpose of conducting low altitude navigation and tactical training under VFR rules below 10,000 feet MSL at airspeeds in excess of 250 kts IAS.

**VFR not recommended**: An advisory provided by an FSS to a pilot during a preflight or inflight weather briefing that flight under visual flight rules is not recommended. To be given when the current and/or forecasted weather conditions are at or below VFR minimums. It does not abrogate the pilot's authority to make his own decision.

**VFR on top**: An IFR clearance term used in lieu of a specific altitude assignment upon pilot's request which authorizes the aircraft to be flown in VFR weather conditions at an appropriate VFR altitude/flight level which is not below the minimum IFR altitude.

**VFR over the top**: The operation of an aircraft over-the-top under VFR when it is not being operated on an IFR flight plan.

**VFR tower/non-approach control tower:** An airport traffic control tower that does not provide approach control service.

**video map:** An electronically displayed map on the radar display that may depict such data as airports, heliports, runway centerline extensions, hospital emergency landing areas, NAVAIDS and fixes, reporting points, airway/route centerlines, boundaries, handoff points, special use tracks, obstructions, prominent geographic features, map alignment indicators, range accuracy marks and minimum vectoring altitudes.

**visibility:** The ability, as determined by atmospheric conditions and expressed in units of distance, to see and identify prominent unlighted objects by day and prominent lighted objects at night. Visibility is reported as statute miles, hundreds of feet or meters.

*Flight visibility* is the average forward horizontal distance, from the cockpit of an aircraft in flight, at which prominent unlighted objects may be seen and identified by day, and prominent lighted objects may be seen and identified by night.

*Ground visibility* is prevailing horizontal visibility near the earth's surface as reported by the U.S. National Weather Service or an accredited observer.

*Prevailing visibility* is the greatest horizontal visibility equaled or exceeded throughout at least half the horizon circle which need not necessarily be continuous.

*Runway Visibility Value*(RVV) is the visibility determined for a particular runway by a transmissometer. A meter provides a continuous indication of the visibility (reported in miles or fractions of miles) for the runway. RVV is used in lieu of prevailing visibility in determining minimums for a particular runway (Fig. G-32).

*Runway Visual Range* (RVR) is an instrumentally derived value, based on standard calibrations, that represents the horizontal distance

Fig. G-32. Some homebuilts, such as the Pazmany PL-1, rival production aircraft in looks, performance and craftsmanship. The structure is designed for amateur builders (courtesy of Peter Bowers).

a pilot will see down the runway from the approach end. It is based on the sighting of either high intensity runway lights or on the visual contrast of other targets, whichever yields the greater visual range. RVR, in contrast to prevailing or runway visibility, is based on what a pilot in a moving aircraft should see looking down the runway. RVR is horizontal visual range, not slant visual range. It is based on the measurement of a transmissometer made near the touchdown point of the instrument runway and is reported in hundreds of feet. RVR is used in lieu of RVV and/or prevailing visibility in determining minimums for a particular runway. Touchdown RVR includes the RVR visibility readout values obtained from RVR equipment serving the runway touchdown zone. *MID RVR* are the RVR readout values obtained from RVR equipment located midfield of the runway. Rollout RVR are the RVR readout values obtained from RVR equipment located nearest the rollout end of the runway.

**visual approach**: An approach wherein an aircraft on an IFR flight plan, operating in VFR conditions under the control of an air traffic control facility and having an air traffic control authorization, may proceed to the airport of destination in VFR conditions.

**visual approach slope indicator**: See *airport lighting*

**visual descent point**: A defined point on the final approach course of a nonprecision straight-in approach procedure from which normal descent from the MDA to the runway touchdown point may be commenced, provided visual reference is established.

**VFR (Visual Flight Rules)**: Rules that govern the procedures for conducting flight under visual conditions. The term "VFR" is also used in the United States to indicate weather conditions that are equal to or greater than minimum VFR requirements. In addition, it is used by pilots and controllers to indicate type of flight plan.

**visual holding**: The holding of aircraft at selected, prominent, geographical fixes which can be easily recognized from the air.

**Visual Meteorological Conditions (VMC)**: Meteorological conditions which can be expressed in terms of visibility, distance from cloud, and ceiling equal to or better than specified minima.

**visual separation**: A means employed by ATC to separate aircraft in terminal areas. There are two ways to effect this separation. The tower controller sees the aircraft involved and issues instructions, as necessary, to ensure that the aircraft avoid each other. A pilot sees the other aircraft involved and upon instructions from the controller provides his own separation by maneuvering his aircraft as necessary to avoid it. This may involve following another aircraft or keeping it in sight until it is no longer a factor.

**VORTAC (VHF omnidirectional range/tactical air navigation)**: A navigation aid providing VOR azimuth, and TACAN distance measuring equipment (DME) at one site.

**vortices/wingtip vortices**: Circular patterns of air created by the movement of an airfoil through the air when generating lift. As an airfoil moves through the atmosphere in sustained flight, an area of high pressure is created beneath it and an area of low pressure is created above it. The air flowing from the high pressure area to the low pressure area around and about the tips of the airfoil tends to roll up into rapidly rotating vortices, cylindrical in shape. These vortices are the predominant parts of aircraft wake turbulence. Their rotational force is dependent upon the wing loading, gross weight and speed of the generating aircraft. The vortices from medium to heavy aircraft can be of extremely high velocity and hazardous to smaller aircraft.

**VOR (very high frequency omniderectional range station)**: A ground-based electronic navigation aid transmitting VHF navigation signals, 360 degrees in azimuth, oriented from magnetic north. VOR is used as the basis for navigation in the national airspace system. The VOR periodically identifies itself by Morse code and may have an additional voice identification feature. Voice features may be used by ATC or FSS for transmitting instructions/information to pilots.

**VOT/VOR test signal**: A ground facility which emits a test signal to check VOR receiver accuracy. The system is limited to ground use only.

**wake turbulence**: Phenomena resulting from the passage of an aircraft through the atmosphere. The term includes vortices, thrust stream turbulence, jet blast, jet wash, propeller wash and rotor wash, both on the ground and in the air.

**warning area**: See *special use airspace.*

**waypoint**: See *area navigation*

**weather advisoty**: See SIGMENT and AIRMET.

**WILCO**: I have received your message, understand it and will comply with it.

**wind shear**: A change in wind speed and/or wind direction in a short distance, resulting in a tearing or shearing effect. It can exist in a horizontal or vertical direction and occasionally in both.

**words twice**: As a request, "Communication is difficult. Please say every phrase twice." As information, "Since communications are difficult, every phrase in this message will be spoken twice."

# Appendix A
# Federal Aviation Administration Headquarters

The Federal Aviation Administration, part of the Department of Transportation, is primarily charged with fostering the development and safety of aviation in the United States (Fig. A-1). It is responsible for the long-range growth of civil aviation, modernization of the airport/airways system, operation of the air traffic control system, use of the United States airspace, both civil and military, and development and enforcement of federal aviation regulations.

The FAA is a decentralized organization with 12 regional offices, plus the multi-purpose Aeronautical Center in Oklahoma City, OK. The address for the main headquarter is Federal Aviation Administration Department of Transportation, 800 Independence Avenue, S.W., Washington, DC 20590, telephone (202) 426-3883. Following are addresses for the 12 FAA regional offices.

*Alabama, Florida, Georgia, Kentucky, Mississippi, N. Carolina, S. Carolina and Tennessee*
FAA
P.O. Box 20636,
Atlanta, GA 30320
(404) 526-7201

*Alaska*
FAA
Hill Building,
632 Sixth Avenue,
Anchorage, AL 99501
(907) 272-5561

*Arizona, California and Nevada*
FAA
5651 West Manchester Ave.,
P.O. Box 92007,
Worldway Postal Center
Los Angeles, CA 90009
(213) 670-7030

*Arkansas, Louisiana, Texas, New Mexico, and Oklahoma:*
FAA
4400 Blue Mound Road,
P.O. Box 1689,
Fort Worth, TX 76101
(817) 624-4911

*Colorado, Montana, Wyoming, N. Dakota, S. Dakota and Utah*
FAA
Park Hill Sta. P.O. Box 7213,
Denver, CO 80207
(303) 837-4992

*Connecticut, Massachusetts, New Hampshire, Rhode Island, Maine and Vermont*
FAA
154 Middlesex Street,
Burlington, MA 01803
(617) 223-6418

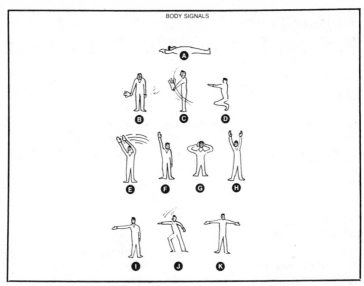

Fig. A-1. Body signals from downed aircraft to search aircraft. (A) Urgently require medical help. (B) Negative. (C) Affirmative. (D) Land here. (E) Do not land. (F) All okay. (G) Our receiver is operating. (H) Pick us up. (I) Can proceed shortly; wait if practicable. (J) Use drop message. (K) Need mechanical help/parts.

*Delaware, District of Columbia, Maryland, New Jersey, New York, Pennsylvania, Virginia and West Virginia*
FAA
Federal Building
JFK International Airport
Jamaica, NY 11430
(212) 995-9684

*Europe, Africa and Middle East*:
FAA
1 Place Madou,
1000 Brussels, Belgium
13.38.30, Ext. 300 or 301

*Idaho, Washington and Oregon*
FAA
FAA Bldg., Boeing Field,
Seattle, WA
98108
(206) 767-2680

*Illinois, Indiana, Ohio, Minnesota, Michigan and Wisconsin*
FAA
2300 East Devon Avenue,
Des Plaines, IL 60018
(312) 775-9000

*Iowa, Kansas, Missouri and Nebraska*
FAA
601 East 12th Street,
Kansas City, MO 64106
(816) 374-5449

*Pacific Region*
FAA
1833 Kalakaua Avenue,
Honolulu, HI 96813
(808) 955-0407

# Appendix B
# National Transportation Safety Board

The National Transportation Safety Board investigates aviation accidents to determine probable cause, issues reports on all civil aviation accidents and promotes aviation safety. It is also concerned with surface transportation, accident cause determination and safety promotion. The NTSB is an autonomous organization that operates independently of the Secretary of Transportation and other offices and officers of the Department of Transportation. The address for the main headquarters is 800 Independence Avenue, S.W., Washington, D.C., 20951, telephone (202) 426-8787. Following are addresses for 10 NTSB offices.

*Anchorage, AL*
NTSB
Hill Bldg., Rm. 454
632 Sixth Avenue,
Anchorage, AK 99501
(907) 277-0593

*Chicago, IL*
NTSB
3166 Des Plaines Avenue,
Des Plaines, IL 60018
(312) 827-8858

*Denver, CO*
NTSB
10255 East 25th Ave.,
Aurora, CO 80010
(303) 837-4492

*Fort Worth, TX*
NTSB
Federal Bldg., Rm. 7A07,
819 Taylor Street,
Fort Worth, TX 76102
(817) 334-2616

*Kansas City, MO*
NTSB
Federal Bldg., Rm. 625,
601 East 12th Street,
Kansas City, MO 64106
(816) 374-3576

*Los Angeles, CA*
NTSB
8939 S. Sepulveda Blvd.,
Suite 426
Los Angeles, CA 90045
(213) 776-0117

*Miami, FL*
NTSB
P.O. Box 1245,
Miami International Airport
Miami, FL 33148
(305) 885-2444

*New York, NY*
NTSB
Federal Bldg., Rm. 102,
JFK International Airport
Jamaica, NY 11430
(212) 995-3716

*Oakland, CA*
NTSB
P.O. Box 2586,
Oakland Airport Station
Oakland, CA 94614
(415) 568-1290

*Seattle, WA*
NTSB
Terminal Bldg., Rm. 202,
King County Airport
Seattle, WA 98108
(206) 763-2810

# Appendix C
# State Aviation Agencies

Most state governments have departments, commissions or agencies that are specifically responsible for aviation matters. The agencies are usually involved in aviation safety, airport planning and development, aerospace education and various other activities related to aviation.

*Alabama Department of Aeronautics*
State Highway Bldg.
11 S. Union St.,
Montgomery, AL 36104
(205) 269-6494

*Alaska Division of Aviation*
Department of Public Works
4510 Intl Airport Road,
Anchorage, AK 99502
(907) 274-1544

*Arizona Department of Aeronautics*
3000 Sky Harbor Blvd.,
Phoenix, AZ 85034
(602) 275-7531

*Arkansas Division of Aeronautics*
Suite 514, 1515 W. 7th St.,
Little Rock, AR 72201
(501) Franklin 1-1471

*California Dept. of Aeronautics*
Business and Transportation
Sacramento Executive Airport
Sacramento, CA 95822
(916) 445-2582

*Colorado (no aviation agency)*
Office of the Governor
136 State Capitol Bldg.,
Denver, CO

*Connecticut Dept. of Transportation*
Bureau of Aeronautics
60 Washington St., Suite 600
Hartford, CT 06115
(203) 566-4594 Ext.95

*Delaware Transportation Dept.*
Aeronautics Section
P.O. Box 778,
Dover, DE 19901
(302) 678-4307

*Florida Dept. of Transportation*
Division of Mass Transit
Tallahassee, FL 32304
(904) 599-6327

*Georgia Dept. of Transportation*
Aviation Unit
2 Capitol Square, S.W.,
Atlanta, GA 30334
(404) 656-5333

*Hawaii Dept. of Transportation*
860 Punchbowl St.
Honolulu, HI 96813
(808) 548-3205

*Idaho Dept. of Aeronautics*
3103 Airport Way,
Boise, ID 83705
(208) 384-3183

*Illinois Dept. of Aeronautics*
Capital Airport
North Walnut Street Rd.,
Springfield, IL 62705
(217) 525-2888

*Indiana Aeronautics Commission*
100 N. Senate Ave.,
Indianapolis, IN 46204
(317) 633-4000

*Iowa Aeronautics Commission*
State House
Des Moines, IA 50319
(515) 285-1551

*Kansas Aviation Division*
Dept. of Economic Development
State Office Bldg.,
Topeka, KS 66612
(913) 296-3481

*Kentucky Dept. of Aeronautics*
Old Capitol Annex,
Frankfort, KY 40601
(502) 564-4480

*Louisiana State Aviation Div.*
Dept. of Public Works
P.O. Box 44155, Capitol Sta.,
Baton Rouge, LA 70804
(504) 389-5549

*Maine Dept. of Aeronautics*
State Airport,
Augusta, ME 04330
(207) 289-3185

*Maryland Aviation Administration*
Friendship Intl Airport
P.O. Box 8755,
Baltimore, MD 21240
(301) 768-9520

*Massachusetts Aero Commission*
Boston-Logan Airport,
E. Boston, MA 02128
(617) 727-5350

*Michigan Aeronautics Commission*
Capital City Airport,
Lansing, MI 48906
(517) 489-2421

*Minnesota Dept. of Aeronautics*
Administration Bldg.,
Downtown Airport
St. Paul, MN 55107
(612) 222-4741

*Mississippi Aero Commission*
P.O. Box 5,
Jackson, MS 39205
(601) 354-7494

*Missouri Aviation Section*
Commerce & Industrial Development
8th Floor, Jefferson Bldg.,
Jefferson City, MO 65101
(314) 636-5133

*Montana Aeronautics Commission*
P.O. Box 1698,
Helena, MT 59601
(406) 449-2506

*Nebraska Aeronautics Commission*
P.O. Box 82088,
Lincoln, NB 68501
(402) 471-2371

*Nevada (no state aviation agency)*

*New Hampshire Aero Commission*
Municipal Airport,
Concord, NH 03301
(603) 271-2551

*New Jersey Div. of Aeronautics*
Department of Transportation
1035 Parkway Ave.,
Trenton, NJ 08625
(609) 292-3020

*New Mexico Aviation Dept.*
P.O. Box 579,
Santa Fe, NM 87501
(505) 827-2861

*New York Aviation Section*
Department of Transportation
1220 Washington Ave.,
Albany, NY 12226
(518) 457-2820

North Carolina Div. of Commerce
P.O. Box 2719,
Raleigh, NC 27602
(919) 829-4151

North Dakota Aero Commission
Box U, Bismark Airport,
Bismark, ND 58501
(707) 224-2748

Ohio Division of Aviation
3130 Case Road,
Columbus, OH 43221
(614) 451-4121

Oklahoma Aeronautics Commission
424 United Founders Tower Bldg.,
Oklahoma City, OK 73112
(405) 521-2377

Oregon Board of Aeronautics
3040-25th St., S.E.,
Salem, OR 97310
(503) 378-4880

Pennsylvania Dept. Transportation
Bureau of Aviation
Capital City Airport,
New Cumberland, PA 17070
(717) 787-8754

Puerto Rico Ports Authority
GPO Box 2829,
San Juan, PR 00936
(809) 723-2260

Rhode Island Div. of Airports
Department of Transportation
Theodore F. Green State Airport,
Warwick, RI 02886
(401) 737-4000

South Carolina Aero Commission
Columbia Metro Airport, Box 88,
West Columbia, SC 29169
(803) 758-2766

South Dakota Aero Commission
State Office Bldg. #1,
Pierre, SD 57501
(605) 224-3575

Tennessee Aeronautics Commission
P.O. Box 3557, Airport Sta.,
Nashville, TN 37217
(615) 741-3208

Texas Aeronautics Commission
111 East 17th St.,
Austin, TX 78711
(512) 475-4768

Utah Division of Aeronautics
135 North 23rd West,
Salt Lake City, UT 84116
(801) 328-2066

Vermont Aeronautics Board
State Administration Bldg.,
Montpelier, VT 05602
(802) 223-2311, Ext. 408

Virginia Dept. of Aeronautics
State Corporation Commission
4508 S. Laburnum Ave.,
P.O. Box 7716,
Richmond, VA 23231
(703) 770-3685

Washington State Aero Commission
8600 Perimeter Rd., Boeing Field,
Seattle, WA 98108
(206) 767-3466

West Virginia State Aero Commission
Kanawha Airport,
Charleston, WV 25311
(304) 348-2689 & 348-3790

Wisconsin Dept. of Transportation
Division of Aeronautics
951 Hill Farms State Office Bldg.,
Madison, WI 53702
(608) 266-3351

Wyoming Aeronautics Commission
200 East 8th Ave.,
P.O. Box 2194,
Cheyenne, WY 82001
(307) 777-7481

# Appendix D
# General Aviation Manufacturers

The General Aviation Manufacturers Association (GAMA) member companies account for more than 95 percent of the general aviation production in the United States. They manufacture engines, avionics, airframes and major components of general aviation aircraft. The address for the GAMA is Suite 1215, 1025 Connecticut Ave., N.W., Washington, D.C. 20036, telephone (202) 296-8848. Following is a list of GAMA member companies.

*Aero Products Research, Inc.*
11210 Hindry Ave.,
Los Angeles, CA 90045
(213) 776-1576

*Analog Training Computers, Inc.*
189 Monmouth Parkway,
W. Long Branch, NJ 07764
(201) 970-9200

*Avco Corporation*
Avco Lycoming Division
652 Oliver Street,
Williamsport, PA 17701
(717) 323-6181

*Beech Aircraft Corporation*
9709 E. Central Ave.,
Wichita, KS 67201
(316) 689-7692

*Bendix Corporation*
Bendix Center,
Southfield, MI 48075
(313) 352-5000

*Cessna Aircraft Company*
P. O. Box 1521,
Wichita, KS 67201
(316) 685-9111

*Champion Spark Plug Company*
P. O. Box 910,
Toledo, OH 43601
(419) 536-3711

*Collins Radio Company*
Collins Road, N.E.,
Cedar Rapids, IA 52406
(319) 395-1000

*Edo-Aire Division*
Edo Corporation
216 Passaic Avenue,
Fairfield, NJ 07006
(201) 228-1880

*Flite-Tronics Co., Inc.*
3314 Burton Avenue,
Burbank, CA 91504
(213) 849-1552

*Garret Corporation*
9851 Sepulveda Blvd.,
Los Angeles, CA 90009
(213)776-1010

*Gates Learjet Corporation*
P. O. Box 7707,
Wichita, KS 67277
(316) 946-2345

*Grumman Aerospace Corporation*
Bethpage, Long Island, NY 11714
(516) 575-0574

*Ub-Flight Devices Corporation*
6601 Huntley Road,
Columbus, OH 43229
(614) 846-4300

*King Radio Corporation*
400 North Rogers Road
Olathe, KS 66061
(913) 782-0405

*Narco Scientific Industries*
Commerce Drive,
Fort Washington, PA 19034
(215) 643-2900

*North American Rockwell Corp.*
General Aviation Divisions
5001 N. Rockwell Ave.,
Bethany, OK 73008
(405) 789-5000

*Northrop Airport Development*
801 Follin Lane,
Vienna, VA 22180
(703) 938-2070

*Oberdorfer Foundries, Inc.*
P. O. Box 1125,
Syracuse, NY 13201
(315) 463-3361

*Pacific Scientific Company*
1346 S. State College Blvd.,
Anaheim, CA 92803
(714) 774-5217

*Piper Aircraft Corporation*
Lock Haven, PA 17745
(717) 748-6711

*PPG Industries, Inc.*
777 State National Bank Bldg.,
Huntsville, AL 35801
(205) 539-8121

*RCA Corporation*
Aviation Equipment Department
8500 Balboa Blvd.,
Van Nuys, CA 91409
(213) 894-8111

*Singer Company*
Aerospace & Marine Systems Group
30 Rockefeller Plaza,
New York, NY 10020
(212) 581-4800

*Sperry Rand Corporation*
Flight Systems Division
P.O. Box 2529,
Phoenix, AZ 85002
(602) 942-2311

*Teledyne Continental Motors*
30500 Van Dyke Avenue,
Warren, MI 48093
(313) 751-7000

*United Aircraft Corporation*
United Aircraft of Canada, Ltd.
P.O. Box 10,
Longueuil, P.Q., Canada
(514) 677-9411

# Appendix E
# Aviation Organizations

Following are some of the largest and most representative of the hundreds of aviation organizations throughout the United States.

Aerobatic Club of America
% EAA
P.O. Box 229,
Hales Corners, WI 53130
(414) 425-4860 or 4871

Aerobatic Club of America
P.O. Box 401,
Roanoke, TX 76262

Aerospace Education Foundation
1750 Pennsylvania Ave., N.W.,
Washington, D.C. 20006
(202) 298-9123

Aerospace Industries Association
of America (AIA
1725 DeSales Street, N.W.,
Washington, D.C. 20036
(202) 347-2315

Aircraft Electronics Association
6310 Gen. Twinning Avenue,
Sarasota, FL 33580
(813) 355-7625

Aircraft Owners & Pilots Assoc.
7315 Wisconsin Avenue,
Bethesda, MD
Mail to: P. O. Box 5800,
Washington, D.C. 20014
(202) 654-0500

Air Force Association
1750 Pennsylvania Ave., N.W.,
Washington, D.C. 20006
(202) 298-9123

Airport Operators Council Intl.
1700 K Street, N.W.,
Washington, D.C. 20006
(202) 296-3270

Air Traffic Control Assoc.
Suite 409, ARBA Bldg.,
525 School Street, S.W.,
Washington, D.C. 20024
(202) 347-5100

Air Transport Association of
America (ATA)
1000 Connecticut Ave., N.W.,
Washington, D.C. 20036
(202) 296-5800

American Aerospace & Military
Museum, Inc.
P.O. Box 1051,
Pomona, CA 91766
(714) 629-8310

American Aviation Historical
Society (AAHS)
P.O. Box 996,
Ojai, CA 93023

American Bonanza Society
Chemung County Airport,
Horseheads, NY 14845
(607) 739-5515

American Helicopter Society
30 E. 42nd St., Suite 1408,
New York, NY 10017
(212)697-5168

American Institute of Aeronautics &
Astronautics (AIAA)
1290 Avenue of the Americas,
New York, NY 10019

Antique Airplane Association
P.O. Box H,
Ottumwa, IA 52501
(515) 938-2773

Association of Aviation Psychologists
(AAP)
Naval Safety Center, Code 1157,
NAS Norfolk, VA 23511

Aviation Distributors &
Manufacturers Association
1900 Arch Street,
Philadelphia, PA 19103
(215) 564-3484

Aviation Hall of Fame, Inc.
Sheraton-Dayton Hotel,
Dayton, OH 45402
(513) 224-9601

Aviation Maintenance Foundation
P.O. Box 739,
Basin, WY 82410
(307) 568-2413 or 2414

Aviation/Space Writers Assoc.
Cliffwood Road,
Chester, NJ 07930
(201) 879-5667

Civil Aviation Medical Assoc.
141 N. Meramec Ave., Suite 4,
Clayton, MO 63105
(314) 862-1122

Experimental Aircraft Assoc.
P.O. Box 229,
Hales Corners, WI 53130
(414) 425-4860 or 4871

First Flight Society
P. O. Box 1903,
Kitty Hawk, NC 27949
(919) 473-2046

Flight Safety Foundation
1800 N. Kent Street,
Arlington, VA 22209
(703) 582-4100

Flying Chiropractors Assn.
528 Franklin Street,
Johnstown, PA 15905
(814) 536-6946

Flying Dentists Association
120-½ N. 5th Street,
Sleepy Eye, MN 56085

Flying Funeral Directors of America
678 S. Snelling Avenue
St. Paul, MN 55116
(612) 689-0895

Flying Physicians Association
801 Green Bay Road,
Lake Bluff, IL 60044
(312) 234-6330

General Aviation Manufacturers
Association (GAMA)
Suite 1215
1025 Connecticut Avenue, N.W.,
Washington, D.C. 20036
(202) 296-8848

Helicopter Assoc. of America
Hangar D,
Westchester County Airport
White Plains, NY 10604
(914) 948-0614

International Flying Bankers
Association
Armour Court
801 Green Bay Road,
Lake Bluff, Il 60044

International Flying Farmers
Municipal Airport
Wichita, KS 67209
(316) 943-4234

National Aero Club
3861 Research Park Drive,
Research Park
Ann Arbor, MI 48103

National Aeronautic Assn.
Suite 610, Shoreham Bldg.
806-15th Street, N.W.,
Washington, D.C. 20005
(202) 347-2808

National Aerospace Education
Council
Suite 310, Shoreham Bldg.
605-15th Street, N.W.,
Washington, D.C. 20005

National Association of State
Aviation Officials
Suite 802
1000 Vermont Ave., N.W.,
Washington, D.C. 20005
(202) 783-0588

National Aviation Trades Assn.
1156 15th Street, N.W.,
Washington, D.C. 20006
(202) 833-8210

National Business Aircraft Assoc.
Suite 401, Pennsylvania Bldg.
425 13th Street, N.W.,
Washington, D.C. 20006
(202) 738-9000

National Intercollegiate Flying
Association (NIFA)
Parks College,
St. Louis University Parks Airport
Cahokia, IL 62206

National Pilots Association (NPA)
806 15th Street, N.W.,
Washington, D.C. 20005
(202) 737-0773

Ninety-Nines
P.O. Box 59964,
Oklahoma City, OK 73159
(405) 685-7969

OX-5 Aviation Pioneers
419 Plaza Bldg.,
Pittsburgh, PA 15219

Pilots International Association
2469 Park Avenue,
Minneapolis, MN 55407
(612) 546-4075

Professional Air Traffic Controllers Organization (PATCO)
2100 M Street, N.W.,
Washington, D.C. 20006
(202) 296-6443 and 6444

Soaring Society of America
P.O. Box 66071,
Los Angeles, CA 90066
(213) 390-4449

Society of Experimental Test Pilots
44814 N. Elm Ave.,
Lancaster, CA 93534
(805) 942-9574

University Aviation Association
Parks College
St. Louis University, Parks Airport
Cahokia, IL 62206

# Appendix F
# FAA General
# Aviation District Offices

*Alaskan Region*
1714 E. 5th Ave., Anchorage, AK 99501
5640 Airport Way, Fairbanks, AK 99701
Star Route 1, Box 592, Juneau, AK 99801

*Central Region*
228 Administration Bldg., Municipal Airport,
Des Moines, IA 50321
Fairfax Municipal Airport, Kansas City, KS 66115
Municipal Airport, Wichita, KS 67209
9275 Glenaire Dr., Berkeley, MO 63134
Municipal Airport, Lincoln, NE 68524

*Eastern Region*
National Airport, Washington, D.C. 20001
Friendship International Airport, Baltimore, MD 21240
510 Industrial Way, Teterboro, NJ 07608
County Airport, Albany, NY 12211
Republic Airport, Farmingdale, NY 11735
Monroe County Airport, Rochester, NY 14517
Allentown-Bethlehem-Easton Airport, Allentown, PA 18103
Harrisburg-York State Airport, New Cumberland, PA 17070
North Philadelphia Airport, PA 19114
Allegheny County Airport, West Mifflin, PA 15122
Aero Industries, 2nd Floor, Sandston, VA 23150
Kanawha County Airport, Charleston, WV 25311

*Great Lakes Region*
P.O. Box H, Dupage County Airport, West Chicago,
IL 60185
R.R. 2, Box 3, Springfield, IL 62705
St. Joseph County Airport, South Bend, IN 46628
5500 44th St., S.E., Grand Rapids, MI 49508
6201 4th Ave., S. Minneapolis MN 55450
4242 Airport Rd., Cincinnati, OH 45226
4393 East 175th Ave., Columbus, OH 43219
General Mitchell Field, Milwaukee, WI 53207

*New England Region*
1001 Westbrook St., Portland ME 14102
Municipal Airport, Box 280, Norwood, MA 02062
P.O. Box 544, Westfield, MA 01085

*Northwest Region*
3113 Airport Way, Boise, ID 83705
5401 NE Marine Dr., Portland OR 97218
FAA Bldg., Boeing Field, Seattle, WA 98108
P.O. Box 247, Parkwater Station, Spokane, WA 99211

*Pacific Region*
Rm. 715, Terminal Bldg., International Airport,
Honolulu, HI 96819

*Rocky Mountain Region*
Jefferson County Airport, Broomsfield, CO 80020
Logan Field, Billings, MT 59101
P.O. Box 1167, Helena, MT 59601
P.O. Box 2128, Fargo, ND 58102
R.R. 2, Box 633B, Rapid City, SD 57701
116 North 23rd West Street, Salt Lake City, UT 84116
Air Terminal, Casper, WY 82601
P.O. Box 2166, Cheyenne, WY 82001

*Southern Region*
6500 43rd Avenue North, Birmingham, AL 35206
P.O. Box 38665, Jacksonville, FL 38665
P.O. Box 365, Opa Locka, FL 33054
Clearwater International Airport, St. Petersburg, FL 33732

Fulton County Airport, Atlanta, GA 30336
Bowman Field, Louisville, KY 40205
P.O. Box 5855, Jackson, MS 39208
Municipal Airport, Charlotte, NC 28208
P.O. Box 1858, Raleigh, NC 27602
Box 200, Metropolitan Airport, West Columbia, SC 29169
P.O. Box 30050, Memphis, TN 38103
Metropolitan Airport, Nashville, TN 37217

*Southwest Region*
Adams Field, Little Rock, AR 72202
Lakefront Airport, New Orleans, LA 70126
Downtown Airport, Shreveport, LA 71107
P.O. Box 9045, Sunport Station, Albuquerque, NM 87119
Wiley Post Airport, Bethany, OK 72008

International Airport, Tulsa, OK 74115
Redbird Airport, Dallas, TX 75232
6795 Convair Rd., El Paso, TX 79925
P.O. Box 1689, Meacham Field, Fort Worth, TX 76016
8345 Telephone Rd., Houston, TX 77017
P.O. Box 5247, Lubbock, TX 79417
1115 Paul Wilkins Rd., San Antonio, TX 78216

*Western Region*
2800 Sky Harbor Blvd., Phoenix, AZ 85034
Air Terminal, Fresno, CA 93727
2815 East Spring St., Long Beach, CA 90806
P.O. Box 2397, Oakland, CA 94614
International Airport, Ontario, CA 91761
Municipal Airport, Sacramento, CA 95822
3750 John J. Montgomery Dr., San Diego, CA 92123
1887 Airport Blvd., San Jose, CA 95110
3200 Airport Ave., Santa Monica, CA 90405
7120 Havenhurst Ave., Van Nuys, CA 91406
5700-C South Haven, Las Vegas, NV 89109
2601 East Plum Lane, Reno, NV 89502

The FAA Aeronautical Center address is P.O. Box 25082, Oklahoma City, OK 73125.

# Appendix G
# Conversion Tables

Table G-1. Metric Conversion Table.

| MULTIPLY | BY | TO GET |
|---|---|---|
| inches | 2.54 | centimeters |
| feet | 30.48 | centimeters |
| yards | 0.91 | meters |
| miles | 1.61 | kilometers |
| millimeters | 0.04 | inches |
| centimeters | 0.39 | inches |
| meters | 3.28 | feet |
| kilometers | 0.62 | miles |
| square inches | 6.45 | square centimeters |
| square feet | 0.09 | square meters |
| square yards | 0.84 | square meters |
| square miles | 2.59 | square kilometers |
| square centimeters | 0.16 | square inches |
| square meters | 0.20 | square yards |
| square kilometers | 0.4 | squar miles |
| fluid ounces | 29.57 | milliliters |
| pints | 0.47 | liters |
| quarts | 0.95 | liters |
| gallons | 3.78 | liters |
| milliliters | 0.03 | ounces |
| liters | 2.11 | pints |
| liters | 1.06 | quarts |
| liters | 0.26 | gallons |
| ounces (weight) | 28.35 | grams |
| pounds | 0.45 | kilograms |
| short tons | 0.9 | tonnes |
| grams | 0.035 | ounces |
| kilograms | 2.20 | pounds |
| tonnes | 1.10 | short tons |

## Table G-2. Temperature Conversion Table.

| CELCIUS | FAHRENHEIT | CELSIUS | FAHRENHEIT |
|---|---|---|---|
| −40 C | −40.0 F | 24 C | 75.2 F |
| −35 C | −31.0 F | 25 C | 77.0 F |
| −30 C | −22.0 F | 26 C | 78.8 F |
| −25 C | −13.0 F | 27 C | 80.6 F |
| −20 C | − 4.0 F | 28 C | 82.4 F |
| −18 C | − 0.4 F | 29 C | 84.2 F |
| −16 C | 3.2 F | 30 C | 86.0 F |
| −14 C | 6.8 F | 31 C | 87.8 F |
| −12 C | 10.4 F | 32 C | 89.6 F |
| −10 C | 14.0 F | 33 C | 91.4 F |
| − 8 C | 17.6 F | 34 C | 93.2 F |
| − 6 C | 21.2 F | 35 C | 95.0 F |
| − 5 C | 23.0 F | 36 C | 96.8 F |
| − 4 C | 24.8 F | 37 C | 98.6 F |
| − 3 C | 26.6 F | 38 C | 100.4 F |
| − 2 C | 28.4 F | 39 C | 102.2 F |
| − 1 C | 30.2 F | 40 C | 104.0 F |
| 0 C | 32.0 F | 42 C | 107.7 F |
| 1 C | 33.8 F | 44 C | 111.2 F |
| 2 C | 35.6 F | 46 C | 114.8 F |
| 3 C | 37.4 F | 48 C | 118.4 F |
| 4 C | 39.2 F | 50°C | 122.0 F |
| 5 C | 41.0 F | 55 C | 131.0 F |
| 6 C | 42.8 F | 60 C | 140.0 F |
| 7C | 44.6 F | 65 C | 149.0 F |
| 8C | 46.4 F | 70 C | 158.0 F |
| 9C | 48.2 F | 75 C | 167.0 F |
| 10 C | 50.0 F | 80 C | 176.0 F |
| 11 C | 51.8 F | 85 C | 185.0 F |
| 12 C | 53.6 F | 90 C | 194.0 F |
| 13 C | 55.4 F | 95 C | 203.0 F |
| 14 C | 57.2 F | 100 C | 212.0 F |
| 15 C | 59.0 F | 125 C | 257.0 F |
| 16 C | 60.8 F | 150 C | 302.0 F |
| 17 C | 62.6 F | 175 C | 347 F |
| 18 C | 64.4 F | 200 C | 392 F |
| 19 C | 66.2 F | 204 C | 400 F |
| 20 C | 68.0 F | 218 C | 425 F |
| 21 C | 69.8 F | 232 C | 450 F |
| 22 C | 71.6 F | 246 C | 475 F |
| 23 C | 73.4 F | 260 C | 500 F |

Eastern Standard = GMT minus five hours
Eastern Daylight = GMT minus four hours
Central Standard = GMT minus six hours
Central Daylight = GMT minus five hours
Mountain Standard = GMT minus seven hours
Mountain Daylight = GMT minus six hours
Pacific Standard = GMT minus eight hours
Pacific Daylight = GMT minus seven hours
Yukon Standard = GMT minus nine hours
Alaska/Hawaii Standard = GMT minus 10 hours

**Table G-3. Time Zones and International Markings. Greenwich Mean Time (GMT) Is the Time At the Prime Meridian In England and Is Used In Aviation Worldwide.**

**Table G-4. Air Navigation Distance/Speed Conversion Table. Multiply Statute Miles by .87 to Get Nautical Miles. Multiply Nautical Miles by 1.15 to Get Statute Miles.**

| KNOTS | MPH/KNOTS | MPH | KNOTS | MPH/KNOTS | MPH |
|-------|-----------|-----|-------|-----------|-----|
| 4 | 5 | 6 | 69 | 80 | 92 |
| 9 | 10 | 12 | 74 | 85 | 93 |
| 13 | 15 | 17 | 78 | 90 | 104 |
| 17 | 20 | 23 | 82 | 95 | 110 |
| 22 | 25 | 29 | 87 | 100 | 115 |
| 26 | 30 | 35 | 91 | 105 | 121 |
| 30 | 35 | 40 | 95 | 110 | 127 |
| 35 | 40 | 46 | 100 | 115 | 132 |
| 39 | 45 | 52 | 104 | 120 | 138 |
| 43 | 50 | 58 | 108 | 125 | 144 |
| 48 | 55 | 63 | 113 | 130 | 150 |
| 52 | 60 | 69 | 117 | 135 | 155 |
| 56 | 65 | 75 | 122 | 140 | 161 |
| 61 | 70 | 81 | 126 | 145 | 167 |
| 65 | 75 | 86 | 130 | 150 | 173 |

**Table G-5. V-Speeds.**

| ABBREVIATION | MEANING |
|--------------|---------|
| $V_a$ | design maneuvering speed |
| $V_b$ | design speed for maximum gust intensity |
| $V_c$ | design cruising speed |
| $V_d$ | design diving speed |
| $V_{df}$ | demonstrated flight diving speed |
| $V_f$ | design flap speed |
| $V_{fc}$ | maximum speed for stability characteristics |
| $V_{fe}$ | maximum flap extended speed |
| $V_h$ | maximum speed in level flight with maximum continuous power |
| $V_{le}$ | maximum landing gear extended speed |
| $V_{lo}$ | maximum landing gear operating speed |
| $V_{lof}$ | lift-off speed |
| $V_{mc}$ | minimum control speed with critical engine inoperative |
| $V_{me}$ | maximum endurance speed |
| $V_{mo}$ | maximum operating speed limit |
| $V_{mu}$ | minimum unstick speed |
| $V_{ne}$ | never exceed speed |
| $V_r$ | rotation speed |
| $V_s$ | stalling speed, or the minimum steady flight speed at which the aircraft is controllable |
| $V_{so}$ | stalling speed or the minimum steady flight speed in the landing configuration |
| $V_{xse}$ | best single-engine angle-of-climb speed |
| $V_y$ | best rate-of-climb speed |
| $V_{yse}$ | best single-engine rate-of-climb speed |
| $V_1$ | critical engine-failure speed |
| $V_2$ | takeoff safety speed |
| $V_{2min}$ | minimum takeoff speed |

## Table G-6. National Aircraft Registration Codes. The Following Letter/Number Codes Identify the Country of Aircraft Registry.

| | | |
|---|---|---|
| AN—Nicaragua | TT—Chad | TR—Gabon |
| AP—Pakistan | TU—Ivory Coast | TS—Tunisia |
| 3A—Monaco | TY—Dahomey | XW—Laos |
| 5A—Lybia | TZ—Mali | XY—Burma |
| B —China | 3C—Equatorial Guinea | XZ—Burma |
| 5B—Cyprus | D —Germany | 3X—Guinea |
| CC—Chile | EC—Spain | 5T—Mauretania |
| CF—Canada | EL—Liberia | 7T—Algeria |
| CN—Morocco | EP—Iran | 5U—Burundi |
| CP—Bolivia | ET—Ethiopia | VH—Australia |
| CR—Portugal | F —France | VT—India |
| CS—Portugal | G —United Kingdom | 5V—Togo |
| CU—Cuba | 9G—Ghana | 6V—Senegal |
| CX—Uraguay | HA—Hungary | 9V—Singapore |
| HC—Ecuador | HB—Liechtenstein | 4W—Yemen |
| HH—Haiti | HB—Switzerland | 5W—Western Samoa |
| HI—Dominican Republic | OO—Belgium | 6W—Senegal |
| HK—Colombia | OY—Denmark | XA—Mexico |
| HL—Republic of Korea | 6OS—Somali | XB—Mexico |
| HP—Panama | PH—Netherlands | XC—Mexico |
| HR—Honduras | PI—Philippines | 9XR—Rwanda |
| HS—Thailand | PJ—Netherlands Antilles | XT—Upper Volta |
| HZ—Saudi Arabia | PK—Indonesia | XU—Cambodia |
| 5H—Tanzania | PP—Brazil | XV—Vietnam |
| 9H—Malta | PT—Brazil | 4X—Israel |
| I —Italy | 7P—Lesotho | 5X—Uganda |
| JA—Japan | 8P—Barbados | YA—Afghanistan |
| 9J—Zambia | 7QY—Malawi | YI—Iraq |
| JY—Jordan | 4R—Ceylon | YK—Suria |
| 9K—Kuwait | 5R—Madagascar | YR—Romania |
| LN—Norway | 9Q—Leopoldville | YS—El Salvador |
| LQ—Argentina | 8R—Guyana | YU—Yugoslavia |
| LV—Argentina | SE—Sweden | YV—Venezuela |
| LX—Luxembourg | SP—Poland | 5Y—Kenya |
| LZ—Bulgaria | ST—Sudan | 6Y—Jamaica |
| 9L—Sierra Leone | SU—United Arab Republic | 9Y—Trinidad and Tobago |
| 9M—Malaysia | SX—Greece | ZK—New Zealand |
| N —United States | TC—Turkey | ZL—New Zealand |
| 5N—Nigeria | TF—Iceland | ZM—New Zealand |
| 9N—Nepal | TG—Guatemala | ZP—Paraguay |
| OB—Peru | TI—Costa Rica | ZS—Union of South Africa |
| OD—Lebanon | TJ—Cameron | ZT—Union of South Africa |
| OE—Austria | TL—Central African Republic | ZU—Union of South Africa |
| OH—Finland | TN—Brazzaville | |
| OK—Czechoslovakia | TO—South Yemen | |

## Table G-7. Radiotelephone Phonetic Alphabet With Morse Code.

| | | |
|---|---|---|
| A - Alpha . - | M - Mike - - | Y - Yankee - . - - |
| B - Bravo - ... | N - November - . | Z - Zulu - - .. |
| C - Charlie - . - | O - Oscar - - - | 0 - Zero - - - - - |
| D - Delta - .. | P - Papa . - - . | 1 - Wun . - - - - |
| E - Echo . | Q - Quebec - - . - (Kebek) | 2 - Too .. - - - |
| F - Foxtrot .. - | R - Romeo . - . | 3 - Tree ... - - |
| G - Gulf - - . | S - Sierra ... | 4 - Fow-er .... - |
| H - Hotel .... | T - Tango - | 5 - Fife ..... |
| I - India .. | U - Uniform ..- | 6 - Six - .... |
| J - Juliett . - - - | V - Victor ... - | 7 - Sev-en - - ... |
| K - Kilo - . - | W - Whiskey . - - | 8 - Ate - - - .. |
| L - Lima . - .. (Leemah) | X - Exray - .. - | 9 - Nin-er - - - - . |

Rytle 1987

# Index